John Keble

Sermons for Ascension Day to Trinity Sunday

John Keble

Sermons for Ascension Day to Trinity Sunday

ISBN/EAN: 9783744742504

Printed in Europe, USA, Canada, Australia, Japan

Cover: Foto ©Lupo / pixelio.de

More available books at **www.hansebooks.com**

SERMONS

FOR

THE CHRISTIAN YEAR

BY THE LATE

REV. JOHN KEBLE,

AUTHOR OF "THE CHRISTIAN YEAR."

SOLD BY

JAMES PARKER AND CO. OXFORD,
AND 377, STRAND, LONDON.

1876.

PRINTED BY THE SOCIETY OF THE HOLY TRINITY,
HOLY ROOD, OXFORD.

SERMONS

FOR

ASCENSION DAY

TO

TRINITY SUNDAY

BY THE LATE
REV. JOHN KEBLE,
AUTHOR OF "THE CHRISTIAN YEAR."

SOLD BY
JAMES PARKER AND CO. OXFORD,
AND 377, STRAND, LONDON.
1876.

CONTENTS.

SERMON I.
CHRIST, THE KING OF ANGELS.
ASCENSION DAY.
1 S. Pet. iii. 22.

"*Who is gone into heaven, and is on the Right Hand of God; Angels and Authorities and Powers being made subject unto Him.*" . . . . pp. 1—11.

SERMON II.
EFFECTS OF CHRIST'S ASCENSION.
ASCENSION DAY.
Ps. lxviii. 18.

"*Thou hast ascended on high, Thou hast led captivity captive: Thou hast received gifts for men; yea, for the rebellious also, that the Lord God might dwell among them.*"
pp. 12—20.

SERMON III.
OUR LORD'S LAST PRAYER.
ASCENSION DAY. 1843.
S. John xvii. 11.

"*And now I am no more in the world, but these are in the world, and I come to Thee. Holy Father, keep through Thine own Name those whom Thou hast given Me, that they may be one, as We are.*" . . . . pp. 21—26.

SERMON IV.

SHOWERS OF BLESSING.

ASCENSION DAY. 1847.

Ezek. xxxiv. 26.

"*I will make them and the places round about My hill a blessing, and I will cause the shower to come down in his season: there shall be showers of blessing.*" pp. 27—33.

SERMON V.

THE DRAWING OF JESUS BY HIS ASCENSION.

ASCENSION DAY. 1849.

Song of Solomon i. 4.

"*Draw me, we will run after Thee: the King hath brought me into His chambers: we will be glad and rejoice in Thee.*" . . . . . . pp. 34—41.

SERMON VI.

THE BENEFIT OF OUR LORD'S INTERCESSION, DEPENDENT ON COMMUNION WITH HIM.

ASCENSION DAY. 1855.

Heb. vii. 25.

"*He is able to save them to the uttermost that come unto God by Him, seeing He ever liveth to make intercession for them.*" . . . . pp. 42—52.

SERMON VII.

RESTRAINT, THE CHRISTIAN'S BLESSING.

SUNDAY AFTER ASCENSION DAY.

DEUT. xii. 8, 9.

" *Ye shall not do after all the things that we do here this day, every man whatsoever is right in his own eyes: for ye are not as yet come to the rest and to the inheritance, which the Lord your God giveth you.*"   . pp. 53—62.

SERMON VIII.

CHRISTIAN CONFIDENCE.

SUNDAY AFTER ASCENSION DAY.

ROM. viii. 33, 34.

" *Who shall lay anything to the charge of God's elect? It is God that justifieth. Who is he that condemneth? It is Christ that died, yea rather, that is risen again, Who is even at the Right Hand of God, Who also maketh intercession for us.*" . . . . . pp. 63—71.

SERMON IX.

A PLACE PREPARED FOR US, AND WE PREPARED FOR IT.

SUNDAY AFTER ASCENSION DAY.

S. JOHN xiv. 2.

" *I go to prepare a place for you.*" . pp. 72—81.

SERMON X.

THE REWARD OF FINISHED WORK.

SUNDAY AFTER ASCENSION DAY.

S. JOHN xvii. 4, 5.

"*I have glorified Thee on the earth: I have finished the work which Thou gavest Me to do: and now, O Father, glorify Thou Me with Thine own self with the glory which I had with Thee before the world was.*" . pp. 82—92.

SERMON XI.

OFFICE OF FERVENT CHARITY TOWARDS OUR FORGIVENESS.

SUNDAY AFTER ASCENSION DAY.

1 S. PET. iv. 8.

"*Above all things have fervent charity among yourselves; for charity shall cover the multitude of sins.*" pp. 93—103.

SERMON XII.

THE NEARNESS OF THE UNSEEN WORLD.

SUNDAY AFTER ASCENSION DAY.

S. MARK xvi. 19.

"*After the Lord had spoken unto them, He was taken up into heaven, and sat on the Right Hand of God.*"

pp. 104—113.

SERMON XIII.
CHRIST FILLING ALL THINGS.
SUNDAY AFTER ASCENSION DAY.
EPH. iv. 10.

"*He that descended is the same also that ascended up far above all heavens, that He might fill all things.*"
pp. 114—123.

SERMON XIV.
THE BLESSING OF PEACE.
SUNDAY AFTER ASCENSION DAY.
Ps. xxix. 9, 10.

"*The Lord sitteth above the water-flood: and the Lord remaineth a King for ever. The Lord shall give strength unto His people; the Lord shall give His people the blessing of peace.*" . . . . pp. 124—134.

SERMON XV.
THE DAYS OF EXPECTATION. I.
WEDNESDAY BEFORE PENTECOST.
ACTS i. 13.

"*And when they were come in, they went up into an upper room.*" . . . . . pp. 135—142.

SERMON XVI.
THE DAYS OF EXPECTATION. II.
FRIDAY BEFORE PENTECOST.
ACTS i. 14.

"*These all continued with one accord in prayer and supplication, with the women, and Mary the Mother of Jesus, and with His brethren.*" . . pp. 143—150.

SERMON XVII.
PATIENT WAITING FOR PROMISES.
WHITSUNTIDE.
Ps. xlviii. 8.

"*We wait for Thy loving-kindness, O God, in the midst of Thy temple.*" . . . . pp. 151—163.

SERMON XVIII.
THE BREATH OF THE MOST HIGH GOD.
WHITSUNTIDE.
Ps. civ. 30.

"*Thou sendest forth Thy Spirit, they are created: and Thou renewest the face of the earth.*" . pp. 164—175.

SERMON XIX.
CHRIST'S BAPTISM, A TOKEN OF PENTECOST.
WHITSUNTIDE.
S. Luke iii. 21, 22.

"*Jesus also being baptized, and praying, the heaven was opened, and the Holy Ghost descended in a bodily shape like a dove upon Him.*" . . pp. 176—186.

SERMON XX.
FORGETFULNESS IN CHRISTIANS, NO EXCUSE.
WHITSUNDAY.
S. John xiv. 26.

"*The Comforter, which is the Holy Ghost, Whom the Father will send in My name, He shall teach you all things, and bring all things to your remembrance, whatsoever I have said unto you.*" . . . . pp. 187—196.

SERMON XXI.
BAPTISM WITH THE HOLY GHOST.
WHITSUNDAY.

Acts i. 5.

"*John truly baptized with water; but ye shall be baptized with the Holy Ghost not many days hence.*"

pp. 197—208.

SERMON XXII.
THE FREE GIFTS OF GOD.
WHITSUNDAY.

1 Cor. ii. 12.

"*We have received, not the spirit of the world, but the Spirit which is of God, that we might know the things which are freely given to us of God.*" . . pp. 209—218.

SERMON XXIII.
FLESH AND SPIRIT.
WHITSUNDAY.

S. John iii. 6.

"*That which is born of the flesh is flesh, and that which is born of the Spirit is spirit.*" pp. 219—227.

SERMON XXIV.
CONFESSION AND SELF-DENIAL, TOKENS OF THE WORK OF THE HOLY GHOST.
WHITSUNDAY.

Acts xix. 20.

"*So mightily grew the Word of God, and prevailed.*"

pp. 228—238.

SERMON XXV.

THE ABIDING PRESENCE OF THE HOLY GHOST, OUR STAY AND OUR COMFORT.

WHITSUNDAY.

HAGGAI ii. 5.

"*According to the word that I covenanted with you when ye came out of Egypt, so My Spirit remaineth among you: fear ye not.*" . . . . . pp. 239—248.

SERMON XXVI.

CHRIST IN ALL.

WHITSUNDAY.

COL. iii. 11.

"*Christ is All, and in all.*" . . pp. 249—258.

SERMON XXVII.

THE WITNESS OF THE SPIRIT.

WHITSUNDAY.

ROM. viii. 16.

"*The Spirit itself beareth witness with our spirit, that we are the children of God.*". . . pp. 259—268.

SERMON XXVIII.

THE UNIVERSALITY OF THE PENTECOST.

WHITSUNDAY.

ACTS ii. 4.

"*And they were all filled with the Holy Ghost.*" pp. 269—280.

SERMON XXIX.
ONE SPIRIT, MANY GIFTS.
WHITMONDAY.
1 Cor. xii. 11.

"But all these worketh that one and the self-same Spirit, dividing to every man severally as He will."
　　　　　　　　　　　　　　　pp. 281—291.

SERMON XXX.
GRACE WELL-USED, ATTRACTS MORE GRACE.
MONDAY IN WHITSUN-WEEK.
Ps. cxix. 55, 56.

"I have thought upon Thy Name, O Lord, in the night-season, and have kept Thy law: this I had, because I kept Thy commandments." . . . . pp. 292—301.

SERMON XXXI.
THE UNIVERSAL LANGUAGE. I.
MONDAY IN WHITSUN-WEEK.
Zeph. iii. 9.

" For then will I turn to the people a pure language, that they may all call upon the Name of the Lord, to serve Him with one consent." . . . . pp. 302—308.

SERMON XXXII.
THE UNIVERSAL LANGUAGE. II.
MONDAY IN WHITSUN-WEEK.
Zeph. iii. 9.

" For then will I turn to the people a pure language, that they may all call upon the Name of the Lord, to serve Him with one consent." . . . . pp. 309—314.

SERMON XXXIII.

FESTIVAL JOY.

TUESDAY IN WHITSUN-WEEK.

ECCLES. ix. 7, 8.

" Go thy way, eat thy bread with joy, and drink thy wine with a merry heart; for God now accepteth thy works. Let thy garments be always white, and let thy head lack no ointment." . . . . . pp. 315—322.

SERMON XXXIV.

CHRISTIAN MINISTERS, TOKENS OF CHRIST'S PRESENCE.

TUESDAY IN WHITSUN-WEEK.

S. JOHN x. 9.

" I am the door: by Me if any man enter in, he shall be saved, and shall go in and out, and find pasture."
pp. 323—331.

SERMON XXXV.

WHY THE WITNESS OF GOD IS REJECTED.

TRINITY SUNDAY.

S. JOHN iii. 11.

" Verily, verily, I say unto thee, We speak that We do know, and testify that We have seen; and ye receive not Our witness." . . . . . pp. 332—342.

SERMON XXXVI.
THE SECRET OF THE LORD.
TRINITY SUNDAY.
Ps. xxv. 13.

"*The secret of the Lord is among them that fear Him, and He will shew them His covenant.*" . pp. 343—353.

SERMON XXXVII.
HEAVEN OPENED.
TRINITY SUNDAY.
Rev. iv. 1.

"*I looked, and behold, a door was opened in heaven.*"
pp. 354—363.

SERMON XXXVIII.
THE ANGELIC HYMN, HOLY, HOLY, HOLY, OUR COMMUNION HYMN.
TRINITY SUNDAY.
Isa. vi. 3.

"*One cried unto another, and said, Holy, Holy, Holy, is the Lord of hosts: the whole earth is full of His glory.*"
pp. 364—373.

SERMON XXXIX.
THE HOLINESS OF GOD, TOWARDS US AND IN US.
TRINITY SUNDAY.
Rev. iv. 8.

"*They rest not day and night, saying, Holy, Holy, Holy, Lord God Almighty, which was, and is, and is to come.*"
pp. 374—383.

SERMON XL.

HEAVEN CREATED FOR US, WE RE-CREATED FOR IT, BY THE HOLY TRINITY.

TRINITY SUNDAY.

Ps. xxxiii. 6.

"*By the Word of the Lord were the heavens made; and all the hosts of them by the Breath of His Mouth.*"

pp. 384—394.

SERMON XLI.

THE THREEFOLD CORD.

TRINITY SUNDAY.

Eccles. iv. 12.

"*A threefold cord is not quickly broken.*" . pp. 395—404.

SERMON 1.

CHRIST, THE KING OF ANGELS.

ASCENSION DAY.

1 S. Pet. iii. 22.

" Who is gone into Heaven, and is on the right hand of God; Angels and Authorities and Powers being made subject unto Him."

It is most certain that, when we have done our best, we cannot lift up our minds and hearts fully to understand the unspeakable glory which the Son of God, as He is also Son of Man, obtained as on this day: when He, who a little more than forty days before had been "[a] a worm and no man, a very scorn of men and the outcast of the people," was set at His Father's Right Hand "[b] in the heavenly places, far above all principality and power, and might, and dominion, and every name that is named, not only in this world, but in that also which is to come:" and had all things put under His feet, and was given to be head over all things. We cannot, I say, realize this in our thoughts, even as we cannot know or imagine the place, where the visible though spiritual Body of our Blessed Lord now is; or how, or which way, He was received up through the air when He hid

[a] Ps. xxii. 6. [b] Eph. i. 20, 21.

Himself in a cloud from the sight of His servants, they stedfastly looking after Him.

They saw Him departing, yet could they no more imagine the manner of His departure than we now can. But did that hinder them from musing and meditating upon it? Nay, their very hearts and minds went after Him, and did in a manner continually dwell with Him. "^c They worshipped Him, and returned to Jerusalem with great joy: and were continually in the temple, praising and blessing God." Christ, ascended into heaven, took up their thoughts day and night. They were never satisfied with the wondering and adoring remembrance of it, and with hymning and praising the Almighty for that last and greatest of miracles. But did they think of it only as a miracle? Or were not their thoughts rather taken up with the portion which they themselves had in it, and all whom Christ came to save?

We indeed are but little able to enter into the thoughts of Apostles, of the favoured friends of Jesus Christ, accustomed to His Divine words and looks, when they saw Him in His very Body, His crucified Body, ascending up into heaven. But we may understand that this was a part of their feelings; that now One, Who is true Man as we are, Who can enter into our joys and sorrows, our hopes and fears, He is set in the highest place, over all created things. And He carries with Him there the same tender love towards the meanest of His faithful servants which He ever vouchsafed to exercise here. He still loves to be called on by the afflicted, with earnest and most

^c S. Luke xxiv. 52, 53.

persevering prayer. He is ready, as of old, to reply to the woman of Canaan, "O woman, great is thy faith, be it unto thee even as thou wilt." There are still families which He loves with distinguishing and peculiar love, as He loved Martha, and her sister, and Lazarus; and there are graves beside which He waits, as He did by that of Lazarus, in deep and tender pity for the sorrows of those who are tried by separation and bereavement.

His going up into heaven was to the Apostles, who remembered these things, a sign that, though absent from us visibly in the Body, He would yet be (if I may say so) more present than ever in spirit with the children of men, in all their cares, and griefs and anxieties. It was a sign of "the Manhood" being so "taken into God," that He would always (so to speak) be on our side, in all our struggles and conflicts, spiritual and temporal, if only we do not cast Him from us.

It was, in some sort, as if one's nearest and dearest relation were made absolute king of the country. If persons who care for earthly things would rejoice in such a change as that, and consider their own fortune made, how much more joy to those who care for heavenly things, when we set our hearts to consider that He Who "is not ashamed to call us brethren," He Who loved us so well that He laid down His life for us in torment, He is made "the great King" in heaven and earth, and has all the treasures of grace and glory put for ever into His hand.

In this, we see at once, is included every good thing. But for the present there is one blessing in particular, on which I wish to say a few words. It is, the subjection of the spiritual world to our Saviour, expressed by S. Peter in the words of the text, that " Angels and Authorities and Powers were made subject" to the Son of Man when He went into heaven, and sat down on the Right Hand of God. That is to say, that not only the things which we see, the sun and moon and stars, the earth and the waters, the bodies of men, their health and sickness, and all that we call the course of this world, is under the command of His Eternal Providence, Who is pledged to make all things work together for good to them that love Him; but also the worlds out of sight, the spiritual and heavenly world, is entirely ordered by Him.

Now, this is a great thing for us to know; a great comfort in our natural fears and misgivings; a great encouragement to well-doing; and a most serious warning against all carelessness and sin.

We naturally think, even from our childhood; at least, all thoughtful children think a good deal of the spiritual world: of beings out of sight, who yet, for aught we know, may often be very near us, and may have great power to do us good, or to hurt us in body and soul. What are the many stories and imaginations about spirits appearing, and tokens from unseen beings, and the like, of which most of us have at times heard so much; what are they all, but signs that we feel, how many things are about us which we do not see? They are providential ways of instructing us, how fearful it would be, were our eyes suddenly opened; and how greatly, therefore, we need some assurance that we are not left alone and helpless, in regard of this unseen world, any more than in regard of that world, which we discern by our bodily senses, and which therefore seems nearer to us.

Now the Ascension of our Lord is such a token. It assures us, that however deep our solitude, however overpowering our sense of spiritual beings possibly near us, One is at hand like-minded with ourselves, Who can pity all our misgivings, as well as protect us in all dangers. In darkness as in light, in desolation as in pleasant places, in melancholy as in cheerful hours, He is still the same. Could we but bring home to ourselves His most mysterious, but most certain Presence, we need not " be afraid for any terror by night," any more than " for the arrow that flieth by day." The whole world unseen, we are sure, is under Him, no less than the world which we see. And committing ourselves to Him, by serious prayer, will ever be as effectual a safeguard against the unknown dangers of our spiritual being, as against those of our natural being, which we can in some measure understand and foresee. Thus the disciples found Jesus at hand to relieve them, as certainly, when supposing Him to be a Spirit, they " cried out for fear," as when in the violent storm on the same lake, they woke Him with the appeal, " Lord save us! we perish."

Consider the matter in this way. The Bible teaches that there are two worlds, in the midst of which we all live, did we but know it and remember it; the one visible, the other invisible: and that there are in the invisible world two sorts of Angels, Authorities and Powers, with both of which we are concerned; with the one, as friends and fellow-servants; with the other, as unrelenting enemies. And the thought of our Lord gone up into heaven, and sitting on the Right Hand of God, is a thought of great power to set us right in our feelings towards both these aweful sorts of Beings.

Consider, first, what a thing it is to know that the good Angels are on our side: that they camp about us to deliver us: that as Christ Himself in His distress had but to pray to His Father, and He would presently have given Him more than twelve legions of Angels, so the members of Christ, in their several agonies of body and mind, have but to pray to the Almighty, and who knows but the same holy messengers, most likely unknown to them, will receive some commission to do them good? As they came to Daniel, to shut the lions' mouths; as they were like an army with horses and chariots of fire round about Elisha; as they opened the prison-doors of Jerusalem, and let out first all the Apostles, then S. Peter, on the eve of martyrdom; as in the book of Revelation they are introduced continually, helping the saints in their prayers, assuring them of blessings, taking their side in their warfare with the world: even so it is now.

In these instances, there is no doubt of the angelical ministry and help: but these are but a few out of many beyond number. In these, the Powers of heaven shewed themselves: but in fact, they are continually acting, continually ministering to such as shall be heirs of salvation. So the prayer of Elisha [d] runs: "Lord," (he does not say, "Send Thine Angel and deliver us," but what he says is,) "Open

[d] 2 Kgs. vi. 17.

the eyes of this young man, that he may see:" as though he might have seen the same at any time, if he would but have opened his eyes.

What a view does this present of the unspeakably watchful and tender care of our Lord and Saviour Jesus Christ, over the very humblest and meanest of His servants! that the whole army of Angels and Archangels, all the hosts of the Lord, are set in array for each one of our defence and salvation: ready and glad to refresh us, the members of Christ, as they did Him Who is our Head, after great and sore temptation: to prompt those who wait on us with thoughts for our good, as the Angel that spake to Joseph in a dream: to strengthen us in agony, as he who appeared to our Lord in the garden: to remove difficulties, and declare good tidings, as he who rolled away the stone, and declared, "the Lord is risen." This certainty of angelical aid, so far as we are on Christ's side, we have by His exaltation into heaven, and the subjection to Him of Angels, Authorities and Powers.

But those words, doubtless, mean the evil angels as well as the good; our unseen enemies, as well as our unseen friends. And is it not worth a great deal to know, that the power of our Saviour is over them also, His restraining power, to keep them from harming us, as His gracious encouraging power is with the good Angels, commissioning them to help us to all kinds of blessings? Of this, also, there were wonderful tokens given in the course of our Lord's abode on the earth: first and chiefly, in the Temptation, when He overcame Satan in the wilderness; and afterwards in the power which He continually exercised over the unclean spirits, not only casting them out Himself, but giving power to His disciples to do the same. And in one very particular instance, He shewed us something of the unseen dangers to which we should be continually exposed, in body and estate as well as in spirit, were it not for His continual care to bind Satan, and keep him in chains. The instance I mean is that of the legion of devils, who were driven out of the men possessed with them, and permitted to take possession of a herd of swine; " and behold, the whole herd ran violently down a steep place into the sea, and perished in the waters."

By this we see what would become of us, if God were to take off the chain, with which Satan, since Christ's coming in the flesh, has been more than ever bound. We see that there are bad angels, powers of mischief and darkness, waiting around us on every side, ready to hurry us away into utter destruction both of soul and body, the moment that He in His anger shall let them loose. It is the power of our Lord Christ, sitting at His Father's Right Hand, that binds them. It is He Who says to them, " Thus far shalt thou go, and no further." Without His permission, we see, they could not hurt so much as a herd of swine; with it, the single case of Job shews, how they may vex and torment even good men; and the case of Judas shews still more fearfully what they are allowed to do with the bad, and with those who will not take Christ's warnings.

And, both as to good and bad angels, we must remember that what they do to us in this world, is but a faint type and shadow of what we may expect from them in the world to come: in that last great day, when the one shall gather together God's elect like wheat into His barn; the other shall be cast, with all impenitent sinners, into the lake of everlasting fire.

In these aweful and overpowering reflections, let this be our stay and our warning: that in the world of Angels as well as of men, Christ ascended into heaven, is supreme, and that He has promised to order and direct their power, and even the malice of the bad ones, so as may best work for the good of them that love Him. Nay, His Holy Scriptures teach that we, being united to Him by His Holy Spirit, are in some mysterious way ascended into heaven with Him; therefore we, through Him, except we have lost our hold of Him by our sins, have power to resist and overcome the bad spirits, and are permitted to depend on the succour and protection of the good.

These thoughts are not mere imaginations: they are great and true realities. They are true and real at all times: only, while we are in light and company, they are harder for us fully to receive. But in a few hours we shall be in the darkness; our day's work will be over; we shall be more alone, and more at leisure to think. Let us recall to our minds, then, what we have been taught of the presence of the two sorts of angels. Let us then fancy to ourselves the evil and unclean spirits lying in wait near our beds, ready to vex us with all sorts of bad thoughts, and torment our very bodies, if God would give them leave. Such imaginations are painful and distressing; yet let us not turn away from them, till they have filled us with a real fear of consenting to any bad thought, for that is the only way in which we can give those evil companions power over us.

Let us not try to put out of our minds the notion of the bad angels being around us, until we have turned in serious prayer to Him Who for our sake holds them in chains. Imagine Christ our Lord on His Throne, to which He this day ascended: imagine Him, how His Eye is ever fixed, both on you in your helpless slumbering condition, and on your adversary waiting to hurt you. And be sure, that if, before you lay down, you seriously and reverently committed yourself to Him in prayer, with sincere penitence for all your sins, He will not let the roaring lion devour you. You may, without presumption, imagine Him, then, saying to some of His good Angels, "Here is one who lay down to rest, desiring to dwell under the defence of the Most High; here is one who hath sought, day and night, to abide under the shadow of the Almighty; he hath set his love upon Me, and tried to know My Name; therefore do you, My good Angels, take charge of him, and keep him from the evil that walketh in darkness." And you may imagine that charge especially given to that one among the good spirits, who was set to watch over you at first, on your becoming one of Christ's little ones. And you may thankfully muse on the joy, with which those blessed spirits set about their loving task, and how it pleases them to cherish in you every good and wholesome thought; and how the tempter, finding you so well guarded, will depart, gnashing his teeth for disappointment, and leave you to your quiet slumber.

Such is the comfortable hope with which a penitent, believing person may lie down in sleep, yea, even in death, ever since Jesus Christ went into heaven, and the Angels, Authorities and Powers were made subject unto Him. I say, a penitent, believing, obedient person. For all these blessings depend on our keeping our hold of Christ: and that depends on our sincerely trying to obey Him, in thought, word, and deed.

SERMON II.

EFFECTS OF CHRIST'S ASCENSION.

ASCENSION DAY.

Ps. lxviii. 18.

"*Thou hast ascended on high, Thou hast led captivity captive: Thou hast received gifts for men; yea, for the rebellious also, that the Lord God might dwell among them.*"

As God Almighty graciously taught us how to pray to Him, in the Lord's prayer, so He had long before set us a pattern how to praise Him, by the divine songs of the Old Testament, which He has instructed us, in the New Nestament, to apply to His mercies shewn us in Christ Jesus. Otherwise, so infinite and unspeakable are those mercies, we never surely should have known how to praise Him for them worthily. We never should have known or thought of a hymn worthy the Ascension of our Saviour, had not the Holy Spirit Himself, by the Prophet David, condescended to provide us with one in that glorious Psalm which is appointed by the Church to be used on Whitsunday: in which, under the figure of the Ark of God, carried up to Mount Sion, the praises of our blessed Lord are sung, going up to heaven as the Head of His Church, and sending down the Holy

Comforter, the fountain of all spiritual blessings, to abide among His chosen in His room.

The Psalm, indeed, goes over the whole reach of God's mercies in redeeming His Church, from the beginning to the end; but the most illustrious verse, perhaps, in it, is this, which relates to our Lord's Ascension: "Thou hast ascended on high, Thou hast led captivity captive, Thou hast received gifts for men; yea, for the rebellious also, that the Lord God might dwell among them."

Here you may observe the several parts of the great triumph of our suffering Redeemer, when His glory was made perfect and He was finally exalted as on this day.

First, there is the simple fact of His Ascension: "Thou hast ascended on high."

Next, the effect on His enemies, and on all the powers of darkness: "Thou hast led captivity captive."

Thirdly, the effect on men, even on the worst of men, "the rebellious." He received for them the most precious gifts, insomuch that the Lord God, the Holy Ghost, the Comforter, was sent down by Him to dwell among them.

First of all, consider the simple fact of our Saviour's Ascension, by itself: you will find that there is no end to the wonderful and glorious prospect which it opens to the children of men. Here is One Who is not ashamed to call us brethren; a true Man, as we are; One Who was born like us in all but sin; Who underwent the pains and infirmities of childhood, the trials and troubles of mature age, the agony of fear, the pain of desertion, the bitterness of extreme anguish both of mind and body, and the pangs of a cruel death: One Who loved us so dearly as to suffer all this for our sakes; here we see Him, with the eye of faith, exalted to the Right Hand of God, having all power given Him both in heaven and in earth. He is gone into heaven, the first of all Adam's children, opening the gates of immortality to all believers. He is gone into heaven, the first-fruits of a whole harvest of His redeemed; and by that glorious Ascension we know something of what is prepared for those who try to ascend thither in heart and mind. We know that nothing possibly can be too high or glorious for faithful Christians to hope for, seeing that He, Who is their pattern and example, is raised to the Right Hand of the Almighty Father.

When we have thought most highly and gloriously of all that can make man happy, spiritually happy; perfect peace, purity unstained, a will to do all that God would have done, and power to act and perform that blessed will, an overflowing charity to all the good creatures of the Almighty, and the certainty that we are ourselves beloved by all; above all, the sight of the Most High God, Father, Son, and Holy Ghost, loving us, and drawing us continually nearer to Him: and all this sure to persevere and improve for ever, so that when thousands of millions of years are past, those who for Christ's sake are graciously accepted, will be no nearer an end of their happiness than when it first began: imagine, as you may, all this and whatever else of joy may be suitable to a pure, holy, divine soul; and you will be infinitely far from comprehending the length and breadth, depth and height, of the promises which are sealed to us by the Ascension of our Saviour, and His having all power given Him in heaven and in earth. We know thereby, that the Father of all will not think anything too good for those who are truly conformed to the image of the Only-begotten Son. And yet we are content to let our minds and hearts creep on here on earth, full of such low cares and fancies, as if we knew nothing of heaven, or had no hope of coming to it. God give us better minds, for His merits and intercession's sake, Who is now on high pleading for us!

We see, then, that the mere fact of our Saviour's exaltation ought in all reason to lift us, heart and soul, on high after Him: and when the effect of His Ascension comes to be considered, our duty, and the way to accomplish it, is so much the plainer. For He has overcome our spiritual enemies, and bound the old serpent in chains. "Thou hast led captivity captive," says the Psalmist: that is, "Thou art now like a great warrior, returning in triumph from the field, with a band of captive enemies." And who are the captives subdued by our Saviour? who, but the devil and his angels, the pomps and vanities of this wicked world, and all the sinful lusts of the flesh, one and all chained as it were to His chariot wheels, and making up His glory and victory.

This gives a fearful notion of what we are in fact doing, when we permit ourselves to forget that we are Christians, serving any lust or unworthy desire, instead of practising those tempers, which only can make us fit for everlasting life. We are then taking the wrong part in the great never-ending warfare, between Christ and the power of darkness. We are serving and honouring those whom Christ is leading captive, the host of enemies dragged at His chariot wheels, instead of serving Him Who, with one act of His will could reduce all such enemies to nothing. What can come of such madness, but utter confusion and ruin ere long?

If, indeed, we could not help ourselves, if we had no power given us to make a better choice, such behaviour were more excusable. But observe what follows next: "Thou hast received gifts for men." What gifts? S. Paul replies in the Epistle to the Ephesians[a]: they are the manifold gifts of the Holy Ghost: "grace given to every man according to the proportion of the gift of Christ." It is in vain then for any man longer to say, "I meant well, but my enemies were too powerful." How should they be more powerful than your Friend and never-failing Helper, the Holy and Almighty Spirit of the Father and the Son?

For of Him, i. e. of the Holy Spirit sent down by the Mediator, the Psalmist is undoubtedly speaking, in the last words of that astonishing verse: "That the Lord God might dwell among them." The Lord God, the Holy Ghost, is personally present in the hearts and bodies of all believers. He dwells in each one of us, as in a temple. The word must be spoken in all reverence, but it may be spoken: What more could Omnipotence itself do for us, than to send an Almighty Helper to dwell in our hearts? We may speak thus, for God Himself has taught us to do so, when He asks concerning His vineyard, the Church: "[b]What could have been done more for My vineyard,

---

[a] Eph. iv. 7.   [b] Is. v. 4.

that I have not done in it?" Were the most perverse and froward of men left to choose what he would have to help him in goodness, what could he ask for more, than the blessed and sanctifying Spirit, for ever present, ready to make clean his very heart, and to purify his inmost thoughts and desires?

When people are outwardly left to themselves, when they lose their parents, elders, and instructors, by death, departure, or otherwise, and then yield to temptation, and go wrong; they are ready enough to plead for themselves, that they had no friend near to warn or advise them. But he who will believe and attend to the Scriptures, as interpreted by the Church in the Prayer Book, that man knows that he cannot plead so; for he has always not only at hand, but dwelling within him, the Parent and Elder, the Friend and Instructor of all reasonable and understanding creatures. He cannot say that he goes wrong unwarned, who has the wisdom of God ever ready to warn him.

And, that no Christian man might imagine himself shut out of this great blessing, and entitled to justify his sins through his want of spiritual aid; observe what is hinted of those, among whom the Lord God, the Holy Ghost, sent down by the Son, vouchsafes to dwell. They are not all good and obedient. Very far from it: they are too many of them rebellious. Christ "received gifts for men, yea, for the rebellious also, that the Lord God might dwell among them."

The Psalmist might mean the word "rebellious," at first, of the stubborn Jews, who kept tempting God, both in the wilderness and in the promised land. "They rebelled and vexed His Holy Spirit,"

Which He had put within them, and sent to dwell among them: they became discontented, lustful, unbelieving, even in sight of the cloud of Glory, by which He shewed Himself from time to time over the door of the tabernacle, checking them for their sins, and telling them the way they should go. Yet He still abode among them: He took not away the Glory from them: although, as long as they refused to be guided by it, it turned not to their blessing, but to their greater punishment.

In like manner, the New Testament teaches, that God's Holy Spirit, the true Cloud of Glory, is given to all Christians in Baptism; but it is at their peril to rebel and vex Him afterwards. If they do, still they cannot drive Him away: He continues among them for judgement and condemnation, if they will not let His gracious Presence conduct them to the mercy which He meant for them. Not indeed visibly, but yet truly, He dwells in every one of us as in a temple, as truly as He dwelt in the whole congregation of the Jews by that bright cloud of His, which declared His presence over the Ark.

As baptized Christians, the Holy Ghost, the Comforter, does truly abide within us. This is too great and fearful a thing to be thought on, if the Scripture of God, the Voice of the same Spirit, had not expressly made it known. S. Paul, speaking to all the Corinthians, who had, of course, various degrees of grace, and of whom some were far gone in things very contrary to God's Spirit; yet, speaking to them all, he says, "c Know ye not that your body is the temple of the Holy Ghost, which is in you?" By

---

c 1 Cor. vi. 19.

this we know for certain, that even from rebellious Christians the Holy Spirit does not so depart, but that they still continue under the special curse of defiling God's Temple, every time that by sinful indulgence they abuse their own or others' bodies, or by sinful desires pollute their souls. Over and above the judgement due to those, who break God's general commandment of purity, they bring on themselves a special judgement, as profaners of God's Ark and Temple. And so of all other sins. Whatever is contrary to God's Holy Spirit, being practised by a Christian man, is a sin against the Temple, is as if it were committed in a Church, and will draw down a sentence accordingly.

Now then, add to all this the most serious thought of all, namely, that we are not speaking of things at a distance: you, and I, and each particular Christian, is the person, of whom these wonderful sayings are written down in the book of God. You are the person to whom God is revealed in His only Son Incarnate; for you Christ died; for you He sits on high, ordering all things both in this world and in that unseen world, so as shall turn undoubtedly to your good, if you truly try to love God. You are the man, in whom the Holy Ghost has condescended, ever since your Baptism, to abide, as in a Temple and Ark of His own. What a thought is this for you to carry about in the daily concerns of your life! What a fountain of humiliation and self-abasing sorrow, when you think over the past! What a spring of holy desires and good resolutions, if you have the courage to make them, for the future!

If the Holy Ghost be dwelling in us, since He is

a pure Spirit, and thoughts, in His sight, are as distinct and as real as actions; then every time you indulge wrong desires, proud, or covetous, or unkind, or lustful imaginations, you are as if you made God's Church a place for actions of the same kind. Who then can remember his own past thoughts, and not be overwhelmed with the mighty sum of his offences committed in this way?

On the other hand, if the Holy Ghost be dwelling in you, since He is an Almighty Friend, there is hope even for the vilest: there is encouragement for those who have been most rebellious, to resolve anew and more earnestly, that they will be such no longer. Therefore, although it is fearful to think of Him so very near us, considering what sort of persons conscience tells us we must be in His sight, yet we dare not pray as S. Peter once did, in hasty alarm, not knowing what he said, "Depart from me, for I am a sinful man, O Lord:" rather we pray every day, as the Church has taught us, in the words of the penitent David, "Cast me not away from Thy presence, and take not Thy Holy Spirit from me." Cast us not away, though we have deserved the worst; and take Him not away, though we have so often grieved and vexed Him by our sins; but for the sake of Him Who is gone into heaven, to plead for rebels and sinners at His Father's Right Hand, grant, O Lord, that the Holy Comforter may still continue with us on earth, and we with Him in Thy Church: that what little good remains in us, and seems often ready to die, may be strengthened; and that our evils, great and manifold as they are, may be purged out by Thy grace and help: that when our King returns from Heaven, we may not be found among "the rebellious."

SERMON III.

OUR LORD'S LAST PRAYER.

ASCENSION DAY.

S. JOHN xvii. 11.

" And now I am no more in the world, but these are in the world, and I come to Thee. Holy Father, keep through Thine own Name those whom Thou hast given Me, that they may be one, as We are."

WHAT Christian would not listen earnestly to the last prayer of Jesus Christ, and account himself very undutiful, if ever he should permit himself to slight what his Lord prayed for, immediately before He departed? Now this prayer in the seventeenth of S. John may be considered in some sense as His last prayer; for it was offered up just before His aweful atoning Sacrifice of Himself on the Cross, and it refers throughout to His Ascension which was to take Him finally from among men, as to something immediately to happen. It is therefore much the same in regard of our Lord, as the last words and prayers of a departing person are in regard of *him*. We may well believe that what He then prayed for on behalf of His Apostles, was the same which He desired for them in that solemn blessing, which He pronounced just before His Ascension. "He led them out as far as to Bethany and lifted up His Hands, and blessed them. And it came to pass while He blessed them, that He was parted from them, and carried up into heaven." We can hardly doubt that one chief point of this blessing was that same heavenly Unity which He had before prayed for on their behalf: that they might be one with Him, and through Him one with the Father, and through the Father and the Son, one with each other: true members of Jesus Christ, and truly making up one holy and mysterious Body, one Church, of which He is the Head.

This blessing He asked, not for the Apostles alone, but for all Christians. "Neither pray I for these alone," saith He, "but for them also which shall believe on Me through their word; that they all may be one; as Thou, Father, art in Me, and I in Thee, that they also may be one in Us." "The glory which Thou gavest Me I have given them; that they may be one, even as We are one: I in them, and Thou in Me, that they may be made perfect in one."

See how the notion of being altogether one, runs through the whole of this Divine prayer: how our Redeemer dwells upon it, as if it were the great point, the great object of all, quite necessary to the accomplishment of the work, for which He came into the world. And observe that the prayer was uttered just before that great and unspeakable Sacrifice of Himself upon the Cross: even as now, when Christians of our Church are making their solemn offering in memory of that Sacrifice, the very first and chiefest blessing they ask is, that God would "inspire continually the universal Church with the spirit of truth, unity, and concord; and that all they that do confess His holy Name may agree, in the truth of His holy

Word, and live in unity and godly love." As that prayer goes before the consecration of the Holy Communion, so our Lord's intercession for Unity went just before His giving His Body to be broken and His Blood shed on the Cross for His people. It seems as if that unity were a great part of our Redemption, or at any rate, very closely connected with it.

And to confirm this, observe on the other hand, that our Lord uttered that wonderful intercession just after He had been ordaining the Sacrament of Unity, the communion of His Body and Blood. How that is a Sacrament of Unity, S. Paul explains in one of his epistles to the Corinthians. "[a] We being many are one bread, and one body; for we are all partakers of that one bread." The pressing together of so many corns into one loaf is a type of the moulding of all Christians, rightly baptized, into one spiritual Body: and the partaking of that one Bread is the partaking of Christ's Body, and incorporates us more and more with Him.

Moreover, all those forty days, from the Resurrection to the Ascension, Christ continued with His Apostles, speaking of the things (no doubt) which were most necessary to be told them, to prepare the way for His return. And what were those things? They were such as pertain to the kingdom of God. The kingdom of God, i.e. the Church universal, took up the greater part of our Lord's instructions now in the portion of time before His departure.

No doubt then, as I said before, this mysterious blessing of Unity had much to do with God's Church and kingdom: rather one may say, it seemed the very same thing.

[a] 1 Cor. x. 17.

And, that the Apostles so understood it, they gave these signs immediately: that after our Lord's departure they all kept together: that the one thing they did before the descent of the Holy Ghost was ordaining one to take Judas' place, and complete the unity of the body, damaged by his fall: that when the Spirit came, He found them "all with one accord in one place."

On returning from the holy Mount, where they had lost sight of our Lord, they did not go apart to seek God each his own several way; but they went, S. Luke tells us, into an upper room, where abode the eleven Apostles, all of them, continuing in prayer and supplication with the women, the devout women who had attended our Lord from Galilee, and with Mary the Mother of Jesus, and with His disciples.

Again, whereas the treachery and death of Judas had made a breach in the Apostolical body, a rent in the Lord's garment, which should be without seam, they knew it to be His will that this should be healed, and the Body made one, as at first, to be ready for the descent of the Holy Spirit: and therefore without losing time they proceeded to elect one, S. Matthias, in the place of Judas. "He was numbered with the eleven Apostles," and so the Mystery of Unity, as far as men could provide for it, being complete, the whole Body continued waiting in prayer for the Baptism of the Holy Ghost. Even as at man's first creation, God formed man out of the dust of the earth, and the entire body was formed, and lay ready to have "breathed into its nostrils the breath of life, and so man became a living soul," after the image of Him Who created him.

Thirdly, the aweful and unspeakable moment itself of the descent of the Blessed Comforter found them all with one accord in one place. They were not scattered abroad in their several habitations, some serving God in one way, some in another; but all were "with one accord in one place." They were "with one accord:" that was, as it were, the soul of their Christian unity: they were "in one place:" that was the body of it. And being thus prepared both in body and soul, they had the third and most glorious part of a Christian man's being, wonderfully added to them. "Suddenly there came a sound from heaven as of a rushing mighty wind, and they were all filled with the Holy Ghost." And so from being only body and soul, they became body and soul and spirit; body and soul and all that they had, began to be sanctified in a heavenly manner, and transformed by the indwelling Spirit into the likeness of Jesus Christ.

This was God's blessing upon the Apostles, the holy women, the Mother of Jesus, and His disciples, they doing all in their power to keep up that heavenly Unity, for which their Lord had prayed so earnestly, and which He recommended to them in so many ways. Surely if ever we are to hope for a return of something like the blessing of Pentecost, a great outpouring of God's gracious Spirit, there is reason to think that some great and earnest longing and prayer for Unity, and self-denial for Unity's sake, must go before it. The body must be made one again, before the breath of that first life can be expected to be breathed into it. I say, *made* one *again*. For where now is that Christian Unity? Where are all, or the greater part, of Christians "with one accord in one place?" No man surely can deny that the Unity, for which our Lord prayed and which was so blessed by His Spirit, is, in a great measure, lost from among Christians. No man can tell how very serious the consequence of that loss may be, to his own soul, and to the Church generally: no man can be sure that his own personal unworthiness has not a great deal to do with the sad darkness and divisions which prevail, where all ought to be light and peace. Alas! how is this glorious and happy day turned into a day of grief and humiliation, because the members of Christ, being stained with many sins, have been permitted by the just Judge to separate themselves, or to cast one another off! "[b]How is the gold become dim, and the most fine gold changed!" To human eyes, all might almost seem lost in confusion. But He in His great mercy still permits us to pray, in humble following our Lord's intercession, that all Christians may again be one, again united in the one true Church, as we hope even now they may be invisibly united. He commands us to pray, and we do so pray, when we say, "Thy kingdom come." He commands us so to live, that that and our other prayers may be heard. He commands us, especially, to love one another; to make allowance for each other's doubts and difficulties; to avoid offence; to fast and pray and labour for peace. So doing, in the end we may trust to find His peace for ourselves: and we may do some little towards obtaining for His whole people the "blessing of Peace."

[b] Lam. iv. 1.

SERMON IV.

SHOWERS OF BLESSING.

ASCENSION DAY.

Ezek. xxxiv. 26.

"I will make them and the places round about My hill a blessing; and I will cause the shower to come down in his season: there shall be showers of blessing."

S. Luke tells us in one of the lessons for to-day, that when the time was fully come for our Lord to depart out of this world unto the Father, "[a] He led" His disciples "out as far as to Bethany, and He lifted up His Hands and blessed them. And it came to pass, that while He blessed them, He was parted from them, and carried up into heaven." It was while He was blessing them: the evangelist repeats the word, as being something to be very much thought of. God the Son departed from His outward and visible home among men in the very act of pronouncing His solemn Benediction. He might have departed in thunder and lightning, in such a storm as might severely punish this whole wicked world, and especially the sinful city which had so rejected Him. He will so depart, when He ascends into heaven the second time, when the last judgement is over. He will leave the world burning under His feet.

[a] S. Luke xxiv. 50, 51.

But on His first Ascension it was far otherwise. All around Him was grace and blessing: so that to Mount Olivet and the disciples kneeling round, and to the precious unspeakable gifts, which our Lord poured down from heaven as He went up, we might very well apply the prophet's saying in the text, "I will make them and the places round My hill a blessing." As if He should say, "These who kneel around Me, as I go up from Mount Olivet: and not only they, but all the places within reach of that mountain, on every side of it, I will make them all a blessing; the Apostles first, and other Christians afterwards. All men that see and notice them shall say, that they are 'the seed whom the Lord hath blessed.'" And "there shall be showers of blessing." God's grace shall come down so abundantly, that it shall supply all men's wants, and satisfy all their desires, as we are taught in our Whitsunday Psalm: "[b] Thou, O God, sentest a gracious rain upon Thine inheritance, and refreshedst it when it was weary." Christ our Saviour went up to His Father's Right Hand, and made haste to send down His "showers of blessing." If you can imagine all the blessings of departing parents, masters, governors, spiritual pastors, gathered together in the greatest possible perfection, and poured out without stint on those whom they leave behind: this will give you some faint idea of the treasures of joy and comfort which our Lord's Ascension opened to all believers.

Observe how He ordered the very outward circumstances of it, making them all as gracious as possible. As true loving friends, departing from their

[b] Ps. lxviii. 9.

friends among men for any length of time, are very regardful of each others' feelings and wishes; they consider how they may leave them pleasant recollections, and contrive the manner of their parting accordingly, so did our Lord. He prepared them by degrees for His going; and when He went, He had provided such store of comforts, that, instead of sorrow filling their hearts, as might be expected when their beloved Master was departing, "they returned to Jerusalem," we read, " with great joy."

Consider the place which He chose for His Ascent. It was on the Mount of Olives, over against Jerusalem, hard by the village of Bethany. In leading them out thither from Jerusalem, He would have in the first place to go over the brook Kedron, and then across or very near the garden of Gethsemane; almost along the same ground as He had trodden with them on the night of His Agony. Think then what joy and comfort it must have been to them, as they went on, recollecting at every step, how sad and bitter the course of things had been, when they were with Him that night: what a happy and glorious change now!

Again, Bethany was the nearest village to the spot of His Ascension: Bethany, the town of Mary and her sister Martha: where He had been used to lodge when He came near to Jerusalem: and where, a few weeks before, He had raised up Lazarus from the dead. From this place He chose to ascend to His Father's Right Hand. There, rather than any where else, He would leave His last footsteps on earth: continuing thus His favours to Martha and Mary and Lazarus, and giving a token to all whom He left behind, that He still loved with an everlasting love His own which were in the world. His favour and gracious remembrance still abode with those places and persons, which had been more especially devoted to His honour and service. The grave from which He had raised Lazarus was very near the spot from which He now ascended, so that the twelve, who were with Him in that miracle, could not fail to think of it: and it would help to carry their minds forward to the day when they should again hear His Voice, and come forth as Lazarus did; not however, as did Lazarus, to return again to corruption, but to ascend after their Lord into heaven with glorified bodies, and abide with Him for ever.

Thus the very place from which it pleased Him to go up was a token of His love to those whom He left behind. But a still more special token was the commission which He gave them to be always employed in His service: "^cye shall be witnesses to Me both in Judæa and Samaria and unto the uttermost parts of the earth." As dutiful children and servants are never so well pleased as when he whom they love and reverence gives them something particular to do for his sake, something which may give them occasion to shew how truly they long to be dutiful and thankful towards him: so must the Apostles have felt greatly honoured and encouraged, when their Lord, at parting, promised them that they should be His true witnesses everywhere: especially as He accompanied the charge with an assurance of the help, without which it could not be fulfilled: "ye shall receive power after the Holy Ghost hath come upon you;" "behold

^c Acts i. 8.

I send" Him, "the Promise of My Father, upon you." "I will not leave you comfortless, I will come unto you." My brethren, these sayings do not belong to those only, who were kneeling round and gazing after our Saviour as He went up. They belong to us also; for we too by our baptismal vow are called on to be witnesses to our Saviour in all the world, and we too have "the Promise of the Father," the Holy Spirit come down to dwell in our hearts. These sayings then of our Lord on His departure are "showers of blessing" for us also; showers of blessing coming down on those who follow Him through Gethsemane to Bethany, through His sufferings to His works of love and mercy: showers of blessing on those who gather around Him in His holy hill, which is the Church, and there on their knees humbly look after Him, trusting in His gracious intercession, and patiently wait His return to take them unto Himself.

To such persons, as well as to the Apostles, His farewell blessing was no doubt pronounced. We are not told the words of that blessing: we only read that "[c] He lifted up His Hands and blessed them." He used the same action, with which before He had been accustomed to seal His gracious benedictions: reaching forth His Divine Hands, and laying them on the sick or the infants who were brought to Him for that purpose; and sometimes without actual touch, only stretching forth His hands towards them: as in the sermon which S. Luke relates, He stretched forth His hands towards His disciples, and said, "[d] Blessed be ye poor, for your's is the kingdom of heaven." This then was the outward sign, with which He ac-

[c] S. Luke xxiv. 50.   [d] Ib. vi. 20.

companied His farewell: thereby sealing as it were afresh, and renewing for ever, all the solemn blessings, which He had at any time pronounced over any one during His abode on earth. And His blessing looked forward also. In that one action of His, and in the solemn words which accompanied it, were gathered together the force and virtue of all the solemn blessings, which His Bishops and Priests have ever since pronounced in His Church. That blessing is continued and repeated to us in every sacramental act: as when the water of our Baptism is sanctified, when we are signed with the Sign of the Cross, when the Priest solemnly blesses us, at home or in Church, in sickness or in health, when he says over us, believing and penitent, the gracious words of Absolution and remission of sins. But what more especially seems to remind us of Christ on Mount Olivet lifting up His Hands to give a blessing, is the lifting up the hands of His servants the Bishops, when persons are confirmed, or ordained, or otherwise solemnly blessed by them. In all such holy and Christian actions, done according to the mind of the Church with true faith in Jesus Christ, we may discern the Presence of Him our only Saviour, blessing us as He goes up, and continuing to bless us after He has gone up. Every one of them, by His mercy, may help to prepare us for that final and eternal blessing, which He will pronounce over His elect at the Last Day: "Come, ye blessed of My Father; inherit the kingdom prepared for you from the beginning of the world." As this was the great farewell, so that will be the great welcome. We have had by His distinguishing mercy our portion in the first; may we so live as not to miss of the second! We know that as our Lord went, so He will return. Be it our care to receive Him then with hearts, if possible, as true and perfect, as were the hearts of His Apostles and followers when they parted from Him. Let us be found of Him on our knees, or at least on the knees of our hearts; looking up steadfastly towards Him by heavenly thoughts and holy prayers. Let us be found in Bethany, in the home of His true servants, such as Mary, Martha and Lazarus: employed in works of Christian love, not in the wild businesses and vanities of the world; or else may He find us in the Mount of Olives, the place of holy and heavenly contemplation, repenting of our sins and humbling ourselves under His Cross. In a word, when His last message, sent at this time by His Angels to His Apostles, is fulfilled, and He shall come again into our sight on His cloud of glory; then may He grant us to be found waiting for Him in His Church, and waiting on Him in His poor and afflicted. So be it, through His mercy, Who is the Alpha and Omega, the Beginning and the End of all blessing! May He bless us now with the gift of His Body and Blood, and hereafter with that perfect unspeakable Union, which He is preparing for us at His Father's Right Hand!

SERMON V.

THE DRAWING OF JESUS BY HIS ASCENSION.

ASCENSION DAY.

The Song of Solomon i. 4.

"*Draw me, we will run after Thee: the King hath brought me into His chambers : we will be glad and rejoice in Thee.*"

WE of Christ's Church are, on this day, as persons out of whose sight a dear friend has just gone, watching the door through which He vanished out of our sight. Jesus Christ has been so long, three and thirty years and more, going in and out among us; and now in a moment He is gone. A cloud receives Him out of our sight. He is gone; and we, His flock and people, may seem to be left alone on earth. We have gone out with Him to the mount of Olives, to the garden, where His sad sufferings had their beginning. He has led us out on this road as far as Bethany, the village where He had last had something like a home on earth : choosing the place of His departure in such a way, as if He would bid farewell at once to all the troubles and all the comforts of this world, and leave His blessing on both. I say, if we have read the Gospels in faith, we have in spirit accompanied our Lord with His Apostles for the last time to that well-known and chosen spot; we have heard His parting commands; He hath lifted up His hands and blessed us, and in adoring wonder we have seen, how in the very act of blessing He was parted from us, and with quiet and gentle motion was lifted up into heaven, and slowly and gradually taken out of our sight, a cloud coming between Him and us, as it comes between the stars and us.

Jesus Christ, our Saviour and Redeemer, is gone away from us into heaven, and we are left here on earth. What shall we do? Shall we wait kneeling here on the hill, watching, as it were, the door through which He vanished? Shall we gaze on that spot of the heavens, until He return, as He promised, again? This indeed to a loving heart might seem most desirable of all things, so to go on contemplating our departed Saviour: even as those who from their hearts are mourning for a deceased parent or friend sometimes feel as if they would gladly go on thinking of him all their lives, and give up every thing else: as the aged Jacob, when he was told that Joseph was lost: "I will go down to the grave to my son mourning."

Something of this sort might well suit the inclinations of some loving hearts. But His will was plainly declared, that His disciples should not so gaze up after Him, nor so mourn His departure, as to withdraw themselves in any degree from the tasks He had set them. By His angels He sent us this message: "[a] Why stand ye gazing up into heaven?" And to His Apostles, when He was preparing them for this

[a] Acts i. 11.

day, He said, "Because I have said these things unto you,—because I have said, I go away, sorrow hath filled your heart. And yet, if ye loved Me, *Me* chiefly and not yourselves, you would rejoice, because I said, I go to the Father." He told them beforehand, true love would make them rejoice when they saw Him go out of their sight: and now, when the time is come, we read that they worshipped Him, and returned to Jerusalem with great joy. It was to them, as it has been to the Church ever since, a matter of the deepest joy and thanksgiving, that Christ is gone up out of sight to His Father's Right Hand.

So the Bride in the Song of Solomon, the mystical Bride in the text, invites us to rejoice. "The King hath brought me into His chambers: we will be glad and rejoice in Thee." Why are we all to be glad and rejoice? Because Jesus Christ, the great Bridegroom, has begun to lift up the Church, His Bride, into Heaven. In the womb of the Blessed Virgin, of her substance, He took to Himself a pure Body, and so first espoused to Himself our human nature: marrying, if I may so speak, the Manhood to the Godhead, so that the two should never more be divided, but for ever united in His most Sacred Person. And now, by His Ascension, He hath unspeakably glorified, and that for ever, His Human Soul and Body, made, as it was at the first, like us in all things, sin only excepted. He humbled it in the garden, at the Cross, and in the grave: and now He hath glorified it far beyond His humiliation. He hath taken His Soul and Body as a spouse into the Bedchamber, and thereby hath given to each soul and body of Adam's seed an invitation and power, to have a share in that glory. Well then may we, as well as the Apostles, be glad and rejoice on Ascension Day!

We are not then merely to gaze after Him; we are not to stand bewailing ourselves for His absence: but this one thing we are to do. For the whole of our time, until He come again or call us into His Presence, we are to set about fulfilling His dying commands. *That* is the point. He is gone, but will come again some day, no one can tell how soon: and in the meantime we are to do all His bidding.

And what is His bidding? That we should run after Him: that we should obtain a place in the same heaven where He is gone before: and in order thereunto, that we should even now ascend thither in heart and mind. But because the Church knows that we cannot by mere wishing obtain such a mind as this, therefore she prays, and teaches us to pray. "Draw me," she humbly and seriously prays, "and we will run after Thee." As if she should say, "I know well that in me, i.e. in my flesh, dwelleth and abideth no good thing: therefore it must be quite changed and renewed; and this is far too hard a task for me: I commend it therefore to Thee, O Lord. Take me in hand, I beseech Thee, and draw me constantly and mightily towards Thee. Fill my heart with a sincere love of Thee, and of that heaven where Thou art gone. Attract and entice it towards Thee, unworthy as it is, by all sorts of loving and affectionate dealings. Draw me towards Thee by Thy good providence, ordering the events of my life; the friends and acquaintance that I meet with; my joys and sorrows, my health and sickness, my employments and diversions, secretly and wonderfully, in such sort as shall most turn my soul from the world and turn it towards Thee. Draw me towards Thee again by the reading and hearing of Thy most holy and heavenly Scriptures: causing me to light in the proper time upon those verses that will do me good: to hang upon them: to taste all their sweetness, or, if need be, all their bitterness; not to let them go till they have become, as it were, part of my mind, and are in a way to do me the whole good Thou intendedst by them. Draw me by the noble and winning examples of the holy men women and children, whom Thou from time to time hast blessed with a double portion of Thy Spirit: shew me Thine own brightness upon them, and incline my heart to delight in it: for, left to myself, I know too well, I shall but neglect or even hate it. Draw me, once more, and most of all, draw me, I pray Thee, by Thy most holy and lifegiving Sacrament. There, above all, help me to taste and see how gracious Thou, O Lord, art: there let me touch Thee, as Thou didst promise to S. Mary Magdalene, now that Thou art ascended to the Father: let me in the Sacrament of Thy love touch but the hem of Thy garment, and by that draw me onward and upward, till, my old impure self being thoroughly put off and cast aside, I being wholly and only Thine, may dwell only and wholly with Thee."

This is the Christian soul's prayer, when she muses earnestly on her Lord's Ascension. Thus day and night she seems to say to Him, "Draw me." But that is not all. She knows well that her holy prayers and heavenly desires, if not embodied as it were in deeds, would soon cease to be holy and heavenly: they would vanish in the air like thin clouds, which never drop down in wholesome dew. This the enlightened soul greatly fears: and therefore she cries out not only, "Draw me;" not only does she pray with all her might for the grace, without which she can do nothing, but she is careful to add always, "We will run after Thee: we will act, and that heartily and zealously, according to the good desires which Thou breathest into us." "Draw me," that is her devout petition: "we will run after Thee," that is her humble and courageous vow, her good resolution made on her knees before God. And we know that these two things must go along with every good prayer, viz. a devout petition, and a humble and courageous purpose. But now mark well the word, in which the devout soul expresses her holy intention. She says, "We will *run* after Thee." She does not say walk, but run. For why? She is full of love: she is like a loving child who has caught sight of his father at a distance, and we see that, when that happens, the child does not creep slowly towards his father, but runs to meet him as fast as ever he can. So should we, permitted, as we are, to behold our Lord with the eye of faith afar off on His Throne in heaven. We must not walk, but run towards Him: or if we cannot run, because we are weak through sin, at least we must endeavour to walk our very best. The child, who for love runs out to meet his parent, does not mind his playthings if they happen to lie in the way: or if he minds them, he does not stop for them. No more should we mind the playthings, the toys of earth, when, according to the Church's invitation, we are hastening after our Lord.

But you will say, "It is so hard to disengage one's-self from these earthly cares; they have so wound themselves about us, like clinging weeds, before we were aware. And in truth it *is* hard: but observe, Jesus Christ, because He knows it is hard, has told us how we may get strength to do it. Because we have to run after Him, and He knows we have little strength, therefore He teaches us to say, "Draw me:" as the little child that wishes to run and cannot, stretches out its arms and asks for help as well as it can. Since then He has taught us to pray, we may not doubt that He will help us to run after Him: any more than the young child doubts the mother's or nurse's will to help him. He will set your heart at liberty, that you may run the way of His commandments. He will help you to untie for ever the bands and chains of evil habit, which fasten you, as yet, more or less down to earth, so that you may be free to ascend to Him in heart and mind, and with Him continually dwell. Morning by morning, and evening by evening, say to Him in earnest, "Draw me;" and day by day you will find yourself better able to run after Him. Again, endeavour day by day to run after Him, to be more alert in His service, and you will be helped morning by morning to pray to Him more earnestly.

And even as those, who are teaching young children to run, very often go before them, and run a little way themselves, and then turn and entice them onwards, beckoning to them with all kinds of affectionate endearments: so our loving Lord before He went up into heaven, had in our sight hastened along the very worst of the rough way which He calls upon us to tread: and now, with unutterable yearning love, He turns towards us from His holy eternal Rest, and beckons us onward by a thousand signs, which we shall see and understand more and more, as our hearts are more open to any kind of goodness. Every hour something happens, by which He speaks to the believing soul, and says, "Behold. Me here preparing a place for you: are you preparing yourself for the place?"

O may we often, very often, think of Him in this manner: of Him and of this His own Ascension Day! May the remembrance of Him, caring for us in heaven, sweeten and allay the troubles of this life, quicken all our languid obedience, and above all, keep us from the horrid ingratitude of affronting Him by wilful sin!

"O holy and merciful Saviour, Thou hast been lifted up from the earth, in order to draw all men unto Thee: Thou knowest how corrupt, how childish we are: draw nigh unto us, O Lord, that we may draw nigh unto Thee!"

SERMON VI.

THE BENEFIT OF OUR LORD'S INTERCESSION, DEPENDENT ON COMMUNION WITH HIM.

ASCENSION DAY.

HEB. vii. 25.

"*He is able to save them to the uttermost that come unto God by Him, seeing He ever liveth to make intercession for them.*"

GREAT indeed, and most blessed, is the mystery of this day: that God our Saviour, He Who suffered for us on earth, should now and evermore be in heaven, at His Father's Right Hand, pleading for us, reigning over us, ruling His Church and preparing it for heavenly glory: and also preparing for it a place, that, in His own good time, He may come and receive it unto Himself, that where the Head is, there the Body may be also. That God the Son should be in heaven, is of course no wonder at all. He was there, of course, through all the time of His affliction and sufferings. Even then He described Himself to Nicodemus as "the Son of Man, Who is in heaven;" and this, by virtue of His Divine Power and Godhead, whereby He is evermore one with the Everlasting Father. But this is the wonder, this the mystery, this is our joy and bliss on Ascension Day, that the Body and Soul which had been humbled to such extremity of pain and shame and death; spit upon, buffeted, stript, scourged, pierced with nails, laid in the grave; the Soul which was exceeding sorrowful, and felt as if the Father had forsaken it; that Soul and Body are now set "at the Father's Right Hand in the heavenly places, far above all principality and power and might and dominion, and every name that is named, not only in this world, but also in that which is to come, and hath all things put under its feet."

The better to enable us to conceive this unspeakable exaltation of the Man Christ Jesus, and the innumerable benefits which we receive thereby, holy Church draws our attention, in the services of this day, to Moses going up to the mount, and to the blessings thereby vouchsafed unto God's people Israel. Moses, we know, was a special type and figure of our Lord: as was promised, "ᵃThe Lord your God shall raise you up a prophet of your brethren like unto me." And Moses was remarkably like unto Christ in his ascension. You know what I mean by Moses' ascension: his going up into Mount Sinai to meet the Lord, while the rest of the people staid below. They were so amazed and affrighted at the fearful sights and sounds, betokening the near approach of the great and dreadful God, that they removed and stood afar off, and their prayer was, "Let not God speak with us, lest we die." They were like all sinners when the Lord touches their hearts: they felt themselves quite unworthy to draw near and speak to God: they longed for a mediator, one

ᵃ Acts iii. 22.

to be between God and them: they said to Moses, "ᵇGo thou near, and hear all that the Lord our God shall say, and speak to us all that the Lord our God shall speak unto thee, and we will hear it and do it." God approved of this. He said, "ᶜThey have well said all that they have spoken." And so it was ordered: Moses went up and was in their stead, before God. Moses, one of themselves: he went up as surety and representative of the whole people, to transact with the Almighty this great business of the covenant between Him and them, on which all their good and happiness depended. So is the Son of God, our Moses, one of ourselves, "of our flesh and of our bones," gone up out of our sight, even to the highest heavens, " to appear in the Presence of God for us."

Then, as Moses went to receive the two Tables of the Law, on which the covenant, even the ten commandments, was written with the Finger of God, so Jesus Christ went up for this among other purposes, "that He might receive gifts for men." What gifts? The New Law, and the Holy Spirit to write it in our hearts; with all His manifold outpourings of grace, "ᵈfor the perfecting of the saints, for the work of the ministry, for the edifying of the Body of Christ." This gift, our Lord plainly tells us, could not, in the counsels of God, be granted, until He had gone up to heaven. "ᵉIt is expedient for you that I go away: for if I go not away, the Comforter will not come unto you." And alas! my brethren, without the Comforter, without the Blessed Spirit of God to write all His laws in our hearts, what profit should we

ᵇ Deut. v. 27.   ᶜ Ib. 28.   ᵈ Eph. iv. 12.   ᵉ S. John xvi. 7.

have either of the blessed laws themselves, or even of His Divine Love in dying to atone for our breach of them? Heaven itself will be no heaven; the Cross will be no salvation to *us*, except our hearts be turned and changed by His Almighty grace. Were it only on this account, then, our Lord's Ascension would be infinitely more to us, than Moses going up to the mount could be to the Israelites; that Moses brought down only the letter of the law, the ten commandments written and engraven in stones; but Christ sent down the living and life-giving Spirit, Who should both instruct us what to do, and also unite us to Him, i. e. to Christ Jesus, through Whom we may have grace and strength, really to do it.

Thirdly, Moses had not only to appear before God for his brethren, and to obtain for them the gift of the holy law, but even before that errand was completed, he had to perform this further work of love for them; to intercede in their behalf, and obtain God's gracious pardon, for that they had already sinned grievously against one of His chiefest laws: they had turned aside quickly out of the way which He had commanded them: they had made them a molten calf. God's sentence had already begun to go out[f]: "Let Me alone, that I may destroy them utterly, and make of thee a great nation." Upon which, Moses, his heart overflowing with love to his backsliding brethren, began to plead most earnestly for them. He besought the Lord, by His great mercies hitherto vouchsafed, by the memory of His servants Abraham Isaac and Jacob, and by His promises made to them; by all this he pleaded with

[f] Ex. xxxii. 10.

God for mercy, and God, in His tender love, heard the intercession of His servant, and both spared those sinners for the present, and afterwards, when Moses came up a second time, to renew the covenant, with the new tables in his hand which he had hewed like unto the first, the Lord accepted his fasting and prayer, continued yet another forty days, and promised to accept the penitence of His people, to forgive them this great sin, and to go up in the midst of them into the land of Canaan. Now what was Moses in this holy and loving work, but a true type of our Saviour in heaven, interceding for our manifold breaches of His sacred law? As S. Paul describes Him in the text, "He ever liveth to make intercession for them that come to God by Him;" and S. John in those golden words, "[g]If any man sin, we have an Advocate with the Father, Jesus Christ the Righteous." He pleads for us with the Father, reminding Him of the perfect Sacrifice which He offered once for all on the Cross: He presents to the Father the Body and Blood, which He, this day, took up with Him to heaven, for a constant memorial of that Sacrifice: and thus, although His bloody atoning Sacrifice is completed, never to be renewed, yet is He for ever offering for us in heaven; He hath an unchangeable Priesthood; He is our High Priest for ever, after the order of Melchizedec. Moses indeed was no priest, but only a great prophet and a sort of king: nevertheless, in his intercession for his sinful and condemned brethren, he was, as I said, a true type of our Lord pleading in heaven for us sinners. A true type and shadow he was, but at an immense distance. His In-

[g] 1 S. John ii. 1.

tercession being as much more effectual than that of Moses, as His Name and Nature is higher: Moses being the servant, Christ the Son; Moses the friend of God, but Christ Himself Very God, God the Son, presenting Himself, as our Priest and Sacrifice, before the Father continually. So that if Moses by his intercession could obtain so great a boon as the sparing of his condemned countrymen, well may they hope to be saved indeed to the uttermost, who truly and heartily come to God by Christ.

Then again, Moses only *wished* that he might be made, if possible, a curse for his people. "[h] If Thou wilt forgive their sin," he says, "well; and if not, blot me, I pray Thee, out of Thy book." Moses, as S. Paul long afterwards, was willing to die for his brethren, the Jewish people: but our Lord actually *did* die. He caused Himself to be "[i] made a curse for us: as it is written, Cursed is everyone that hangeth on a tree." As the Apostle saith of God the Father, "[k] He that spared not His own Son, but delivered Him up for us all, how shall He not with Him also freely give us all things?" so we may say of the Son Himself, "He that spared not His own life or body, but poured out His soul to death for us all; how shall He not by earnest intercession fully obtain for us all good things?"

Thus you see that our Lord's Ascension, besides other and infinite blessings which belong to it, did according to the counsel of God provide you and me and all Christians with a perpetual Mediator, Intercessor, Advocate at the Right Hand of the Father in heaven; One Whose word cannot return to

[h] Ex. xxxii. 32.   [i] Gal. iii. 13.   [k] Rom. viii. 32.

Him void; of Whom we are certain that, whatsoever He blesseth, is blessed. Now what I wish you particularly to observe, dear brethren, is this: that our Risen and Ascended Lord's Mediation for us with the Father, whether it rightly be called prayer or no, depends almost or altogether on the memorial which (as I said just now) He perpetually maketh before His Father, of the Sacrifice of His Death on the Cross: even as the high priest of the Jews, when he entered once a year into the most holy Place, always took with him the blood of the atoning sacrifice, which he had just been offering without. So S. Paul informs us[1]: "Into the most holy place, or inner tabernacle, entereth the high priest alone, once every year, not without blood, which he offereth" for sins and errors: "[m] but Christ being come, High Priest of the good things to come—not by the blood of bulls and goats, but by His own Blood, entered once for all into the sanctuary, having obtained eternal redemption for us;" "He hath entered into heaven itself, now to appear in the Presence of God for us." "This Man, having offered one Sacrifice for sins for ever, sat down on the Right Hand of God." Thus Jesus Christ in heaven, presenting to the Father His own Body and Blood, maketh continual remembrance of the Sacrifice of His death, and thereby obtaineth for us "remission of our sins and all other benefits of His Passion," saveth us, (as the Apostle says) "to the uttermost."

For *us*, (so the Scripture speaks) not for *all*, but for *us*. And who are *we*? It is a most serious question: but He leaves us in no doubt about the answer.

[1] Heb. ix. 7.   [m] Ib. 11, 12, 24. x. 12.

"He is able to save to the uttermost those who come to God by Him." If we really and earnestly keep on coming to God by Him, then are we the persons for whom all these blessings are prepared. He intercedes for us now; He will save us to the uttermost. Now, do you not perceive, my brethren, even before I have named it to you, that there is one special appointed way of coming to God by Jesus Christ, I mean the Holy Sacrament of the Lord's Body and Blood, to which these promises especially relate? For even as our Lord in heaven is day and night presenting to the Father the very Body with its Wounds, and the Sacred Blood, which was once for all offered on the Cross: so He hath appointed His Church on earth to join in that Sacrifice of His, and present it to the Father, uniting thereby the services of earth and heaven. "This do," He said, " in remembrance of Me:" and that very thing the Church does. We join in that very Sacrifice, which He offered in the upper room the night before His Death, and which He is now continuing day and night before His Father in heaven, in the place to which He this day ascended. In that very Sacrifice we join, as often as we duly receive the Holy Communion. The Holy Communion is our Lord's heavenly memorial transferred to earth: there is the same Priest as in heaven, Jesus Christ, only out of sight; and there is the same Sacrifice, His very Body and Blood. It comes then to be a very serious question, whether they who slight Holy Communion have really any part in our Lord's Intercession; whether their prayers are good for any thing. Certainly it was a saying of Bishop Wilson's, "If I were not a communicant, I should be afraid to say my prayers."

I suppose he meant, not simply that it is a great fault to neglect Holy Communion, and, like any other great fault unrepented of, would make a person unfit to appear before God. I suppose he meant something more particular than this. He meant that, in order to pray acceptably, we must be joined to Him Who is our only High Priest and Mediator: our prayers must be joined to His continual Intercession; that this can only be through that Sacrifice of Holy Communion, which keepeth us one with Him and He with us; and that therefore the prayers of a wilful non-communicant are indeed no Christian prayers. There is no promise, that in them the Holy Spirit will be interceding for us, or that they will go up to be presented as a memorial before God by our great Melchisedec in heaven. My brethren, I want to make this quite plain to you. There is reason to fear that a Christian person, who might come to Holy Communion and does not, is wilfully separating between himself and his God; he is putting himself in such a condition that his prayers will be no prayers; they will do him no good at all, because they are not *really* said in Christ's Name: they are not put into the Mediator's hands, to be offered by Him as part of His perpetual Sacrifice to His Father.

And what if a person come unworthily, I mean in wilful, impenitent unworthiness? We know, alas! too well, what such an one is in the way to bring on himself; "he eateth and drinketh his own damnation." It is a fearful instance of taking God's Name in vain, drawing near to Him only to affront Him.

What then is a poor sinner to do? It is very plain. He must not stay away, for this is putting from him the only remedy for his sins: he must not come hastily, for this is turning the remedy into poison: but he must come *penitently;* that is the word. He must come to Christ's Altar; for that is the Throne of grace, where He is to be found Who is our true King and Priest, from Whom we are sure to obtain both mercy for the past and grace for the future, to help in time of need. Come unto Him in this way, all ye that travail and are heavy laden, and He will give you rest; as surely as, at the prayer of Moses, He forgave His people Israel, and helped them on the way to Canaan, their earthly rest. Through all the forty days and forty nights, the whole time which yet remains for the trial and exercise of His Church on earth, He will be interceding at His Father's Right Hand, in virtue of that Body and Blood which He this day took with Him into heaven. He will be interceding both for the whole Church and for each one of its members. And O, my brethren, how can we think enough of it? If we are trying in earnest to be worthy communicants, this blessed, this perfect Saviour is ours. He is our Saviour and He will save us; He is our God, and He will save us to the uttermost. Through Him we may lie down every night of our lives in peace, in comfortable hope that, for His Intercession's sake, we are absolved from our past sins, how grievous soever; and that our daily repentance is accepted for our daily slips and infirmities, we watching and praying against them. And we may present before Him, and put under His care, the cares and troubles, the needs and infirmities and dangers, temporal and spiritual, of all our dear friends and relations and benefactors, all for whom we are anxious, and of whom we are bound to take charge. Finally, this our great and good High Priest will accept at our hands and present to His Father, in union with His own Flesh and Blood, our earnest prayers and wishes and longings for the whole Christian people, the whole of Christendom in its fallen and divided state; that, according to His own parable of the barren tree, He may spare it yet awhile, "let it alone this year also," if so be, by our Lord's merciful grace, " digging about it and dunging it," it may bear fruit, and not be cut down.

For all, even for the worst, we may pray in hope; since for all our Melchisedec liveth to make special intercession, if only they will come to God by Him. He liveth, not for a time, but for ever: He offereth, not now and then, but perpetually. As He is able therefore, so He is willing to save us to the uttermost. Only have the same will to be saved, that He hath to save you, and there is no end to the blessing you may hope for.

SERMON VII.

RESTRAINT, THE CHRISTIAN'S BLESSING.

SUNDAY AFTER ASCENSION DAY.

DEUT. xii. 8, 9.

"*Ye shall not do after all the things that we do here this day, every man whatsoever is right in his own eyes: for ye are not as yet come to the rest and to the inheritance, which the Lord your God giveth you.*"

THESE words are part of Moses' last admonition to the children of Israel in the wilderness. They had just ended their forty years' wanderings, and were on the point of entering on that promised land, which for so long a time had been the great object of their hopes and prayers. He, like a wise and affectionate friend, well knowing the stubbornness of their hearts, and what danger they were in of being spoiled by prosperity; while he speaks to them at large of the blessings of their new home, its corn, wine, and oil, its flowing with milk and honey, the wealth, peace, and glory, which they might expect in it; warns them also, no less carefully, of God's constant Presence there, and of the exact obedience they would have to pay Him, as ever they hoped to enjoy these blessings. He warns them, here in the text, that it would be a great mistake, if they supposed themselves more at their own ease and liberty, as to what they would do and what they would leave undone, when they were in Canaan, than when they were in the wilderness. He mentions it as one of the advantages of Canaan, that they would have it in their power, and it would be their duty, to live by a stricter and more exact rule there, than they could possibly do, whilst they were moving about in the wilderness. " Ye shall not do after all the things that we do here this day, every man whatsoever is right in his own eyes: for ye are not as yet come to the rest and to the inheritance, which the Lord your God giveth you."

Now, there is a striking resemblance between the condition of the Jews, brought safely to the borders of Canaan, and waiting for God's signal to go in and possess it, and the condition of Christians, after our Saviour had made perfect our redemption by His death and was ascended into heaven, but before He had sent down His Spirit to make us fully partakers of the blessings of the Gospel. And, accordingly, the Church has ordained this part of the admonitions of Moses to be read at this solemn time, as most useful towards helping us to judge rightly of the great change, which the coming of the Holy Ghost has made, both in our blessings, and in our duties.

The blessing, of which it is proposed now to speak more particularly, is that of being more under control, of having our lives and ways more exactly ordered, than as if we were not Christians. We are now come to the rest and to the inheritance, which the Lord our God was so long preparing for us; and therefore we are no longer to think of doing, every man what is right in his own eyes. If it might be excusable in Jews or heathens to do so, it does not follow that it is excusable in us.

And therefore the gate, into which we must strive to enter, is called " strait," and the way which leadeth unto life, " narrow." And our Saviour, inviting us to the blessings of the Gospel, describes them as a yoke and a burthen; easy indeed and light, yet still a yoke and a burthen.

And this very circumstance He mentions as a blessing; as the very reason why, coming to Him, the weary and heavy laden might find rest: " Come unto Me, all ye that labour and are heavy laden, and I will give you rest. Take My yoke upon you, and learn of Me, for I am meek and lowly in heart, and ye shall find rest unto your souls."

So that it appears, that both the Law and the Gospel, both Moses and Jesus Christ, consider it a great blessing, a great increase of comfort and happiness, to be kept under strict rules. The Gospel was more strict than the Law; and on that very account its subjects were happier. Canaan was a place, where men could not do what pleased themselves, so much as they could in the wilderness: and it was the more entirely and truly a place of rest.

But now, this way of thinking is by no means the way of the world. People in general like nothing so much, as having their own choice in all things. They account it a burthen, and not a privilege, to be under the government of others. And there is not, one may venture to say, one man in a thousand, who would not rather be rich than poor, for this very reason; that a rich man is much more his own master, has much more of his own way in choosing how to spend his time, what company to keep, what employments and diversions to follow, than a poor man generally can have.

Again, every one has observed, I might say has experienced, the hurry which children are usually in, to get out of the state of childhood, and to be left to judge and act for themselves. There are few, it may be feared, who have not to charge themselves with some undutifulness towards their first and best friends, their own parents, on this account. Like the prodigal son, young persons are too often found so unthankful, as to hurry on the time of separation from their parents, and say, "Give me the portion of goods that falleth to me:" as if it were a piece of preferment and happiness, to get away, as early as possible, from one's father and mother.

Further: as most of us are, or have been, under authority of some kind, either as servants, or as scholars, or in some other way, we cannot be ignorant how jealous we were of being interfered with by any but our own masters; how unwilling to take advice even from the wisest, lest we should seem to give him a right to direct us; and how impatient of control even from our masters themselves, in matters, which, as we imagined, lay beyond their authority. All of us, as it may seem, naturally sharing, more or less, in the temper of that peevish Hebrew, who would not let Moses interfere with him, though it was only as a friend, to save him from a great sin. We put off our best friends, with "Who made thee a ruler and a judge over us?"

But the worst, and, unfortunately, the most common instance of this ungovernable temper in mankind is, our unwillingness to let God choose for us, and our impatience under the burthens He lays upon us. How very commonly does it happen, that the very condition people chose beforehand, the very place they wished to live in, and the persons they wished to live among, being obtained, becomes the ground of continual complaint and vexation. If they could but change at will, they say, they should like their situation well enough; but now they are tied down to it, they cannot, that is, they will not, help being fretful and impatient.

Yet this very circumstance, of being tied down to rules, and not having the power to change at will, is, as we have seen, reckoned a great blessing, both in the Old and New Testament, both by Moses and Jesus Christ. And the contrary (the having to choose for ourselves, and to do what is right in our own eyes) is spoken of as a great disadvantage. So different is the judgement of God from the judgement of men.

It is true, Moses is speaking of a particular point of conduct; but we shall presently see, that what he says will apply, just as reasonably, to every other part of our duty, and may serve to shew us the benefit of subjection, and not being left to ourselves in any.

He was speaking of the question, where the Israelites should offer their sacrifices and solemn prayers to Almighty God. Whilst they were in the wilderness, they sacrificed where they would; but when they should have come into the land of promise, his word of caution is this: "Take heed to thyself, that thou offer not thy burnt-offerings in every place that thou seest: but in the place which the Lord shall choose in one of thy tribes: there thou shalt offer thy burnt-offerings, and there thou shalt do all that I command thee."

We may be apt sometimes to wonder, that the Israelites should have so generally disobeyed this easy command, and should have sacrificed as they did in the high places, even in some of their best days; when God had said, "You shall worship before this altar in Jerusalem." But if we would look at home, we might find something very like it amongst ourselves. For many men, even now, are rather too jealous of being ordered and directed in their performance of the outward duties of religion. They had rather choose out churches, ministers, prayers for themselves, than be content and thankful with what God's providence has appointed for them.

It is a great happiness in our condition, that we need not be at any loss in these respects. We have no reason to doubt that the clergy are God's ministers, really appointed by Jesus Christ to stand in His place, and to bless in His Name. We are certain that Baptism and the Lord's Supper are His Sacraments; the Bible, His word; and the Lord's Prayer, His prayer. We may be more certain than the Jews could be, which side He would have us take in all doubtful and difficult points of practice. Suppose the question to be between patient suffering and violent and eager resistance, we need not be at a loss for want of a voice from heaven, as the Jews sometimes were. We know beforehand; the New Testament teaches us, in every page, how much better it is to submit quietly, than to do ourselves right by any hasty or passionate ways. Or suppose that two ways appear equally reasonable, but that our inclinations and fancy are rather too passionately inclined towards one of them: we may be sure the safer and better way is rather to incline to the other. "[a] For even Christ pleased not Himself."

I say, it is a great happiness which Christians enjoy, in being thus over-ruled and guided in every step, and not left to their own ways. It is impossible to consider the thing at all seriously, without perceiving that it is so; unpleasant as we too often find it to own as much, even to ourselves. The advantage is as plain, as when we say that it is good for a child, that cannot stand alone, to have hold of a kind and careful nurse, instead of being left to totter about by itself. It is, in the strict sense of the words, a blessing infinite and unspeakable. It is as great as the difference between what God knows and what we know: between eternal, unbounded wisdom, and our frail and short-sighted understanding.

To have this thought steadily fixed within us, will prove, indeed, the greatest of all blessings: both as to our *rest* in this world, and as to our *inheritance* in that which is to come. In whatever counsel and pursuit we are sure we are guided by God, that, we are equally sure, must turn out well in the end: and soberly speaking, what can we wish for more? Now, (whatever may be said about the ways and means) the issues and events of things, we know, are absolutly and entirely in God's hand; and therefore it very ill becomes us to be careful and anxious about

[a] Rom. xv. 3.

them. Let us leave them quietly to be managed by Him, Who cannot do us wrong, and cannot wish us harm. Do but reflect on the meaning of these words, and you cannot but wish to keep it always in your mind, as an anchor of the soul, sure and steadfast, against the most tormenting of all the evils of this mortal life; those which arise from too anxious thoughts about the morrow. Once make up your mind to this most certain truth, that what is right in God's eyes is far better for you, than what is right in your own eyes; and you will have but one care in the whole world: i. e. how to please God in making the best use of the present time: a care in which, by His gracious assistance, you are sure not to fail.

But it was further said, that this temper of not choosing for ourselves leads directly to our everlasting inheritance in the other world, as well as making sure of our rest and refreshment in this. For it helps us greatly in the performance of our duty, because, in truth, it leaves us nothing else to do. The moment we set our heart on any worldly object, however innocent it may be in itself, that moment we are, in that respect, in more danger than we were before. We are embarrassed, from having set ourselves another task, besides pleasing God. This is of course a snare and a trouble to us, and it requires great help on God's part, and most commonly a painful struggle on our own, to keep out of sin, under such circumstances. To guard against which we must be so far free from passions, as to indulge them no more than we are thoroughly convinced is pleasing to God. In the spirit of S. Paul's wise and kind warning: "[b]This

---

[b] 1 Cor. vii. 29, 30.

I say, brethren, the time is short: it remaineth, that both they that have wives be as though they had none; and they that weep, as though they wept not; and they that rejoice, as though they rejoiced not; and they that buy, as though they possessed not; and they that use this world, as not abusing it: for the fashion of this world passeth away."

"ᶜ The world passeth away, and the lust thereof: but he that doeth the will of God endureth for ever." These words of the beloved disciple, S. John, point out to us the great and final blessing of such a temper as has now been recommended: a temper which had rather be under wise and good guidance, than be left to choose for itself. It prepares and trains us for everlasting happiness in heaven. For the very secret of our enjoyment there will be, that God's Will shall be ours. We shall behold His works and ways, especially the Glory which He has given to His beloved Son our Saviour, and shall rejoice in them, as in so much good done to ourselves, more and more thankfully for ever.

What a beautiful and comfortable thought is this, of the high and noble uses to which, if we will, we may turn all our worst disappointments, the bitterest thoughts of shame and remorse, which ever come upon us! We may consider them as part of our heavenly Father's way of breaking us in, as it were, and training us to the desire and enjoyment of His own blessed Presence in heaven. They are so many lessons in His school, each intended to make us a little more perfect in that divine art of having the same will that He has. Look upon your feelings of shame

ᶜ 1 S. John ii. 17.

and self-reproach in this way, and you will compose yourself to receive them calmly, however grievous for the time, in cheerful hope that they may prove hereafter, for Christ's sake, the happy means of your amendment and forgiveness.

And if even the bitter thought of our past sins may be accompanied with so much of what is comfortable and hopeful, surely we may well leave it to Almighty God, to do what He will with us in every other respect. Only let us think over, fairly and seriously, what has hitherto passed in our own life. Let us recollect what we have experienced in ourselves, seen in our friends, heard of in the world, and read in our Bible. We cannot think it over in earnest, without seeing the great evil of being left to our own way; and the security, the comfort, and happiness, of having God to choose for us.

Once possess yourself with this truth, and you will be fit for every condition that God may send upon you. You will be humble in prosperity, because then God seems to leave you to yourself, and this temper has made you very much afraid of yourself. In sorrow you will be cheerful, because then you feel for certain that God does not leave you to yourself. And in all conditions, you will keep up a constant and thankful sense of the presence and providence of the Almighty God, of God our Saviour; in Whom if we once learn to delight ourselves, He is sure to give us our heart's desire.

SERMON VIII.

CHRISTIAN CONFIDENCE.

SUNDAY AFTER ASCENSION DAY.

Rom. viii. 33, 34.

" Who shall lay anything to the charge of God's elect? It is God that justifieth. Who is he that condemneth? It is Christ that died, yea rather that is risen again, Who is even at the Right Hand of God, Who also maketh intercession for us."

It would not perhaps be wrong to suppose that the holy Apostle in these courageous words was thinking particularly of the troubles which he and all Christians were then suffering at the hands of the Roman and other heathen magistrates and people. Wherever S. Paul went, he was bitterly reviled, because he was a Christian, and the most false and impossible stories were spread abroad concerning him. In many towns the people rose against him, and he was in danger of being torn in pieces. His own words are, "[a] We are made as the filth of the world, and are the offscouring of all things, unto this day:" words, which shew how deeply he felt the scorn and censure of men, yet how little he cared for it when in the way of duty. And why did

[a] 1 Cor. iv. 13.

he care little for it? What was the thought that bore him up? It was the hope of being accounted righteous before God: it was the remembrance of all that our merciful Saviour has done for us, and more especially of His Ascension into heaven, and constant appearance before His Father in our behalf. "Who dare lay any thing," asks the Apostle, "to the charge of God's elect?" God Almighty forgives and acquits us: He pronounces us not guilty of these grievous things which our enemies report against us. He justifies: who dare condemn? He accounts us innocent: who dare call us guilty? What signifies how men judge us and treat us, if we have such a friend in heaven? He that alone has power finally to condemn is Jesus Christ; and Jesus Christ is the very Person Who has done and suffered so great things for us. He died; yea rather, let us say, He is risen again. The Apostle speaks so, because His Resurrection was the sign of our forgiveness; we knew by it, that God was willing to accept His Sacrifice. His Death purchased our deliverance; His Resurrection sealed it. But there is something beyond them both to be mentioned, making our condition still more blessed. He "is even at the Right Hand of God; He also maketh intercession for us." The Man Christ Jesus, the very same Who was conceived of the Holy Ghost and born of the Virgin Mary, Who suffered under Pontius Pilate, was crucified, dead and buried, Who rose again the third day from the dead: He is taken up, both soul and body, to the Right Hand of His Father, where, being still perfect Man as we are, "of a reasonable soul and human flesh subsisting," He reigns over all in heaven and earth: Angels and Authorities and Powers, as well as all the children of men, being made subject unto Him.

Again, He maketh intercession for us; He is not only our King in Heaven, but also our Priest. As King, He sits on the Throne of God: as Priest, He stands at God's Right Hand, making intercession for us: offering up (so Scripture seems to teach) our prayers and fastings, our doings and sufferings, our sacrifices and self-denials, to be accepted of His Father, as being united to His only precious Sacrifice of Himself on the Cross. And all this He does, not as one who merely pitied us, though he could not exactly enter into our feelings: not as an Angel might be merciful to us, although he could not possibly understand by his own experience what our sufferings were. It is not so with Jesus Christ. He can be touched with a feeling of our infirmities; for He, in all points but sinfulness, has been tried as we are. Now we know what a difference it usually makes in people's compassion and kindness for one another, if they have ever themselves felt the calamity which they are called on to pity and relieve. The Almighty Himself appeals to this feeling repeatedly. E.g., He bids His people remember and leave gleanings in the fields for the stranger, and love him as themselves, and allow him the rest of the Sabbath: "for," saith God, "[b]ye know the heart of a stranger, seeing ye were strangers in the land of Egypt." In like manner He knows our hearts: He feels for us when death parts us from relations and friends; for He wept at the grave of Lazarus. He com-

[b] Ex. xxiii. 9.

passionates the destitute in their hunger and thirst, for He was an hungred after His forty days' fast; He on His Cross felt the thirst that goes before death. And thus, as persons who have been sick themselves, make the most compassionate and thoughtful nurses, so is our Lord the very fountain of all true compassion for every affliction and misery, that man can suffer. He feels for us and with us, being, as He is, one of us, both body and soul. What a reason is here, if we had but faith to consider it, for our bearing calmly and patiently all the pains and frailties of this present life, and whatsoever "the devil or man worketh against us!" If it be sweet and soothing to every sufferer, when he feels the sympathy and kind concern of some affectionate person, on whom he can depend here in this life: how much more, to be certain, as all Christian men may, that Christ Who died and rose again is at the Right Hand of God, making intercession for us with that unspeakable Love, which caused Him to lay down His life for us!

In this way then the Apostle comforts himself and all his persecuted brethren when they were condemned by the world. "God," he says, "justifieth." He has made you members of Himself: He sees not now your old sins which you committed in your heathen state, but He sees you as you are in Jesus Christ, with His robe thrown over you: your sinful habits dead and cast away, and the righteousness of Christ filling your life and heart and transforming you more and more into the likeness of Him. If so it be with you, little need you care for the suspicions and revilings, the condemnation and persecutions of men.

But further: we may with humble hope and thankfulness apply this same blessed sentence to the assuaging the reproaches of our own hearts, when they are too much cast down by fear and shame at the thought of our many sins and infirmities. Conscience may too reasonably say to most of us, "True, these are great and precious promises; but what have you to do with them, whose life has been blemished, since your baptismal justification, by so many serious faults; whose heart is still so imperfect before God, so far from being throughly renewed after His glorious Image?" And the Evil spirit may taunt us, as it were, and try to reduce us to despair, and make us say with the Jewish sinners before the captivity, "There is no hope; I may as well go after my sins." Nay, my brethren: we, by God's mercy, will never give way to such thoughts as these: we will not cast away our hope in Him, Who justified us by His free grace, making us members of Himself before we could know any thing: "Who died, yea rather Who is risen again, Who is even at the right hand of God, Who also maketh intercession for us." Too surely we have sinned, some of us grievously; and if He should deal strictly with us, we cannot deny that we have broken the covenant, and forfeited His pardon and grace. But He allows repentance, He invites us to confess our sins, to humble and punish ourselves for them: to be watchful and busy in all sorts of well-doing: to seek Absolution in all ways, where He has appointed it to be found: and so doing, He permits us to hope that we are still in communion with Him; that the blessings of our Baptism are not forfeited; that He Who will come to be our Judge has not ceased to make intercession for us. We may still say to our own hearts, "[c] Put thy trust in God, for I will yet thank Him for the help of His countenance;" and to the Evil one we may say, "[d] Away from me; I will keep the commandments of my God."

See how the words of the text both encourage us to cherish such good hope, and warn us on what it must depend, on our own part. We must be such as not to have forfeited the title of God's elect: for concerning them only the question is asked, "Who shall lay any thing to their charge?" They only have the promise of justification. And again we must be such as not to have quite lost the gracious Intercession of our crucified and glorified Lord. Now "God's elect" or chosen means of course those whom He has called out of the world to be His own peculiar people: as the Jews were called from among all other nations. So the catechism instructs every baptized child to regard himself as one of the "elect people of God." So S. Paul, in this epistle to the Romans, speaking of the elect among the Jews, plainly means those who had received the Gospel, whom Christ had taken to Himself, and put His mark on them in Baptism. So our Lord Himself in His parables speaks of the elect, as of persons who should, first of all, come to His spiritual feast, and next, should keep their wedding-garment, true holiness, so as not to be cast out. Against such it will be in vain for bad men or bad angels to bring any kind of charge. Until they have cast themselves out of the kingdom, or by staining their robes have made themselves unworthy to abide in it, they are, by God's mercy, safe.

So again, as to Christ's Intercession: the many frailties, negligences and ignorances, with which even

[c] Ps. xlii. 7. add 15.   [d] Ib. cxix. 115.

the best man's conscience must accuse him, need not utterly cast him down, though they should make him daily more diligent and watchful. For they do not hinder, but that he is still in a state of justification: such a state, that our Lord in heaven is still making intercession for him. But if he be in wilful sin, then his justification so far ceases: then Christ's intercession is not for such as he. So S. John expressly teaches. "ᵉIf any man see his brother sin a sin which is not unto death, he shall ask, and He shall give him life for them that sin not unto death. There is a sin unto death: I do not say that he shall pray for it. All unrighteousness is sin, and there is a sin not unto death." Wilful sin persisted in, and that only, can forfeit God's justifying grace, and our Saviour's Intercession. If you are conscious of it, lose no time, break it off by the ways of true penitence. Nothing else can ruin us. "Neither tribulation nor distress nor persecution nor anguish nor nakedness nor peril nor sword: neither death nor life, nor Angels, nor principalities nor powers, nor things present nor things to come, nor height nor depth nor any other creature, shall be able to separate us from the love of God, which is in Christ Jesus our Lord." None of these can separate us; but sin may. S. Paul, you observe, does not say a word as to the elect being safe from sin in this life. What he does say is, that as long as they continue elect, that is, until by wilful sin they have separated themselves from among God's people, none of these outward things can hurt them.

We see then most plainly, which way all our cares and labours should tend: to keep ourselves from

ᵉ 1 S. John v. 16.

what we know displeases Almighty God, lest we lose our part in Christ Jesus, to which He elected us in our infancy by His free grace. And here, that no man may deceive himself, let it be well understood and always remembered, that nothing displeases God more, and forfeits our part in His Son more entirely, than lukewarmness and indifference in His service. Thousands, at the last day, I fear, will be found, who have cast themselves out of the kingdom of heaven, not by positive sin, but by leaving undone the things which they ought to have done. Do not then say, "I am neither thief nor murderer, I bear no malice to any one, I do not live in adultery nor in fornication, I take no false oaths; why should I be uneasy about myself?" But say rather, "How have I spent my time from my youth upward? How have I attended to my prayers? Which way has my heart turned? How strictly have I denied myself? How anxiously have I kept in order my thoughts, my passions, and my tongue?" And if you permit your conscience to answer these questions truly, it will be a wonder if you do not sentence yourself to be a humble penitent all your life, instead of indulging any kind of boastfulness.

In a word, the token of God's continued election is a man's truly loving God, as S. Paul indeed had intimated a little before. "All things work together for good," he says, "to them who love God: who are the called according to His purpose:" and of these same he speaks afterwards as justified, and as being those for whom Christ died, and arose, and intercedes. If a man love God, he may trust to be still a partaker of these blessings: not else. Now "this is the love of God, that we keep His commandments." Where true love is, it is impossible that a man should be easy or careless, and soon satisfied in his duties. Look e. g. at an affectionate mother with her child: can she ever think she has done quite enough for it? Is she not still watching and contriving, how to make her love and service more perfect? So is it with the love of God and of our Saviour Jesus Christ: it is a restless ever-active principle: of all things it never will permit a man to be soon pleased with himself.

I conclude therefore, that although every one who has been baptized into Jesus Christ has been called to a part in these glorious promises, yet those only have a present portion in them, who so unfeignedly love God, as to be habitually endeavouring to keep *all* His commandments and do *all* His Will: who love Him as truly and constantly as a dutiful child loves his father or mother, and who shew their love in like manner, by regularly striving to please and obey Him more and more.

Such a person will be the last to say to himself, that he *has* such love in him: yet in some unknown way God will make him partaker of His peace, that "peace which passeth all understanding." Worldly want, distress, pain and vexation will come lightly in comparison upon him, because he never depended on this world. In doubt and perplexity he may hope for safe guidance: and should his education, or other circumstances, lead him into error, or continue him in it, through no wilful fault of his own, his charity, his true love of God, will cover a multitude of such sins. The Divine goodness will overflow towards him: all things will work together for his good: and in the end he shall see, with joy and for ever, the Face of the Beloved.

SERMON IX.

A PLACE PREPARED FOR US, AND WE PREPARED FOR IT.

SUNDAY AFTER ASCENSION DAY.

S. JOHN xiv. 2.

"I go to prepare a place for you."

THE Holy Scripture bids us particularly remark the constant love of our blessed Lord and Saviour, now about to ascend into heaven, towards His chosen disciples and Apostles. S. John's saying is, "[a] when His hour was come, that He should depart out of this world unto the Father, having loved His own which were in the world, He loved them unto the end." And this, His great and enduring love, He particularly shewed, the night before His death, by the many comfortable words which He poured into their ears, to prepare them for His departure: at the very mention of which, as He well knew, sorrow was sure to fill their heart. But He would not have them be so cast down. He, the great Lord of heaven and earth, humbles Himself to behold and to pity the thoughts and misgivings, which He knows will arise in the hearts of His poor frail creatures, when death and separation are spoken of. "[b] Let not your heart

[a] S. John xiii. 1.   [b] Ib. xiv. 1, 2.

be troubled: ye believe in God, believe also in Me. In My Father's house are many mansions:" i. e. "in the great eternal heaven, where God lives and rules for ever, is abundance of room for you all." The promise indeed had just before been made to S. Peter especially; "[c] Whither I go, thou canst not follow Me now, but thou shalt follow Me afterwards." But it was by no means confined to S. Peter. On the contrary, all the twelve, and through them all the disciples, are here given to understand that in the happy home, to which our Lord has returned, every one may find a place. He is the Head of the Body, the Church: and where the Head is, there the members, in due course of time, may hope to be. Not a few only of the most honourable, but every one, the meaner as well as the more glorious, may hope to be raised with the Head to everlasting joy.

This surely is infinite love and condescension. But our gracious Lord goes even beyond this. Hear how His discourse proceeds. "In My Father's house are many mansions: He has room enough and glory enough for all His family both in heaven and earth: but even were it otherwise, were there room for a few only, I would have said to you, 'I go to prepare a place for you.' Whatever became of others, to you at least, My chosen Apostles, I should have given a special promise of a home in heaven, suited for each one of you. Much more may you depend upon that greatest of all blessings, now that you know by My sure word how large heaven is, and how the gates of that happy place are thrown open, by God's mercy, to all who draw near Me with true hearts!"

[c] S. John xiii. 36.

This being, as it appears by holy writers of old time, the true way of understanding our Saviour's words in the text, we may well take them as containing an assurance, to the Apostles first and through them to all believers, of the great mercy which our Lord intended us at His going up into heaven. He goes to prepare a place for us, to make ready a happy home, where we may dwell with Him to all eternity.

And this He does, first, by offering Himself, His own sacrificed Body and Blood, day and night to His heavenly Father, as a true and perfect atonement and satisfaction for our sins. S. Paul tells us so, plainly, in the epistle to the Hebrews. "[d]Christ being come a High Priest of good things to come, by a greater and more perfect tabernacle, not made with hands... neither by the blood of goats and calves, but by His own Blood, hath entered once for all into the holy place, having obtained eternal redemption for us." That is, as there was a division in the tabernacle of Moses first, and afterwards in Solomon's Temple, and the outer court was called simply holy, the other Holy of Holies, or holiest of all: so is God's heavenly kingdom separated from His kingdom on earth, and far, very far more holy and glorious than it. And as the priests went always into the outer tabernacle, accomplishing the service of God, but into the second went the High Priest alone, once only in every year, and without this all the rest would have been nothing: so all the services and offerings, which are made to God here on earth, have respect to that one meritorious Offer-

[d] Heb. ix. 11, 12.

ing, which our Lord carried up into heaven and presented as at this time to His Father: the Offering of His own crucified Body and Blood. He has taken It with Him through the veil into that unseen world of glory: and there He exhibits and offers it, in some heavenly and mysterious way, to His Father and our Father, His God and our God, Who is so well pleased with it, that for the sake thereof He is content to remit the punishment which all we have deserved, and to allow us a passage through the veil into the most high and holy court of heaven. Thus, as Joseph went in and obtained leave of Pharaoh that his father and his brethren might dwell in the best of the land of Egypt, so Jesus Christ our Lord, Who verily made Himself a brother, a true Joseph to us, has gone in and obtained leave of the great King of heaven and earth, that we may dwell with Him in heaven. He has redeemed us by His own Blood on the Cross, and He never ceases to plead the virtue of that Blood. "He ever liveth to make intercession for us." By His painful death He overcame the sharpness of death, and by His Resurrection and Ascension He opened the kingdom of heaven to all believers. Once for all, He did then prepare a place for us; Heaven for sinners, the Throne of God for worms of the earth, the Holy of Holies for us who were unclean from the womb. How can we ever think enough of it? And yet, beyond this infinite deep of mercy, opens another deep no less infinite.

For our Lord ascended, not only to present Himself for us, as our true sin-offering, before His Father's mercy-seat, but also to send down the Holy Ghost the Comforter, the Co-equal, Co-eternal Spirit, to be with us, and dwell in us: to make and keep us, in very deed, members of Christ, children of God, and inheritors of the kingdom of heaven. That is, He not only prepares a place there for us, but sends also from thence to prepare us for the place. For after all that He has done and suffered for us, though, by His mercy, the gates of heaven stand open, yet we could not pass through them, so long as our hearts continue unclean and unprepared. Therefore to all His other favours He has mercifully added this one, that He hath given us His grace, His good Spirit to live and rule in us, changing our hearts, and giving us true faith and love; putting on us the wedding-garment, that the Angels may not turn us back and bid us depart into outer darkness, when we are crying, "Lord, Lord, open to us." This is what He continually spake of to His disciples, as His hour came on, to make them contented with His going. "ᵉIt is expedient for you that I go away; for, if I go not away, the Comforter will not come unto you: but if I depart, I will send Him unto you." Christ sends the Comforter to us, to teach us and guide us into all truth: to bring all things to our remembrance, which He hath taught us from the beginning: to shew us things to come, turning our hearts to dwell on the great unspeakable matters of eternity: to be His true witness, putting us in mind of Him continually: to help us especially when we pray, making "ᶠintercession for us with groanings which cannot be uttered:" but most especially of all, to regenerate and sanctify us, uniting us to our Redeemer in Holy Baptism, and then

---

ᵉ S. John xvi. 7.   ᶠ Rom. viii. 26.

dwelling in our hearts and bodies, to make us grow up from day to day in more entire and perfect communion with Him. Thus our Lord prepares a place for us, by sending His Spirit to prepare us for it.

And thirdly, Christ is preparing our heavenly home, by that which He does as our King, sitting on the Right Hand of God, with all power committed unto Him in heaven and in earth. He, Who is now bone of our bone, and flesh of our flesh: He, Who is not ashamed to call us brethren: He is now and for evermore King of kings and Lord of lords, having "[g] given unto Him dominion and glory and a kingdom, that all people, nations and languages, may serve Him." All kings are to fall down before Him, all nations are to do Him service. And He has distinctly told us to what end, and by what rule, He will order this His empire. "[h] All things shall work together for good to them that love God, to them who are the called according to His purpose." He gives to all the changes of this mortal life such a turn as He knows to be best for His Church and kingdom, His Body here on earth. He is gradually bringing matters into that condition, which He knows will best prepare this His earthly Jerusalem, the Church, to be taken up again into that heaven, from which at first she came down, and to become a heavenly Jerusalem again. By His royal power, out of sight, He is preparing heaven for the Church, and by the same royal power and providence, continually governing all things here in sight, He is preparing the Church for heaven. And all these His great and gracious works, visible and in-

[g] Dan. vii. 14.   [h] Rom. viii. 28.

visible; His sending His Spirit, His offering Himself, as our Priest, His ordering all as our King: all are to go on, until the time arrive when He shall come again, and receive His own to Himself, that where He is, there we may be also. Thus you see, in a few short words our Saviour here gives His disciples a sufficient account of His doings unto the end of the world. All was to be ordered by Him, and all ordered with an eye especially to the Church, His Spouse; that she might in His good time come to be where He is.

We are, every single one of us, members of that holy Church: every single one among us, be it man, woman, or child, has a portion in these great promises. Let us turn this over in our minds.

Every one among us may know for certain, that our Lord went up to be an Intercessor and Mediator for the sins not of the whole world only, but also for each one of us in particular. He had each one in His thought, when He entered within the veil. He knew there would be in His Church, at such a time, such persons as we are, and that we should be tempted to commit such and such sins. Knowing it all, knowing all those secret and horrible circumstances of our sins, which make them so intolerable to our consciences, our Lord Christ did nevertheless vouchsafe to carry into the Holy of Holies, and there present before His Father, His own Blood, for the washing away of those sins. He knew the worst of us, yet He laid down His life for us. Think of it again and again, for you can never think enough of it. From the beginning, from the moment of our Lord's Ascension to His Father's Right Hand, even to this very hour, Christ has been preparing a place for us. What a pity, should we now forfeit that place! And for aught we know, we may forfeit it for ever, the very next known sin we commit.

Then again, our Lord sent the Comforter, not to quicken whole Churches only, or other large bodies of Christians, but also to dwell in *your* heart, in *my* heart, in the hearts of all His baptized: for this special end, that He may prepare us for our place in heaven. This again is a very aweful, as well as a very comfortable thought. The great God of heaven and earth abides and dwells, not only near us, not only around us, not only about our path and about our bed, and so as to spy out all our ways, but within us, in our very heart, to be, as it were, the soul of our souls, dwelling in them as they dwell in our bodies. And to what end? That we may be not unworthy to enter in and dwell in the room which the same great God, in another Person, is getting ready to receive us in heaven. Reflect on this: that in every wilful sin we commit, we are actually and immediately fighting against God the Holy Ghost, Who strives against that sin in our hearts: and we are so far disappointing and undoing the work which God the Son, our Saviour, is even now working for us in heaven. To our corrupt hearts, alas, it seems a light, simple, natural thing, a mere matter of course, that we should one hour tell a lie, to keep ourselves from some little trouble or disgrace; another hour, suffer our thoughts and eyes to wander after impurity and sin; another, that we should in a deliberate way speak and judge unkindly of some neighbour: and so on with other sins. To us, alas! it all seems but too natural. But what says the Scripture to all Christians? By every such indulgence in wrong, though it be but in thought, you resist the Holy Ghost here on earth, and you vex and scorn your Saviour, pleading for you in heaven. Who can ever feel as if he were watchful enough, when he considers in this way the immense importance of every thought word and work, in which God gives him a choice between right and wrong?

And again, who ever can be thankful and courageous enough, when he considers that other fruit of our Blessed Lord's Ascension, that we know Him now to be reigning not only as King over the whole Church, but as Shepherd and Guide over each one of us in particular, ordering all and putting all together, in such sort as may most help us, if we will, in the way to heaven? So that as every known sin is unspeakably dreadful in a Christian, being a direct act of warfare against those two Divine Persons, God the Son and God the Holy Ghost, so every common indifferent matter may be, if we will, turned into an unspeakable blessing. For if it is set about in God's faith and fear, our Lord and King will know how to make it work in some way for our everlasting good.

And now, what shall we say, on the whole, to this astonishing course of love and mercy, which our Lord sets forth to us in those few plain words, "I go to prepare a place for you?" What can we say or feel, my brethren, but this—that we are the meanest and worst of beings, if such love is lost upon us: if, while God the Son is so busy in heaven, preparing us there an everlasting home, and God the Holy Ghost no less busy on earth, preparing us for that home, we still go on brutishly set upon the things which we see around us, bodily and earthly things, which are but for a day? It ought not to be a question; but it is a most serious question. Christ is gone to prepare a place for us: are we preparing ourselves for that place? Christ has suffered and is doing all things to provide us with a happy eternity: are we in any true sense training ourselves for that eternity? He is in heaven as our Priest, Intercessor, and Advocate, to offer up our prayers like sweet incense to His Father: how often, and how earnestly, do we send up prayers for Him to offer? He never forgets our souls: do we ever seriously think of them? What that heaven is, which He is preparing for us, we know not yet fully: but thus much He has told us; that His Presence there, the Presence of the Most Holy Trinity, is all in all: that His saints and servants are to be happy with one another and with Him, serving Him continually, as in a perfect and glorious Church: that nothing wicked or unclean can come there, and that such as abide there will go on eternally from glory to glory, becoming more and more like Him. We know not yet what we shall be, but "[i] we know that, when He shall appear, we shall be like Him, for we shall see Him as He is." O that we may be wise! that we may consider these things! that we may turn ourselves once for all, away from the world, towards Christ in heaven, and having done so, may never forget to keep our hearts pure, lest we forfeit the place prepared for us!

[i] 1 S. John iii. 2.

SERMON X.

THE REWARD OF FINISHED WORK.

SUNDAY AFTER ASCENSION DAY.

S. JOHN xvii. 4, 5.

" I have glorified Thee on the earth: I have finished the work which Thou gavest Me to do: and now, O Father, glorify Thou Me with Thine own self, with the glory which I had with Thee before the world was."

GOD Almighty gives every one a work, and prepares for every one a reward. So it has been with all the children of men, ever since the time of Adam. Adam had his work given him, to dress and to keep the garden of Eden, keeping himself with religious care from going near the Tree of knowledge. His reward also was prepared for him; freely to eat of the trees of the garden, and especially of the Tree of Life, the fruit whereof would cause him to live for ever. In like manner we children of Adam, all the men and women upon earth, have had their task assigned them one by one at the will of the heavenly Work-master, the great Householder, the Lord and Owner of us all: and He is not a hard nor an unfair man: He never appoints any one a piece of work without providing for him beforehand an ample recompense. We belong indeed absolutely to Him. He gives us life and health and all things, so that we should be bound to do His work without any recompense at all: yet still He is so bountiful, that He offers us large and abundant wages. "[a] Man goeth forth to his work and to his labour until the evening." He works on, or neglects his work, until the shadows of death fall: and then begins the time of reward: then the Lord of the vineyard says, "[b] Call the labourers, and give them their hire:" then he that hath wrought, receiveth wages and gathereth fruit unto life eternal: and he that would not work, but chose rather to be unprofitable, receives his sentence, to be cast into outer darkness.

All this is so well known to us, that, if we have any serious consideration at all, we think of it, I suppose, very often: and especially as often as any person dies. As we stand by our neighbour's death-bed, or by his grave, whoever and whatever he was, these are the two thoughts which naturally come into our minds, " his work is done," and, " he is gone to his reward." And we begin, according to our knowledge of the man and the interest we take in him, to consider *how* he did his work, and what *sort* of a reward it is likely his will be.

Now in this, as in other respects, the great Almighty Son of God, our Lord and Saviour, made Himself one of us. He too, when He came on earth, had His ordained work, and when He departed from earth, He too went to His ordained reward, to His own place, as any of us, His poor earthly creatures, might do. Of this work He often spoke, while He was

[a] Ps. civ. 23.   [b] S. Matt. xx. 8.

going about in accomplishment of it. "ᶜMy meat" and drink "is to do the will of Him that sent Me, and to finish His work." And in another place, "ᵈI must work the work of Him that sent Me, while it is day: the night cometh, when no man can work." This was our Lord's way of speaking: just as one continually hears hard-working labourers say, "they are not their own masters, they have not their own choice, they would like to do so and so, but they cannot, because they have a task to finish before night." We say such words, too often, in a dissatisfied, complaining way. At least, let us learn to say them with patience, seeing that our good God and Saviour had to say the very same, when He was among men. He too was in that condition, that neither His time nor His labour was His own. He was as a servant or slave among men, not pleasing Himself, not doing His own will, but bound to do a certain work before His life ended. He too denied and humbled Himself for the Glory's sake, into which He was bye and bye to enter: as He tells us by His Apostle, "ᵉ For the joy that was set before Him, He endured the Cross, despising the shame." Let us not grudge one against another, nor vex ourselves at the restraint we live in, but rather let us try at least to be very thankful for our Lord's exceeding mercy in so coming among us, and vouchsafing to be one of us; to have a work and a reward, as we have.

Our Lord's work was His perfect Sacrifice: that Will of His Father, which He came into the world to do. He began it by taking to Himself that Body, which the Holy Spirit prepared for Him in the womb

---

ᶜ S. John iv. 34.   ᵈ Ib. ix. 4.   ᵉ Heb. xii. 2.

of the Blessed Virgin, and He ended it by offering up that same Body on the Cross, and commending His Soul into the hands of the Father, with the words, "It is finished." Looking forward to that moment, He had said a few hours before, "I have glorified Thee on the earth : I have finished the work which Thou gavest Me to do : " reckoning it already finished, because its accomplishment was now so very near. Indeed His Passion had now in a manner begun, for Judas had gone out to betray Him, and He had offered Himself sacramentally in that first Holy Communion. Now therefore we hear Him saying, "I have finished My work: it is time for Me to receive My reward." And what is His reward? To be glorified by His Father, with the glory which He had had with Him before the world was. That is, that His very Body, that humbled, scourged, crucified, buried Body, should be taken up into heaven, and with His Human Soul made partaker of that Infinite glory, which His Divine Person had with the Father before the world was, and from which, as God, He could never be separated for a moment. This, we know, took place at His Ascension. That was the great Day of our Lord's Glorification, as the Crucifixion was the great day of finishing His work. His work was, to save us from hell by the Sacrifice of Himself, and His reward, if we may so call it, was that His crucified Body should go up into heaven, and sit there in the highest place; on the Right Hand of God, in the Glory of the Father.

This was the work, and this the reward, of Jesus Christ, our Head and our pattern. And though, as the heavens are higher than the earth, and as God is greater than man, so infinitely high are His work and His reward above ours, yet is the one in some sort the pattern of the other. As His day's work was, to offer Himself in Sacrifice for the souls and bodies of all men: so our day's work is, to save each one his own soul, and the souls committed in any way to his care. Not that we can, properly speaking, save ourselves, any more than we can create ourselves, or raise ourselves from the dead. But the Scripture calls it saving ourselves, if we do what in us lies, not to destroy our own souls, not to forfeit and cast away God's mercy. Therefore, as I said, our day's work is, to save each one his own soul and the souls committed to him. *That* is the common work or calling of us all: the priest and the labourer, the king and the wandering beggar, have so far the same task. But then God Almighty has given also to each of us a separate work, task or calling of his own, for which we have bye and bye to give in our separate accounts. Thus, the labourer has to save his soul, by dutiful, diligent, religious care in his day-labour; the priest, in his ministry; the rich man, in the spending of his money; the sick man, in enduring his affliction: and so of all others. God has given them a work to do: and the great question hereafter will be, How was that work done?

Our work is a shadow of our Lord's work, because whatever it is outwardly, in the end it will be found to pertain to the salvation of souls. And our reward, if we be found faithful, will be a shadow of our Lord's reward. It will be some portion, more or less, of His bright unspeakable glory: as in the pictures of our Lord with His saints we commonly see a sort of lesser brightness round the heads of those whom we know He delights to honour; not in any degree so wide nor so dazzling as the glory which is around His Head, yet still enough to shew that they are partakers of His light, and by it shine forth far more brightly than ordinary men. And this, in fulfilment of His own most gracious promise, when, speaking to His Father, He says, "The glory which Thou gavest Me, I have given them, that they may be one as We are." In some heavenly and wonderful manner, Christians are even now, at a great distance, partakers of their Lord's glory. How much more, when they come to the other world: when our vile bodies shall be changed, and made like unto His glorious Body: when "'the righteous shall shine forth as the sun in the kingdom of their Father:" when we shall be made like unto Him: "for we shall see Him as He is!"

This is our exceeding great reward: and our day's work is, to prepare ourselves duly for it. We have to work under Jesus Christ in this world, that He may give us a crown of life in the next. You see at once, surely, that there is no proportion between the work and the reward. A few days or years in this world is nothing, yea less than nothing, and vanity, compared with a happy and glorious eternity. A joyful and pleasant thing it is, at any time, to look back on our hours of work, and feel that they have not been spent in vain: that we have, in some tolerable manner, fulfilled our task in its proper time. Joseph, for instance, must have felt a great and peculiar delight, when he had finished storing up the corn

ᶠ S. Matt. xiii. 43.

which was to feed all the country in the famine: and Moses, when he had completed the tabernacle; and Joshua, when he had brought the whole land of Canaan into subjection to the Israelites; and Solomon, when he had made an end of building the temple: and S. John, when he had baptized our Saviour. All men have special satisfaction in having finished their work, although, strictly speaking, none ever did finish his work entirely, except Jesus Christ, Who said on the Cross, "It is finished." Still each one of us has a special delight in thinking over what he has gone through with, though it be done but indifferently well. How much more, when, by God's mercy, he has to look back on his whole life, with the certainty that it has not been a failure: that in some way, by innocence or by penitence, his task is in God's sight accomplished, and his soul saved for Christ's sake! Consider. Imagine but for one moment what the joy and the sweetness will be, should the merciful Lord at the last Day meet you with the words of approving love: "Well done, good and faithful servant." Then all doubt, all regret, will vanish in a moment: then will Christians no more disquiet themselves, as now they may and do but too reasonably, with the conscience of their manifold infirmities. This one thought, "God now accepteth my works," will fill and entrance the soul, and carry her out of herself; she will never more have leisure, as one may say, to grieve that she has not acted more entirely up to the rule which God had set her. The overflowing transport of that one moment will spread into a deep and wide sea of pleasure, which will bear us on to all eternity, and bring us nearer and nearer Him, in

Whom, though now we see Him not, we "[g] rejoice with joy unspeakable and full of glory."

All of us know *something*, some little, of these unspeakable encouragements, held out in God's Word to those who do but seriously endeavour to finish their work. How then does it happen, that any of us should wilfully leave his day's work undone? It is, because, though we know of the great reward, to be given us at the end of our day, we do not earnestly care enough for it, to think often of it. It would be well for each one of us to examine ourselves this night, before we lie down to rest, on this one matter: "How have I been keeping the Day, on which our Lord went up into heaven? How often have I thought to-day of the happiness of heaven? How often have I thought of seeing His Face with joy? of hearing from Him, 'Come, ye blessed of My Father?' of beholding Him, not '[h] through a glass darkly,' but 'face to face,' even as He is? Did I think of it, when I waked from my sleep this morning? Did I think of it, when I said my prayers? Did the blessed remembrance ever come into my mind, to assist me in bearing the burden and heat of the day?" Alas! I fear, were all to ask themselves such plain questions as these, very many, perhaps the greater part, would be compelled to reply that they had not once thought of the matter. And if we have not really thought of eternity, what else was there, to make us do our work well, so much of it at least, as is not done in sight of man? Then, if we have spent this one day without thinking of heaven, how did we spend yesterday? and the day before that? and

[g] 1 S. Pet. i. 8. [h] 1 Cor. xiii. 12.

the third day again, and all our past days? Must we not confess before our God, that we have hitherto slighted His promises? We have said, over and over in His hearing, the words which He meant to put us in mind of heaven, such as, "Thy kingdom come, Thy will be done;" "Thine is the kingdom, the power and the glory:" or again the words of the Creed, "He ascended into heaven, and sitteth on the Right Hand of God, the Father Almighty," or, "I believe in the life everlasting." These words we have said over and over in the hearing of our God, and all the while He saw that our hearts and minds were far away from Him, set on any thing but His promises. It is high time, surely, that this were amended; for as long as we are in this mind, I do not see how we can say a single prayer well: and then what is to become of us?

Perhaps, however, we are not so bad as this: we do sometimes recollect the happy place prepared for us; nay even, we wish ourselves there, especially (for such is the profane way of some) when anything goes wrong and discomposes us. But in how many instances have we given up anything for this blessed reward's sake? What sins have we broken ourselves of, to make the reward sure? What imperfections have we fought against, to make it purer and more precious? Too commonly, I fear, every little worldly trifle has more power to draw us away from remembrances of heaven, than all Christ's words to invite us. We kneel down to pray, and time after time, before the prayer is half over, our frail thoughts fly off, and we scarcely know where they are. Instead of being with God in heaven, and with that good

Saviour Who is waiting there to present them before His throne, they are busy with some ordinary affair of work or amusement: and the saddest part of the matter is, that Christians content themselves with this, and take it as a matter of course, and quite leave off striving against it.

When our prayers are over, and we go out into the world, and set about our day's work, temptations of course come in our way. Sometimes people are very provoking, and anger and ill-blood begin to stir within us. Now if we were in a way of striving in earnest to think often of Christ in heaven, we might presently put down the unkind thought, before it had broken into words, by just wishing in earnest that He would help us to do so. But we are not used to this, and so unhappily we soon become used to give way to our evil tempers, and we spoil our dealings with our brother by all manner of cross words, angry looks, and harsh imaginations. Or it may be, a different sort of temptation comes across a man. The devil brings before him some object, from which Christ has commanded him to turn away his eyes and his heart. If now he were used to look upward, to think of that heaven where no unclean thing can enter, and of that Saviour Who is always watching him there, this would give him strength to pray in earnest that very moment: and no unclean spirit, no evil desire or fancy, can ever prevail against real and serious prayer. Pray with the heart, and courageously turn away the eyes, and you will, by God's blessing, win in a moment a great spiritual victory, which may do you unspeakable good as long as you live. But such prayer and such self-command will not come of themselves to a person who has gone on idly and carelessly, without any regular endeavour to muse and meditate on heavenly things.

Therefore, my brethren, in one word I say to you, *Try*. There is no good to be had without serious *trying*. Try to think earnestly, at least twice a day, of the work which your Father has given you to do, and of the reward which He has prepared for you. Try to remember these your earnest thoughts at other times of the day or night, and especially when temptation of any sort comes on. Try to-day, try to-morrow, try every day, try again and again. God is merciful: He will surely lend you a hand. God is true, and He has promised to help you. Holiness and heaven are great things; but through His unspeakable love, they may be had for trying!

SERMON XI.

OFFICE OF FERVENT CHARITY TOWARDS OUR FORGIVENESS.

SUNDAY AFTER ASCENSION DAY.

1 S. Pet. iv. 8.

"Above all things have fervent charity among your-selves, for charity shall cover the multitude of sins."

During these days of waiting, the days between Holy Thursday and Whitsunday, the Church will not allow us to forget the warning words, in the sound of which He departed. He will come again in "ᵃlike manner, as ye have seen Him go into heaven." She gives us therefore a lesson for the week, which takes us on to the Last Day. "The end of all things is at hand." As surely as the heavens opened on Ascension Day to let the Son of Man, our Redeemer, pass through into heaven; so surely, and that before long, will the same heavens open again, and He will pass outwards once more, not now alone, and in humility, but in power and glory, His Angels and saints all with Him. And that will be the end of all things: the end of all these things that we see, and live amongst, here on earth: the end of caring and labouring for the body: the end of earthly

ᵃ Acts i. 11.

schemes, fancies, and passions; of eating and drinking, marrying and giving in marriage, buying and selling, planting and building. It will be the end of all these, and the beginning of heaven and of hell. It will surely be, and that before long. It is at hand: the thunders are gathering in the air. What are we to do? "Be sober, and watch unto prayer." There be will an end of eating and drinking; therefore be sober. Give not yourself over to base and filthy satisfactions, which make a man uneasy beforehand, which are gone in a moment, and are loathsome when they are over. Be sober, and be awake: "watch unto prayer." Observe, it is S. Peter who speaks: one of those who being told to watch, while his Lord was praying in the Garden, fell asleep, and *that* three times over: and who afterwards fell into the more grievous fault of denying his Saviour *just three times.* It is S. Peter who bids us all "watch unto prayer," for he knows better than most, how dearly we must pay for it, if we refuse to watch. Our Lord had said to him, "Watch, and pray," and he had not watched, and had fallen into temptation: but having recovered, he now delivers on the message to us. Our Lord had said, "he that betrayeth Me is at hand;" S. Peter says, "the end of all things is at hand." And then it is as if he added, "I did not altogether watch, and great indeed was my danger, and my escape narrow: do you try and do better than I did." Watch and pray: and before all things, be found of Him in love: take care that, when He comes, you may go out to meet Him with fervent love towards one another in your hearts. You must love: your hearts must be full of love: love to Him, love to one another: and you must love with all fervency: the fire must be kept clear and bright, or it will surely go out. Have fervent charity towards one another: keep it up, feed it, fan it, purify and quicken it. It is not to be *bright* only, to make a fair shew to persons at a distance, and make them think we are alive and busy: but it must have in it warmth also, genial and continual warmth, for the support and comfort of those who are close at hand. As those who have to spend the night abroad in the hot countries where lions and tigers are found, take care to make a good fire before they lie down to rest, and take turns also to watch the fire at night, this being the best way to keep off the ravenous beasts until the morning: so it behoves us, one and all, to keep up the fire of Christian love, inwardly in our hearts and outwardly in our behaviour, as long as we are in this wilderness, in the darkness or dim twilight of this dangerous world: and so to keep off that roaring lion, who goeth about, seeking whom he may devour. Our one care should be, that when He cometh, Who will come as a thief in the night, He may find us with oil in our lamps, i. e. with charity in our hearts and behaviour.

Now, mark the reason alleged for this: observe the special cause set down by the chief Apostle, why we should labour above all to have fervent charity among ourselves. Of course many, very many, and very true and good reasons might have been mentioned. He might have said, "Have fervent charity, for it is the only sufficient sign of faith: have fervent charity, else you will be unlike your Lord: have fervent charity, else heaven itself, could you go there, would not make you happy." But in this place he does not say either one of these things; but the Holy Spirit guides him to say another thing equally true, and equally needful for us all to remember: "have fervent charity among yourselves, for charity shall cover the multitude of sins:" i. e. "if you have true love for God and for one another in your hearts; if you have kept this holy fire up by the constant practice of your lives, and so are found at the last Day really loving, fervently loving both your God and your neighbour, this love will in some way or other cover and hide your sins, and shelter you from the wrath to come. The Almighty Father for Christ's sake will accept it: Christ will present it, as He does our prayers and good works, joining all to His one only perfect Sacrifice: Christ will present it, for He is our Advocate, ever living to make intercession for us: and thus although not in the way of merit, properly so called, for in nothing can we sinful creatures make God our debtor, but according to the true way of His most merciful covenant by the Gospel, our charity will really help us to obtain pardon for our sins. The Almighty, pleased with us, will cast all our sins behind His back: i. e. He will remember them no more, He will make as though He did not see them, they shall be fully and freely forgiven.

Plainly this is the meaning of the words, "charity shall cover the multitude of sins:" plainly they refer to what will be at the last day; for the Apostle's thoughts in this place are all upon the last day. He is speaking of the end of all things; of our having to give an account as stewards; of the joyful revelation of Christ's glory. This is what the Apostle is speaking of; and not of any lesser comfort and satisfaction, how real soever, allowed us by the way. We are to draw a picture in our mind, as we read, of our Lord on His Judgement seat, and the Books opened, and the hidden things revealed according to what is there written. How then shall any man stand, since we are all born in sin, and in many things we offend all? The gracious Judge will cast, as it were, His own royal mantle over those who shall have been found in Him, in faith and in fervent charity: He will spread His skirt over His servants, accounting them His near kinsmen: He will blot out all the handwriting, all the entries that would otherwise stand against them in His account-books. Thus their charity will cover the multitude of their sins. For His Son's sake He forgave them in their Baptism their original sin, the sinful taint inherited from Adam. If they have since grievously sinned, yet upon their true confession, and turning to Him in loving penitence, He again forgave them, and gave them entire Absolution; still for His dear Son's sake. Again, as to their daily sins of infirmity, which, if despised, would grow to a most heavy burthen, like grains of sand, each one little in itself, but when heaped together, enough to sink a large vessel: these also, being daily confessed, daily renounced and striven against, will be found at the Last Day to be covered with that atoning veil of charity: as an old Father and Bishop says, "First is confession, then charity: for of charity what saith the Scripture? It covereth the multitude of sins."

But here we must be careful not to deceive ourselves. A man may think that he has this charity, and so that he will find his sins forgiven, while he is very far from it. Fervent charity is a precious medicine, made up of many ingredients: and persons may easily mistake and think it is all right, when perhaps some chief portion of the healing draught is left out. One man may depend on his good-temper, another on his warm and affectionate feelings, another on his freely parting with his money. Therefore Holy Scripture does not only tell us, as here in general, that we must have fervent charity, but mentions also in several places the chiefest and surest tokens of charity, for men to try themselves by. E. g. it is full of penitent thoughts: true love cannot bear itself for having behaved so ill to the beloved; it is not ashamed to confess; it grudges not to bear pain and self-denial; like the woman who washed our Lord's feet with her tears, and wiped them with the hairs of her head: and for her reward, He Who is the Truth said of her, "[b] Her sins which are many, are forgiven, for she loved much." My brethren, are not our sins many? And how shall we ever obtain forgiveness for them, except by loving Him much, Who hath paid so dear that they might be capable of pardon? And again another Apostle, S. James, has used the very form of speaking in the text, about covering a multitude of sins. They are remarkable words, the very last words of his epistle. "[c] If any of you do err from the truth, and one convert him: let him know, that he which converteth a sinner from the error of his ways, shall save a soul from death, and shall hide a multitude of sins." Here forgiveness is promised especially to one especial work of charity; converting sinners: doing good

[b] S. Luke vii. 47.   [c] S. James v. 19, 20.

to perishing souls. Which of us all is tender and humbled in heart, from the recollection of wrong things weighing down his conscience, mingling in his prayers, chilling and damping his endeavours to please his Saviour? Let him with all his heart apply himself more and more, far more than he has done yet, to the profiting of his brethren's souls: let him not mind going out of his way, denying himself, giving more than he can well spare, if by any means he may attain to that highest honour, of being really God's instrument for the saving of one of Christ's redeemed. O how can we ever think enough of our merciful Lord's most tender and fatherly providence, in that He not only offers us pardon, but appoints, as one chief way of obtaining it, our helping, in good earnest, to the conversion of our fellow sinners! What happy meetings, to be looked forward to, hereafter in heaven! What double joy to the Angels, even now watching us on earth, when they behold each returning penitent making his own pardon sure by labouring to bring back others to repentance, and those again others, in a blessed chain, reaching, no one can tell how far! And for this among other reasons I would seriously advise every one of you, my friends, (for which of us all has not more than enough sins to be forgiven?) to give some little of his substance: to his power, yea, and beyond his power, to the missionary collections which we make half yearly among you. It is one way of helping to convert sinners from the error of their ways. Doubt not, then, that according to the Scripture it will help to hide your multitude of sins.

There are other works of charity mentioned especially, by our Blessed Lord in His Sermon on the Mount, with express promise of the forgiveness of sins. One, you all know, since He has put it in your mouth to be spoken of, every time you say a prayer to Him. When ye pray, say, "Forgive us our trespasses, as we forgive them that trespass against us." "[d] For if ye forgive men their trespasses, your heavenly Father will also forgive you." O, bear this in mind, ye sinners: take care to be very very forgiving: it will greatly help your own repentance and pardon. The Merciful One will not keep His anger for ever against you; He will chasten you, maybe, but only in love, if you, while you turn from your own faults, are free and speedy in pardoning others. Have pity on your fellow-servants, and He will have pity on you.

Again our Lawgiver said on the Mount, "[e] Judge not, that ye be not judged." Here is another most gracious help to pardon. Be candid, favourable, kind, in your sentences on others : slow to make yourself their judge: unwilling to believe or speak amiss of them. So will the Almighty more readily accept your endeavours to repent, and not be extreme to mark what is done amiss. Alas ! how plain it is that Christians in general think little, far too little of their own sins; they are so very free in censuring their brethren, and making out bad meanings in all that they say and do ! But why should it be always so with us ? Surely we have a heavy burden of transgressions of our own; we cannot afford to part with any means of release. Christ has appointed, as one help and mean to our release, that

[d] S. Matt. vi. 14.   [e] Ib. vii. 1.

we should not judge, should not be eager to find fault. If we judge not, He has promised that we shall not be judged. He has pointed out this as one work of that heavenly charity, which will be found at the last Day to cover a multitude of sins.

By this time, dear brethren, if you have been able to mind what was said, you will understand how that every where in Scripture forgiveness is offered to love, and to the fruits of love: and yet not a word is said, as though we by our good works could deserve or purchase it. No: the deserving and purchasing of our pardon depends, we know, on our Lord Jesus Christ entirely. "It cost more to redeem our souls:" "it is higher than heaven, what can we do? deeper than earth, where should we go?" And when Scripture speaks of love covering sins, it does not of course mean that *our* love, *our* faith, *our* works, any thing of *ours* could be a sacrifice, so as to do away with one sin. But it does mean that there are things, without which the pardon so dearly bought will not in the end be ours: it means that charity, forgiveness, conversion of other sinners, judging gently, and other good ways and works, do really help, in some way known to God, to make our pardon and cure more perfect: and, that although these things could never have obtained heaven for us, yet the neglect of these things may and will forfeit heaven, and fasten our sins freshly upon us. We could not have saved ourselves; but, being saved, we may ruin ourselves. We could not have called and elected ourselves: but we may make our calling and election sure, or we may unthankfully cast it away. Sin casts it away; love and charity make it sure. Are you then troubled at past sins? Pray and endeavour to love: busy yourself in all the works of love. Or is your care on account of your own present infirmities? Yet do all as well as you can; still love on, and be active in deeds of love; and of all things abhor known and wilful sin; for that absolutely excludes love. Your love must be fervent. You know how it is with regard to those for whom you have a partial kindness. Such in some measure ought to be your love of God: such also your charity to your brethren, as members of Christ. Those whom you love, you delight to think of: so, if you love our Lord, you will often draw nigh to Him by devout meditation and prayer. You will think of Him till your heart is full; and then you will look round and see, who of your brethren are now within your reach, to whom you have it in your power to do good. Make sure that in helping any such you are in fact helping the Lord; for each one of them is in the Lord's stead: of each one of them He will say, "Doing it unto him, ye did it unto Me[f]." Especially, He charges you, do what you can for the perishing souls of your brethren. Be very covetous, very ambitious to help in saving, if it may be, a soul from death. If you care little for the souls of men, be sure there is some very serious defect in your charity. You had need go over your doings again and again, and compare them with the Word of God and the love of Christ, until you are thoroughly vexed and ashamed of yourself: thoroughly touched with His love, Who is ready to pardon you all. This will help you to be really lov-

[f] S. Matt. xxv. 40.

ing to your neighbour: a humble, contrite heart will help you to forbear and to forgive: a loving heart will desire that other hearts should be loving also. You will try to awaken them, that they and you may do good to one another: and so bye and bye, when you look for the account of your past sins, there will be no entry in that page: the Lord will have cast them all behind His back, they will have melted away "like the ice in the fair warm weather," and you, and those whom you charitably helped, will be on the Right Hand, will hear Christ's final Absolution, and will enter after Him into the Kingdom of Love.

SERMON XII.

THE NEARNESS OF THE UNSEEN WORLD.

SUNDAY AFTER ASCENSION DAY.

S. MARK xvi. 19.

"After the Lord had spoken unto them, He was taken up into heaven, and sat down on the Right Hand of God."

It is well that at such times as this, Christian persons earnestly trying to meditate on the great things which happened to our Lord, should put themselves as well as they can in the place of the holy Apostles, and consider what their feelings must have been, who saw with their very eyes the wonderful and fearful events which we only read or hear of. The difference between seeing and only hearing is very great. Job speaks of it, as if it made *all* the difference. "[a] I have heard of Thee by the hearing of the ear: but now mine eye seeth Thee." Which of us has not found something like this? When God, e. g. has given us back a dear friend, whom we perhaps expected never to see alive again: or when on the other hand He has taken away some one whom we could ill spare: which of us but found such joy and such sorrow far different from what he had before expected? It might be more tolerable to us, or it might be

[a] Job xlii. 5.

heavier; at any rate it was not the same as our imagination had told us of.

We cannot therefore suppose, do what we will, that we draw accurately to ourselves in thought the picture of the great event, which the Scripture draws for us in words at this time, the Ascension of our Lord and Saviour into the heavens. But some points in it we may be sufficiently sure of, and may feel in our hearts enough to do us much good. I will now take one, and that the simplest and most obvious. Only think how the beholding of that sight must have brought home to them the thought, how near earth is to heaven; what a narrow line, what a mere hair's breadth, separates us from the eternal world. Here is a Person Who, down to a certain moment on the day answering to last Thursday, the fortieth day after the Paschal Sunday, had been living and conversing bodily among His friends, going in and out, eating and drinking in their presence. For so many years, except at certain short intervals, He had been their constant companion; day after day and all day long, it had been a matter of course to them to think of Him, to expect His interference, to order all their ways with an eye to Him, as visibly present. Their whole life, their whole being in the world, had been in a manner mixed up with Him. And behold, He disappears at once: not gradually, by slow decay and death, as one worn out, from whom people part by degrees; but in a moment. They see Him go, their eyes follow Him, as He is taken up and parted from them, rising up from the earth on which He was standing, the level land on the top of Mount Olivet, very near the village of Bethany. From that spot, a familiar spot, a neighbourhood where they had been used to see Him employed in His daily work; while in the act of lifting up His Hands to bless them, they behold Him slowly drawn up as by an invisible power, through the air. He is going: He will soon be gone. See now, a cloud begins to receive Him, a bright cloud probably, like that which came and overshadowed the three disciples on mount Tabor; the special token, perhaps, of the presence of His Holy Spirit. In this cloud His disciples lose sight first of His glorious and Divine Countenance and all the upper part of His person, and then of the rest; and while they are gazing, He is gone. His very Feet slowly disappear and are lost within that bright cloud. He is gone: they feel that He is no more on earth. "But where is He? How is He employed? How may we now think and imagine of Him? We cannot forget Him, we cannot do without Him:" so we may be sure, would each Apostle feel in his heart, "Who will tell us what has become of Him?" They saw His Footsteps; the very spot from which He ascended was specially marked with the print of His retiring Feet, which indeed some affirm to be visible even at this time: at any rate, the saying shews the feeling of the Church about our Lord's example and pattern left on earth, that we, treading in His steps, may ascend after Him to heaven. They saw His Footsteps, but Himself they saw no more, and a thousand times a day, we may be sure, did they ask themselves, "Where is He now? In what work of love is He engaged for us?"

We may the better enter into the feelings of our

Saviour's Apostles at that moment, if we consider how it is with ourselves, and with those whom we know, when they are taken from us by death; when that final, cold, dark cloud receives them altogether out of our sight. They had been gradually, perhaps, but slowly, fading away; their friends had staid with them watching them, and had said over and over again to themselves, "they *must soon* be released: they *cannot* last much longer." We knew they would go; we watched them, as we saw that they were going: and now they are gone: and where are they? What is their place in the world out of sight?

Yes, brethren: the death of each person among us, as we part with each one in turn, reads so far the same lesson as the glorious event of our Lord's own Ascension. It puts *home* to us, brings forcibly before us, this most certain, most aweful, most blessed circumstance, the nearness of the next world to this: so that as we read in the Burial service, "in the midst of life we are in death," so at sight of the Ascension, were it not for our sad unworthiness, we might say to ourselves, "in the midst of earth we are in heaven." There is, as I said, but a hair's breadth, the narrowest possible span, between the condition of Lazarus, lying at the rich man's gate full of sores, yet full of patience and faith, and the condition of the same Lazarus, carried of the Angels into Abraham's bosom. One moment *this*, the other moment *that*, is his condition. To see our Lord disappear as He did, must have fixed this aweful thought in the Apostles' minds, so as nothing else could fix it; except indeed they had been caused by Providence to witness with their eyes a case of the contrary kind, a case like that of Dathan and Abiram, when the earth opened her mouth suddenly, and swallowed them up, with their wives and children and all that appertained unto them. "[b]They and all that appertained unto them went down alive into the pit, and the earth closed upon them: and they perished from among the congregation." If we had been by to see this, surely, my brethren, it would have been to us a most overpowering proof, how close we are to eternity; how near to this present world is that fearful pit into which those sinners sank; quite as near on the one side, as the heaven which was opened on Ascension Day is on the other side.

Truly it is so: had we been by to witness these great things, they would have been to us astonishing testimonies from the great Lord, Creator and Owner of all, that we are on the edge of both heaven and hell. There are but those two, heaven and hell, appointed for us, and one or other we must take; there is but heaven for us to ascend into with our Saviour, or the pit for us to go down alive into, with Korah. And the end of all things, this double end, is close at hand: one moment, and it may be here. Before one more breath is drawn, the one or the other of these may be our unchangeable portion for ever: and if we are spared, it is but a question of time. Sooner or later that last breath will come, and we shall find ourselves—we, who are now here, as yet by God's mercy with more or less of hope—shall find ourselves actually sinking into the deep with the Evil one, or in the act of being carried up with our Lord into heaven itself.

[b] Num. xvi. 33.

It is even so, brethren: if you have any faith at all, you surely believe this: I know you do not doubt nor deny it. You believe it: but what do you think of it? Or is it too fearful, too astounding, for you willingly to think on it at all? Well, you *may* put it off; I mean, you may put off the thought of it, if you please. Nothing at present forces you against your will to turn your minds towards eternity. As it is in any person's power, when he hears of such things in Church, to stop his ears, and hinder himself from so much as receiving the sounds which bring with them disagreeable unwelcome thoughts; like the deaf adder spoken of in the Psalm, "which refuseth to hear the voice of the charmer:" so the just God leaves us all free, if we will, to decline listening in our hearts to His calls and warnings at any time. There are plenty of things in this world to think about, if we choose, every day and all day long: mere play for children and childish people, mere business for grown-up men and women, mere ease and refreshment for the aged whose work is over. There are lusts for the sensual, vanities for the proud, quarrels for the quarrelsome, grievances for the discontented and envious. Verily it is a world, not wanting in objects to take up a man's mind, if he chooses to give himself wholly to them. No doubt, you may, if you will, come to great perfection in the art of shutting out from your soul uneasy disquieting thoughts about the next world: and there is one who will always be too ready at hand, too glad to help you to such irreligious forgetfulness.

But then, my brethren, you must take the consequences. You may effectually shut out the apprehensions of eternity for the present: but then you must make up your mind to what may happen bye and bye. This is a war, in which there is no discharge. If a man take the devil's wages, if he consent, for his present enjoyment's sake, to turn away his heart from his Saviour and his salvation; then he must abide the same sentence, which the master and captain whom he has chosen will abide at last. You may refuse to think of the next world, saying, "it is too dismal; you had rather enjoy yourself: you will let nothing daunt you:" but whatever comes in the next world of such a course of conduct, to that you must make up your mind.

But, my brethren, my children in Christ, I hope better things than this of you, one and all. I hope that there is not one here, who will obstinately refuse to face the thought—terrible as it surely is for all who have sinned; that to you, to me, to each one of us severally, the Almighty Judge will ere long openly and bodily appear, and say a word which will send us either upwards or downwards for ever. Now, He speaks many words to us, and leaves us our choice whether we will mind them: but that word will leave us no choice. As soon as we hear of it, we shall obey it[c]. He will either say, "Come, ye blessed of My Father," or "Go, ye cursed:" and presently each one of us will find himself either drawn upwards, as our Lord on the day of His Ascension, or cast down and swallowed, as Dathan and Abiram when the earth opened her mouth.

Supposing there were any doubt of these things, yet a wise man would do his best to be safe, even

[c] Ps. xviii. 44.

from the chance of so terrible a lot as falling into hell, and to secure but the chance of so blessed a place as Heaven. But there is really no doubtfulness in the matter: you know there is not. Think only of what happened on Holy Thursday. Twelve men saw their Lord, Whom they had before seen crucified and risen again, go bodily up into heaven: they gave up everything they had in the world, and spent their time in labouring and suffering, and at last laid down their lives, in testimony of what they had seen, "God also bearing them witness with signs and wonders and gifts of the Holy Ghost." And as surely as they saw Him go into heaven, so surely they know, and have told us, where He is in heaven. Not in any Angel's place, but above the highest Angels: "on the Right Hand of God, Angels and Authorities and Powers being made subject unto Him:" according to His own prophecy, uttered indeed to His enemies, the high priests and elders, but in the hearing also of S. Peter and S. John, and perhaps also of some other of His friends: " Hereafter shall ye see the Son of Man sitting on the right hand of power, and coming in the clouds of heaven." That is, " ye shall see Him both as King and as Judge: as King, for it is said 'sitting on the right hand of power:' as Judge, for it is said 'coming in the clouds of heaven.'" Plain therefore it was to the Apostles, and no less plain is it to us and to all Christians, what is become of our Lord, and how highly He is exalted. Now this of course, if a man have common sense, to say nothing now of duty, and gratitude, and love, settles what ought to be the whole course of our lives. If Christ is exalted above all, if He has all power in heaven and in earth, what madness is it to disobey Him; what entire safety, peace, and comfort, to be under His protection and favoured by Him! But there is another thing which touches us yet more nearly. This Almighty King, this righteous and unerring Judge, is no stranger, no alien to our nature, under whose dominion we find ourselves placed, and so are bound to submit ourselves to him, but without having any special interest, he in us and we in him. Not at all so. He is no stranger: He is our bone and our flesh; of the same blood, of the same nature that we are, only without spot of sin. He is so near to us, so entirely one with us, that in His exaltation we all are exalted. We are exalted as men, children of Adam: because One Who is also a child of Adam is lifted up to so high a place. One Who is really, as men speak, our blood-relation; really, outwardly, bodily, akin to each one of us: is set down on the right hand of the throne of the Majesty in the heavens. He has all our natural tendencies to love and indulgent pity: He loves us because we are His kindred, with a love far more perfect than any one of us loveth another: indeed our love for one another is altogether taught and inspired by Him. If you had a brother who loved you, in the Queen's court, entrusted with all the good things of the state: should you not account your fortune made? How much more, now you know that your brother Who loves you and died for you is at the Right Hand of God!

Can there be anything more than this? There is something more, yea, and beyond comparison greater and more blessed. We are not only, as men, brothers of our Lord and Saviour, but as Christian men, we are actual members of Him, mystically yet really united to Him, partakers through Him of the Divine Nature: as it is written, "[d] He called them gods, to whom the Word of God," the Incarnate Saviour, "came." Since then we are each one members of Him, not only is our common human nature exalted in Him, but each of us also personally. He is the Head: you, I, the rest, are members: and where the Head is, there God intends the members should be also; there, by mysterious communion, they are already. He is the great King; therefore we are all of us kings. Through the Sacrament of our new-birth, Holy Baptism, we are inheritors of His royal blood; and by His grace we are entrusted and enabled to reign as kings here on earth; to reign over our own wild passions and keep our bodies and souls in order; and also to reign over outward things, to command even the changes and chances of this mortal life, that they do us no harm but everlasting good, because, being either borne patiently or used faithfully, they help us to become better, and to do God service, in His kingdom: as it is declared to all Christians; "[e] All things are yours: whether... the world, or life, or death, or things present, or things to come; all are yours; and ye are Christ's; and Christ is God's."

Away then with all little and low thoughts. Who would not be very courageous in Christ's work! And on the other hand, down with all proud thoughts: for the more highly we are exalted in Christ, the more reason is there we should abase ourselves in the very dust, remembering past backslidings and present infirmities, and the strict account we have to give.

[d] S. John x. 35.   [e] 1 Cor. iii. 21—23.

SERMON XIII.

CHRIST-FILLING ALL THINGS.

SUNDAY AFTER ASCENSION DAY.

EPH. iv. 10.

"He that descended is the same also that ascended up far above all heavens, that He might fill all things."

S. PAUL, in this part of the epistle to the Ephesians, is preaching us a short sermon on a verse in the sixty-eighth Psalm. The verse on which he is preaching is, "When He ascended up on high, He led captivity captive, and received gifts for men;" and of course his sermon is well suited to this holy season, in which we remember Christ's Ascension. Observe here, says the Apostle, how David, speaking of the Lord his God, says, "He is gone up on high." Well, but for God to go up, He must first have come down among men. For His place and abode is naturally up on high. He must descend, before He can ascend. Therefore, proceeds the Apostle, "this word, ascended, what else can it signify, but that He had also descended first?" He had in a mysterious way come down from His high place in heaven: and whither had He come down? Not simply to earth, but into the lower parts of the earth. And whither hath He gone up? Not simply to heaven, but far above all heavens. There is a descent first, and an ascent afterwards: the descent as low, the ascent as high as it could be. That there might be no mistake, he bids all take notice, that it was the same Person Who first came down and afterwards went up. "He that descended is the same also that ascended up far above all heavens." And lastly, he explains in one word the merciful purpose of this most astonishing dispensation. The Lord, the very same Lord and Son of God, first came down, then went up, and His end in doing so was, "that He might fill all things." The whole answers in a remarkable way to the second and third portions of the Apostles' Creed. The great God descends to earth, that is, Jesus Christ made Man, "conceived by the Holy Ghost, born of the Virgin Mary." He descends not only to earth but to the lower parts of the earth: i. e. He suffers "under Pontius Pilate; is crucified, dead, and buried, He descended into hell." For of this descent into hell, more especially, we are to think, when we read of His going down to the lower parts of the earth. During the hours from the moment that He gave up the ghost to the moment of His glorious Resurrection, His Body lay in the grave, and His Divine Soul went down "[a]and preached to the spirits in prison." As low as could be was His descent: and when He began to ascend again, He staid not till He came to the Right Hand of God. First, from the lower parts of the earth, from the grave and from the prison of departed souls He came to the surface of the earth again, on Easter morning,

[a] 1 S. Pet. iii. 19.

to abide in men's sight forty days. That was His Resurrection: the beginning, in fact, of His Ascension. Afterwards, at the end of the forty days, He ascended into heaven, and not into heaven only, but far above all heavens, to the very Right Hand of God the Father Almighty; where He sitteth as a King on His throne; and from whence He shall come to judge the quick and the dead. Thus the saying, He descended and ascended, is in short the second portion of our Creed. And the other saying, that He might fill all things, answers to the third or concluding portion of the same Creed. For how doth our Incarnate and Risen Lord fill all things? Surely by His Holy Spirit; of which it is written in the book of Wisdom, "[b]The Spirit of the Lord filleth the world." And did not the Holy Comforter on the first Whitsunday begin to fill the world with Christ, uniting sinners to Him one by one, and making them saints, till the whole earth should be full of His glory, and that glory should be more and more glorious, until in its fulness it should become the "Resurrection of the body, and the life everlasting?" Of all which He gave a token, in that He came down at the first "[c]with a sudden great sound as of a rushing mighty wind, and *filled* all the house where" the Apostles " were sitting." They heard Him, above, beneath, on every side of them, at once: as their fathers had seen His visible glory when the cloud filled the Temple. That mighty sound, that bright cloud, were the sure tokens of the Spirit of the Father and of Christ, abiding everywhere and at all times in the Holy Catholic Church; shewing its present work in the "Communion of saints,

[b] Wisd. i. 7.   [c] Acts ii. 2.

and the Forgiveness of sins," and certain bye and bye to fulfil, as I said, its future work in the "Resurrection of the body, and the life everlasting." Thus the final portion of our Creed explains how He Who first descended and then ascended did so, that He might fill all things. Had He not descended, by taking our nature upon Him, there could have been no Body of Christ, of which we might be made members. Had He not afterwards ascended into heaven, He could not afterwards have sent down His Spirit to fill all things with Himself by making all members of Him.

This is the special point, my brethren, on which I would desire that we may all meditate to-day: our Lord and Saviour filling all things. Reflect how entirely He does fill all things in every sense of that word. All things, according to their measure, are full of Him. In that He is true God, One with the Father, He filleth all places, all regions, one as much as another, with His Divine Presence. In that He is God made Man, God our Saviour, God crucified, dead, and buried, risen and glorified and partaken of by His people, He filleth all His holy ones, whether in earth, in paradise, or in heaven, as each one is capable of receiving Him. Look at a little child just baptized. There is no outward change in it, it sleeps and wakes, takes its nourishment and utters its little cries as before; we *see* no particular difference, and yet faith tells us, that little one is full of Christ, and were it to die this moment, would be sure, quite sure, to go to Christ. Consider that same little child as it grows older. It is still full of Christ; for it hath still Christ's Spirit within it, enabling it, if it will, to live in its degree the life of Christ upon earth. Too true it is, that by a certain amount of sin, known to God, unknown to us, any one of us may, if he will, cease to be a partaker of Christ; he may finally drive the good Spirit away from him, and become the mere shadow of a Christian, a walking dead body, empty and void of Christ our life. Yet still the great truth remains, that it is the purpose and will of our Redeemer to fill us all with Himself by His Spirit; and even with regard to those who seem most entirely to have forfeited the gift, we are not allowed to despair. It may be some friend's sad case, it may be our own; we may have come fearfully near to the point of final ruin, we may be trembling on the very edge of the pit, but it is not too late: if we yet hear the voice of Christ, if we yet have the heart to turn towards it when we hear it, He may return and fill us with Himself again. Only remember, and never let the thought go, that every moment of wilful delay is lost for ever: and what if we should be lost with it?

Christ is in each Christian, filling each more and more with Himself, in such measure as we try to keep Him with us; but He is not in all alike. The gifts of His Holy Spirit are of many kinds, and are given in divers degrees, as the rewards will be hereafter; and so holy men have compared the condition of glorified spirits in heaven to so many vessels ranged in some rich man's treasure house, each to be made quite full, yet of course holding more or less according to their unequal sizes. All good Christians will be called together to sit down at the feast in the kingdom of heaven, to "be satisfied with the plenteousness of His house, and to have drink given them of His pleasures as out of a river [d]:" but some will be able to taste and receive more than others. Every star will shine in unclouded brightness, yet "[e] one star" will differ "from another star in glory." And as the rewards prepared in heaven, such must the trials be here on earth: various and unequal, as He knoweth best for each. As a man's limbs are all of the same body, all quickened with one life from the same soul, which belongs to one limb as entirely as it does to another, so you and I, this Christian and that Christian, all alike are of Christ, all quickened with one and the self-same Spirit, which is the life, the Christian life, of one of us as entirely as of another. And yet our offices and our gifts are not the same, any more than the eye has the same work with the hand, or the head with the feet. Christ filleth all, therefore all are one: therefore none must look down upon another, or refuse to sympathize with it. You know S. Paul's parable: "[f] the eye cannot say unto the hand, I have no need of thee; neither again the head to the feet, I have no need of you." Those who have higher or more favoured places are not to look down upon others, or think they could do without them. And again: Christ filleth all, and in the strength of Christ each one doth his work, whatever it is. Why repinest thou, as if thou wert forgotten, as if thy Lord took no account of thee, whoever thou art who occupiest the room of a lower and less honoured limb in the great body? Do thou thy mean ordinary work throughly well, entirely in Christ's Spirit, and see whether He will not treat thee with such a reward as will take

[d] Ps. xxxvi. 8.   [e] 1 Cor. xv. 41.   [f] Ib. xii. 21.

away all temptation to envy thy neighbour. It is not, depend upon it, it is not so much *what* we do, as how we do it, with what mind and purpose, which will make the great difference in the accounts of eternity. Your Lord has set you in such a place: one care you have, to do your duty in that place: you may safely trust your good Saviour to take care of your reward. It is *your own* duty, moreover, which you have to mind, not the duty of other people: *that* also, except so far as you can help them, you had best leave to the common Master Who hath set each one his task. If you cannot help seeing faults in your brethren's work, pray for them, but do not despise them, nor indulge a fretful wish that you were in their place, under the notion that you could manage better. Force yourself still to recollect that Christ is in them and in you: for His sake be gentle to them; for His sake be strict with yourself.

One other thought I will mention: a very deep and aweful one, and very natural to come into a serious mind on this great day of Ascension; that as Christ is in all Christians, one and the same to all, so He is, and ever must be, one and the same with His former self. He is one and the same Christ now in Glory, Who humbled Himself in the dust at Gethsemane, and permitted men to nail Him to the Cross on Calvary. He is, as S. Paul says, "[g] Jesus Christ, the Same yesterday, and to-day, and for ever." "He that descended is the same also that ascended up far above all heavens, that He might fill all things." Now as Christ is one with Himself always, so we, who are Christ's. We are not so bad perhaps, or not

[g] Heb. xiii. 8.

so good, as we were at some former time, but we are the very same persons that we were at our Baptism, may be, or so many years ago. This seems a simple thing: but have you ever considered it in earnest, my brethren? Have you considered, that as our Lord Jesus Christ is the very same Person, now above all the heavens, as He was when His condition was lowest; hid in the womb, and laid in the grave: so shall you and I be the same persons, bye and bye, in the next world, as we have been since our first beginning? You and I, and those who are next to us, on our right hand and our left, and all the rest of the congregation, every one of them, are and will be the same persons for ever. "[h] My Redeemer liveth," saith holy Job: "and in my flesh shall I see God: Whom mine eyes shall behold and not another." And another, with very different expectations, said, even the covetous prophet Balaam said, "[i] I shall see Him but not now; I shall behold Him but not nigh." Every wicked Christian may expect with Balaam to see Him one day with the eye of flesh, Whom he refuses now to see with the eye of faith. Such as Balaam will see Christ, but not nigh; for the word will be given in that moment, "Depart from Me." And on the other hand patient believers, like Job, who have waited on Him, though their reins were consumed within them, they also shall see Him, they shall see His Face with joy, plainly with their very bodily eyes, wherewith they behold one another in their life-time: as it is written, "[k] thine eyes shall behold the King in His beauty." We shall see Him, we shall all behold Him: with the same keen and

[h] Job xix. 25, 26, 27.   [i] Num. xxiv. 17.   [k] Isa. xxxiii. 17.

aweful distinctness, the same sense of utter reality, as the Apostles felt when they saw Him rise from the earth, and disappear behind the cloud on the top of the mount of Olives. We shall all see Him, we shall behold Him; but with how different aspects, and with what opposite results! What a cloud will that be, behind which He will hide His glory from those who shall be left behind, when in the Body He shall return to heaven again! For it will not be then, you know, as in His first Ascension. He will not leave His faithful ones gazing after Him, but they shall be caught up to meet Him in the air, shall be received into His own cloud, and so shall they ever be with the Lord[1]. But those that are left behind; the Balaams and Korahs and Judas's, the unclean and covetous, the unruly and unbelieving; which way will *they* move? What sort of a cloud will receive them, and with whom will they be for ever?

And *we* shall see it, *that* is the point: *we* shall be there, and have our portion on the one side or on the other, *we*, the very same persons that are here now, shall be there then: on the right hand or on the left; and we shall have our memories with us and our consciousness, only a thousand times keener and more lively than ever they were on earth. Here, from mere lapse of time, unless people watch against it, they really forget that they are the same persons who did such and such wicked things many years ago. I have often found it so. Without any special repentance, they go on as if the sins of their youth were blotted out, merely because it is twenty, thirty or forty years since they were committed; and they

---

[1] 1 Thess. iv. 17.

are as much affronted at being reminded of them, as if you were charging them with the sins of some other person. But it is not so: they *are* the same persons, and so they will find at last. God grant they may find it in time!

We shall be the same persons, when we stand up to be judged: and what is yet more aweful, more beyond thought, we shall be the same persons afterwards. On and on through all eternity, *we*, we ourselves shall abide, knowing ourselves to be, in heaven or in hell, unspeakably near to God or unspeakably far from Him. Very different, no doubt, we shall be, both in soul and in body, from what we are now: but still in God's sight and in our sight we shall be the same individual beings. How unlike is a little new-born child to a tall strong full-grown man, full of wisdom and counsel, and knowing so much of many things: and yet the little child, if he lives and prospers, may become such a man. So, after this our childhood on earth, we shall be full-grown in goodness or in badness, when we come to the other world; yet knowing ourselves to be the same. We must be moving upwards or downwards: starving the good seed, which is Christ in us, or growing more in His fulness. Which way are you moving? I beseech you, lay it to heart. Prove yourselves, examine yourselves, try yourselves thoroughly this very week: for next Sunday is one of the great Seasons, in which God cometh to try and judge His people for their correction; and as you employ or neglect those Seasons here on earth, so will He honour you or cast you away, when He cometh finally to judge you for reward or punishment.

SERMON XIV.

THE BLESSING OF PEACE.

SUNDAY AFTER ASCENSION DAY[a].

Ps. xxix. 9, 10.

"*The Lord sitteth above the water-flood: and the Lord remaineth a King for ever: The Lord shall give strength unto His people; the Lord shall give His people the blessing of peace.*"

THIS time last year, my brethren, and for months before and after, we were (so to speak) in a great storm: like our Lord's disciples that night on the sea of Galilee, when "[b] there arose a great tempest in the sea, and the waves beat into the ship, so that it was now full." And what did the disciples then? They had our Saviour on board, and they knew it, but He was sleeping. In that He was the Son of Man, weariness had come upon Him after His hard day's work, and it pleased Him in His Divine providence to give way to it at that time, so trying the faith of His followers; and our faith too, my brethren, whether we will really turn to Him on the like occasions, as His disciples then did; for they "came to Him, and awoke Him saying, Lord save us: we perish." So

[a] Being also the day of thanksgiving for peace at the close of the war with Russia.   [b] S. Matt. viii. 24.

did our mother the holy Church, all the time of that storm of war, which we thought so much of, while it was going on. Three times a week the Church prayed in the Litany, "that it may please Thee to give unto all nations, unity, peace, and concord;" and when there was no Litany, then we prayed for all Christian nations especially, that they might hold the Faith not only "in the unity of the spirit," but also "in the bond of peace." And more than all this, as often as we offered the Sacrifice of praise and thanksgiving, the Body and Blood of Christ in Holy Communion, we offered it for all that confess His Holy Name, that they might "live in unity and godly love." Thus the Church prayed; and who can tell how many prayed at home also, alone or with their families, that God would bring the war speedily to a right and lasting peace? And now He Who was in the ship with us, sleeping as it were, and unseen all the while, He hath heard us, unworthy, according to the greatness of His mercy, and when we least expected it, hath stayed the winds and the sea; according to that power which He shewed in so many miracles, wherein the Voice of the Lord hath been upon the waters, preserving Noah in the ark, abating the Deluge, dividing the Red Sea, quieting the ocean when Jonah had been cast into it, and the sea whereon S. Peter walked to meet Him; and delivering S. Paul and his companions from shipwreck according to His promise. We are to make no question of it, that He Who thus stilleth the raging of the sea, He, and no other it is, Who stilleth the madness of the people also: subduing men's violent passions, and making peace, when so many were eager for war.

How can we ever thank Him enough, first for the public blessing, that we are no longer at war, especially no longer at war with a nation of Christians, our brethren in the Faith; and that, so far as there may have been unfair aggression and injustice, it seems to be sincerely and effectually withdrawn and ended? And again, how can we thank Him enough for the consolation restored to so many of our fellow-creatures, who may now lie down at night and rise up in the morning, without the aching, heart-wearing thought of those who are dearest to them being in pain and danger, and they unable to wait on them or help them: who are now freed from the sad anxiety of listening after what every day may bring forth, lest they should find themselves on a sudden widowed, orphaned, or otherwise made mourners? We had so sadly abused the blessings of our long continued peace, that surely we deserved to have them entirely taken away from us. But He, Whose Name is Merciful, has had mercy upon us. He has given us another trial. God grant, that, in this time of restored peace, we may be more earnest in setting a good example to the heathen, and in praying and labouring for their conversion, than we proved ourselves to be before the war!

We cannot thank Him enough. But there is a way of thanking Him which He will surely receive: and God our Saviour calls upon us to take this way, by the very season, on which our thanksgiving falls. It is not without reason, depend upon it, that the good providence of God calls upon us thus to thank Him for the blessing of peace, in the very season of Peace, the time between our Lord's Ascension and the coming of the Holy Ghost. He went away, lifting up His Hands and blessing us, and what His words of blessing were, we know. When He came among His disciples, He was accustomed to say, "Peace be unto you:" and when He took leave of them, the night before His Death, some of His last words were, "Peace I leave with you, My Peace I give unto you." And when His Holy Spirit came down, sent down by Himself from heaven, He came to be our Peace, making both one, Jews and Gentiles to be one in Christ. Therefore, as I said, this particular season is indeed a suitable season for us to think worthily of the outward and temporal peace, with which it has pleased God to bless us. The very time itself instructs us to receive that peace as a true and great blessing, yet to think nothing of it in comparison with the heavenly Peace of which it is a shadow. And how are we to thank Him? Surely in the same way, in which He of His great love requires us to thank Him for all His mercies: by humbly receiving fresh mercies from Him. Such is His tender, parental mind towards us. "[c] What reward shall I render unto the Lord for all the benefits that He hath done unto me?" So asks the Psalmist: and what is the reply fit for God's true servants to make? "[d] I will receive the cup of salvation, and call upon the Name of the Lord." The reward He looks for at our hands is, that we should consent to receive another and greater blessing from Him. We, English Christians, are to thank Him for this deliverance from the dangers and miseries of war, by drawing near with a true heart and full assurance of faith,

[c] Ps. cxvi. 11.   [d] Ib. 12.

and humbly accepting from His Hands the spiritual and eternal good things which He, our Ascended. Lord, is inviting us to.

What those good things are, the Psalmist in the text tells us. The first is, spiritual strength : for "the Lord will give strength unto His people;" and the second is, spiritual peace: for "the Lord will give His people the blessing of peace." And they both depend on His Ascension; for what had gone before them is this, "The Lord sitteth above the water-flood, and the Lord remaineth a King for ever."

"The Lord sitteth above the water-flood." He poured out the flood in the time of Noah, and stayed it when it had done its work. He ordereth the nations, who are as mighty waters. They think they are having their own way: but indeed it is His way in which they are moving, His work which they are accomplishing, without knowing it. And again, in the spiritual world also : it is as in the twenty-fourth Psalm, "The earth is the Lord's and the fulness thereof; the world, and they that dwell therein. He hath founded it upon the seas, and established it upon the floods." At the first creation, Christ, the Word of the Lord, by Whom the heavens were made, laid out the earth above the waters: and at the new creation, the great deliverance of the world, He founded His new heaven and His new earth, the holy Church, His heavenly kingdom, on the waters of holy Baptism.

And again, "The Lord remaineth a King for ever." The kingdoms of this world change continually and pass away: not so the kingdom of Christ, that kingdom which began on Ascension Day, and under which we are now living. His "ᵉkingdom is an everlasting kingdom, and His dominion endureth throughout all generations." It is the stone hewn out of the mountain without hands, against which nothing can stand: it will dash in pieces, one after the other, all the kingdoms of this world and the glory of them, be it more or less: iron, brass, silver or gold: but as for Christ's kingdom itself, the Holy Church Universal, it shall never be dashed in pieces, for it is founded upon the Rock, Christ. And let this be our comfort and our stay in all the changes and chances of the kingdoms of men here below; in all human and earthly politics. England may pass away, as Egypt and Babylon, Greece and Rome, have passed away before her; but the Church of Christ, the heavenly Jerusalem, shall never pass away. "The Lord remaineth a King for ever:" and therefore His promises are for ever; and His people whom He hath formed for Himself, they also are for ever.

And what are His promises? Every good thing: but at this time, as I said, two more especially are set before us:—spiritual strength, and spiritual peace. "The Lord will give strength unto His people," strength, to stand firm in the place wherein He shall set them; strength, to accomplish the work which He shall appoint for them; strength, to prevail against the enemies whom He shall at any time permit to rise up against them. Such strength He promised to His holy Apostles, when, as at this time, He gave them His parting benediction. "ᶠYe shall receive power, i. e. "strength," "after that the Holy Ghost is come upon you." "ᵍTarry ye in the city of Jerusalem, until

ᵉ Ps. cxlv. 13.   ᶠ Acts i. 8.   ᵍ S. Luke xxiv. 49.
K

ye be endued with power from on high." They waited as He bade them, and in ten days time, as we shall hear on Whitsunday, " they were all filled with the Holy Ghost," Who made them bold to stand fast in the Faith, gave them a tongue and a heart to do their work in preaching it, and in due time victory over death and hell, won as their Master's had been before, by dying. Thus the Lord gave, and is ever giving, strength unto His people.

He gave also, and is ever giving, to the same people that other blessing of peace: peace with God, peace with their brethren, peace and consolation each in his own heart. Of these three, peace with God is the first and best, and on it the others depend; for as one asks, who had it in perfection, "if God be for us, who can be against us?" The peace of God is to have God Almighty, the Father the Son and the Holy Ghost, for our friend and not our enemy; to be on our part and not against us. It is the blessing of all blessings: but as S. Paul says again, it "[h]passeth all understanding;" for it is hidden in God Himself. But it maketh itself known usually by the two other kinds of peace, peace with our fellow men, and peace with our own hearts; by our being in love and charity with our neighbours, and by the witness of a man's own heart, that he constantly and humbly endeavours to please and obey his Divine Master, and when he falls, makes haste by His aid to recover.

Now both this holy peace, and the strength which enables us to preserve it, are promised, you see, to Christ's people, and to Christ's people only. Christ's people are His, not only as any other people may be

[h] Phil. iv. 7.

said to belong to their king; as Cæsar's, or Pharaoh's or Cyrus' subjects might be called their people; but in a nearer and dearer sense, because they are His members; really though mysteriously united to Him by His Holy Spirit; "[i] members of His Body, of His flesh, and of His bones." This strength and peace, strength to obey Him, and peace so long as they really strive to do so, are therefore made sure to them; for, as they live by Christ's life, not they but Christ living in them, so they are strong by Christ's strength, and at peace by Christ's peace: as He said in His gracious Farewell, "Peace I leave with you, My Peace I give unto you." And therefore, as soon as ever we quit our hold of Christ, we lose both our strength and our peace. Without Him we can do nothing: neither can any man come to the Father but by Him.

My brethren, let no man deceive himself. There are many who try to persuade themselves that all is right with them, because they have no enemies, and all around are on good terms with them. But this is merely outward peace: a heathen or an unbeliever might have it. It is no safe mark of your being one of God's people; and you hear what He says, His people only have the gift and the blessing of peace. So it is with nations, so it is with the soul of each one. We know by God's sure word of prophecy, that "[k] the nation and kingdom, which will not serve" God's Church, however it may prosper for a time, "shall perish; yea, those nations shall be utterly wasted." And too well, I fear, may most of us know by our own sad experience, that so far as a man cuts

[i] Eph. v. 30. [k] Is. lx. 12.

himself off even from his Saviour by wilful neglect of any of his duties, so far he shuts himself out from true peace, and joy, and consolation.

Surely, it is so, my brethren, and you cannot deny it. Any one great duty, wilfully neglected, deprives a man of true peace, because it deprives him of Christ. Now then, my brethren, let me speak to you (the subject and the time itself even call on me for it): let me speak freely to you on one matter, which most nearly concerns the peace of us all. We have just been celebrating the Ascension of our Saviour to His Father's Right Hand: we have known and believed the hope laid up in store for us, in that Christ Jesus our King and our Priest is gone up into heaven, in order to be both our Strength and our Peace. Now as we know that He cannot be our Strength, unless we are members of Him, and therefore, we would not on any account remain unbaptized: so let us for God's sake consider, that neither can He be our Peace, unless we apply to ourselves what He hath done and is doing, to make our peace with God: unless we take our part in His atoning Sacrifice. And how are we to do this? In the Sacrament of Holy Communion. If we wilfully neglect or abuse that Sacrament, we refuse to have Christ for our Priest. And who then is to reconcile us? How can we ever have peace with God?

My brethren, do let me beseech you to lay this to heart; for indeed it is of more consequence than any of us can well imagine. One of the great feasts of the Church, Whitsuntide, as you know, is fast coming on: and may I acknowledge it to you, I look forward to it with dread: for it will bring with it a trial, in which I fear too many of Christ's flock in this place will fail. It is a sad and a humbling confession to make, for one who has the care of souls; but I must confess to-day before you, that in this parish we can count those who have at some time communicated and have withdrawn themselves from Holy Communion, we can count them, I say, by twenties, almost by fifties : and if we add to them the many who having been instructed and promised, yet go on week by week, and month by month, and year by year, breaking their promise, then we shall have to count them by hundreds. And moreover, my brethren, who can help fearing that some may perhaps be partaking unworthily ? Sad things have happened, which may well cause us to fear it. And they are not cases of ignorance. It is not as if men had not been told the meaning and the consequence of what they do and leave undone. They have been told what Christ said, and how to set about obeying Him.

Alas ! if one were able to think of these mischiefs as they really are, in their full effect on men's souls, it would be enough to break a Christian Pastor's heart, unless God in His great mercy were to shew him also at the same time the great, the almost angelical, blessings vouchsafed to those who communicate duly with a humble and contrite heart. The Lord increase their number, and make us more fit to be among them ! For of such it is written, "[1] Thus saith the high and lofty One that inhabiteth eternity, Whose Name is Holy : I dwell in the high and holy place, with him also that is of a con-

[1] Isa. lvii. 15.

trite and humble spirit, to revive the spirit of the humble, and to revive the heart of the contrite ones."

"[m] I have seen his ways and will heal him: I will restore comforts unto him and to his mourners. I create the fruit of the lips: Peace, peace to him that is far off, and to him that is near, saith the Lord; and I will heal him."

O blessed words! Which of you would not wish to have them spoken to his own self? And they will be, if you lose no time, but come seriously to Christ in His ordained way. But if not, you may read in the next verses, what God hath decided concerning you: "[n] The wicked are like the troubled sea, when it cannot rest, whose waters cast up mire and dirt. There is no peace, saith my God, to the wicked."

[m] Is. lvii. 18, 19.   [n] Ib. 20, 21.

SERMON XV.

THE DAYS OF EXPECTATION.

WEDNESDAY BEFORE PENTECOST.

Acts i. 13.

"And when they were come in, they went into the upper room."

THESE ten days, which come between Ascension Day and Whitsunday, are called, sometimes, the days of Expectation: because, you know, the disciples were so long waiting for our Lord to fulfil His promise of sending them another Comforter. They are, in some respects, like the time of betrothal before a marriage, or like the time which passes, when any dear friend, father or mother, son or daughter, wife or husband, brother or sister, is gone away, and has fixed the day to come back. At such times, we know, affectionate spirits are fully taken up with the one thought, how happy they shall be when the promised blessing comes: and so, we may be quite sure, the disciples' minds were quite full, during those ten days, of our Lord's promise to come to them by His Spirit. They lived, as it were, all those days upon that one thought. In all they did, they were preparing themselves to receive the Holy Ghost.

Now we are in a manner, as the Apostles then

were. Christ our Lord did in a manner depart from us last Thursday, and we are waiting to receive the Holy Ghost, by His great mercy, in next Sunday's Communion. How can we do better than try to spend these days, these ten holy days of joyful yet longing expectation, in the same way as the friends and Apostles of the Holy Jesus spent their ten days? The fulness of the blessing, we know, came upon *them:* on *us*, who call ourselves His friends and disciples now, it will come in such measure as we try to be like them. For that unspeakable blessing, the Gift of the Holy Ghost, is not in any wise wasted or worn away. The Lord's hand is not shortened; the holy Fire is not burned out, nor the holy Water dried up, neither has the Breath of the Lord ceased to breathe. The promise was unto those first Christians and to their children, and to all that were afar off: and to us, by His great mercy, among the rest. Therefore we have but to prepare ourselves as the first friends of our Saviour did, and we shall have the same blessing to crown our Pentecost that they had. The Holy Ghost will come upon *us* also, and we in our several ways shall be enabled to glorify God far more worthily than we have yet done.

Now as Jesus Christ after His Resurrection kept Himself apart and out of sight of ordinary men, only appearing from time to time to His chosen witnesses as His and their work required, so it appears that these ten days were spent by His friends and disciples in religious retirement. Before His death, when He sent them out, and was for a while to be parted from them, He sent them out for a course of active employment, to be much among their fellow-men, and to work in their sight: to preach the kingdom of God, and to heal the sick. Then they were to make a circuit of all the chief towns and villages of Judea and Galilee: now His express command was, "Tarry ye in the city of Jerusalem, until ye be endued with power from on high." Some of them, it is likely, after all the wonderful things they had seen, would be eager to publish His great Name, and to tell friends and relations at a distance, how He had died for them and risen again and ascended up to heaven in their sight. But they put by all such inclinations for the present, and staid joyfully and contentedly where He bade them.

They staid where He bade them, and did exactly as He bade them. That was their main and most necessary preparation for receiving the gift of the Holy Ghost. Let it be our preparation also. If we would have grace, we must, as well as we can, put ourselves in the way of it. It is true, no man, properly speaking, can deserve grace: yet our Lord speaks of some who are fit and some who are unfit for the kingdom of God; of some who are near to it and some who are far from it: and what little we can do, to put ourselves in His way, we are sure He will graciously accept, and help us to do more. If but for these few days we set ourselves a strict rule, to watch all our ways, and do nothing that we know will displease Him: to think of Him as much as we can, at all leisure times, and to look away from the world; no one can say how much good that little effort, if sincere, may do us: how abundantly the good Spirit may bless us when He comes down next Sunday: how He may cause that little leaven to leaven the whole mass of our earthly time and doings, and give unto the whole the taste of eternal life.

Observe, where the Apostles tarried. Not in any place chosen by themselves, but in the city of Jerusalem, which still continued to be the chosen place of God's temple and worship. So must we tarry and abide in His Church, if we expect Him to come among us by His Spirit. Our own Bishops and Priests, and our own Prayer-Book; with them and in them, our Lord has promised to be: even as to the Israelites He had promised to be at Jerusalem; and that from Mount Sion and no other place, His Word, full of His Spirit, should go forth. As they then had to wait in Jerusalem for the gift of the Holy Ghost, so we have to wait for the same gift in the holy Catholic Church, in communion with our own Church, and in devout use of the Prayer-Book.

Moreover, see where the disciples went in Jerusalem. As soon as they returned from Mount Olivet, as it were on Thursday afternoon last week, they went to the house where, before our Lord's death, and in all likelihood many times since, they had assembled together with Him: a house somewhere on Mount Sion; the house to which, on the day of the Passover, they had been directed by a man bearing a pitcher of water. Thither, S. Luke seems to tell us, they returned straight from the scene of His wonderful Ascension, full of great joy: and when they were come in, they went into the Upper-room. What Upper-room? No doubt the very same, in which on that other holy Thursday they had sat down with our Lord to His last Passover; in which room, whilst they were eating, He took bread and blessed and brake it, and solemnly ordained the Sacrament of His Body and Blood. *That* was the room which He had most highly honoured: *there* He had been and had promised to be in the midst of them in an unspeakable manner, so as the world cannot receive Him. He had promised to be among them and within them by the power of His Holy Spirit. There He had spoken all those comfortable words, to cheer their hearts nearly broken at the thought of His departure from them: there He had promised them another Comforter, Who should abide with them for ever, and by Whom the Father and the Son should come unto them and make Their abode with them. There, again, He had stood in the midst of them, and had lifted up His eyes to heaven, and had offered in their and in our behalf that most merciful prayer to the Father, which we read in the seventeenth of S. John: thereby fulfilling His Word just given, "I will pray the Father, and He shall give you another Comforter:" "I will pray the Father for you." From that same Upper-room He had led them forth into the garden by the Mount, where His Passion was to begin. There, most likely, it was that He shewed Himself to them on the night of His Resurrection, coming in while the doors were shut, and on Low Sunday: and thence, we may well believe, He had led them out to Bethany and the Mount of Olives the second time, that very Thursday morning, not to suffer, but to be glorified. Whither else then should they return, or what other place on earth could be so like a home to them, as that Upper-room? Where else might they so naturally abide, waiting for the great Gift which was so soon to come upon them?

They might not stay in the mountain, gazing after Him: they were expressly forbidden to do that; and they were also commanded to stay in Jerusalem: and this was their home in Jerusalem, the home of their hearts. Here therefore they abode together. Their place of waiting for the Holy Ghost was the Upper chamber where their First Communion had been given them: where, besides, all their Lord's farewell sayings and doings, His heavenly words and looks and actions would seem yet fresh and present to them. Where they had most helps to remember Him, there they waited for His Spirit.

And does not this tell us something of the best way in which we can prepare for Whitsunday? Surely, as the friends and followers of Christ, the Apostles and holy women, loved to be in that Upper-room, so it is good for us at this time to be as much as we can in those places, where our Lord has at any time specially come to us by His grace and spiritual favour: and if the places be too far from us, or we hindered from visiting them, it is good that we should muse on them and be there in spirit. What I mean is like this: we should be as much as we can in Church, because the Church is *the* special place where He has met us again and again: and if we cannot go to Church, we should think, all we can, of it and of Him Who is there. In thought we should do well to go back to our Baptism, wherever that took place, and to consider again and again the inestimable love of God our Saviour in so taking us into His arms, and washing us from our sins in His own Blood. If there are any of us, who have unhappily fallen into grievous sin, for a short or a long time, and by God's exceeding mercy have truly repented and confessed and received Christ's Absolution, now is a good time to recollect with all possible thankfulness that miraculous loving-kindness of our Judge: now, I say, whilst we are humbly waiting for Him to seal it by a new gift of His sanctifying Spirit. And the mention of that Upper-room seems to remind us, that very much of these ten days might well be spent in meditation on Holy Communion: in recollecting, as we may, all His mercies vouchsafed unto us in that Sacrament from our Confirmation until now: in fear and trembling to think, how little our hearts and lives have answered to this great love of His: and in earnest consideration, how we may now become and continue, ever after, more worthy communicants. Any Christian who should so employ himself would, I suppose, be in God's sight spending this time of expectation, as the Apostles spent it in that blessed Upper-room: and when the Day of Pentecost shall be fully come, such an one may humbly hope that the heavenly Gift then vouchsafed to the Apostles will be poured out even on him, unworthy as he feels himself, and grievous as his sins may have been.

I would particularly suggest, as a sort of spiritual exercise likely to be very useful to many of us, that we should at this time go over in our thoughts the providential dealings of our God, whereby He has helped us all along hitherto. As, for example, if at any time we have had dear friends and relations, who, having been lovely in their lives, did in their last sickness and departure draw nearer than ever to their Saviour: if we have heard them speak words which sounded almost as messages of Angels in our ears: now is the time to remember them, and think over all that happened, all the signs and tokens which God gave us when we were waiting on them, that He is indeed very near, and that our way to Him is to follow their faith, as the disciples in that Upper-room remembered all Christ's parting words. If we have been ourselves at any time brought very low, deeply distressed in body or in mind, or both; and after many thoughts and misgivings, sore agony and wondering what would become of us, it pleased the Lord to raise us up, and give us more time and strength to serve Him: now is a good time seriously to review both our trouble and His mercy: as S. Peter and the rest, no doubt, reviewed all that passed on the night of our Lord's Agony: how near they were casting themselves away, and how graciously He interfered to save them.

By such thoughts as these, my brethren, I advise you to prepare for Whitsunday. I would we might all put ourselves in the way of grace; for that is the way to have grace come abundantly to us. Retire as much as you well can from the world: sit alone and keep silence: go over in your minds our Lord's gracious dealings towards you: remember past Communions, how unworthy you were, and how merciful He was. Thus may you abide in the Upper-room, the place of high and heavenly meditation, until His Spirit be poured upon you, to strengthen and refresh you more abundantly than ever for all that you have to do and suffer for His Sake.

SERMON XVI.

THE DAYS OF EXPECTATION.

FRIDAY BEFORE PENTECOST.

ACTS i. 14.

"*These all continued with one accord in prayer and supplication, with the women, and Mary the Mother of Jesus, and with His brethren.*"

WE are told over and over in Holy Scripture, that if we really desire the grace of God, we ought to put ourselves in the way of it: we shall do so of course, just as we look after any thing which we desire to find, or ask for any thing which we wish to have, or knock at any door which we want to have opened. Our Lord has taught us all this in the Sermon on the Mount. "[a] Ask, and ye shall have; seek, and ye shall find; knock, and it shall be opened unto you." As if He should say, "You must not think of obtaining what you want, if you will not give yourself the trouble of doing what little in you lies for it." And lest any one should say, " the Holy Spirit is so great a Gift: our doings are nothing at all towards it: surely in vain shall we give ourselves any such trouble:" hear how, in the same breath, He distinctly makes our obtaining the Holy Spirit a thing to depend on our prayers. "[b] If ye, being evil, know

[a] S. Luke xi. 9.   [b] Ib. 13.

how to give good gifts unto your children : how much more shall your Father which is in heaven give the Holy Spirit to them that ask Him!" Fathers give their children what they ask, not for any profit that they have of their children's asking, but because they are their fathers, and love them. So the Lord God will hear our petitions, when we say, "Take not Thy Holy Spirit from us," not for any worth in those prayers of ours, but because He is our loving Lord, and from Him alone flows out all fatherly and motherly love. As our parents, for our good, often made us ask respectfully for a thing before they gave it, so our Lord would have us pray to Him, or ever His gifts of grace shall descend upon us.

He will have us pray; and there are also other things which He will have us do. One of them, as I shewed you the other day, is to make much of the very places, where God has at any time shewed us any particular mercy: where He has at all wrought wondrously with us. I shewed you, how the disciples of our Lord, having to wait in Jerusalem for the gift of the Holy Ghost, waited in that very Upper-room, in which they had seen so much of Christ before His departure : where He had given them the First Holy Communion, and where also, as we may well believe, He had often met them, after He was risen. So may we prepare ourselves for a new gift of the Holy Ghost, by going back in spirit to the places, times, and ways, in which He has, before now, graciously given Himself to us. We may come to Church, or if we cannot come always, we may think of the holy place : we may in spirit kneel at God's altar, and remember what Holy Communion has been to us, and how much more it might have been. All this we may ponder upon, whilst we are at home or at our work: and this will be like abiding in the Upper-chamber, in the place where Christ has met us aforetime, in hope of another happy meeting.

But there was another thing which the friends and followers of Christ crucified did at that time; they not only staid in the place which Christ had blessed, but they continued also in company with those, whom they knew to be dearest to Christ. Each Apostle continued with the other Apostles: they did not go apart, each to his own place of devotion, but all went up together to the same Upper-room, and there abode the whole ten days. They did not part; why should they? They were all alike thinking of the same departed Saviour, they were all alike waiting for the same Blessed Spirit: that sacred Upper-room belonged to one of them as much as to another: there they had been all alike used to meet their Lord; and to see one another there, would help as much as anything to keep them well in mind of Him. And so, I suppose, my brethren, we all feel, when in obedience to our mother, the Church, we try to prepare ourselves for great and holy seasons, such as this of Whitsuntide which is coming. As it helps us to be here in Church, so it helps us to see one another here. Those few who are able to come, more or less regularly, on other days besides Sundays, know well, if they come thoughtfully, how good it is for them to be here; here, in the immediate Presence of Christ; here, where they have so many times had great spiritual mercies; here, where their hearts have burned within them at hearing His holy

Word, and where He has afterwards shewn Himself to them in breaking of bread. They know how much good the very place by itself seems to do them: how the very air and shadow of it is felt the moment they come in, as a shelter from the bleak rude wearisome world without. And are they not also able to say something of the comfort it is to them to meet the same people there continually? how much help it sometimes gives them in their own prayers, if their eyes fall on some devout old man or innocent child making the most of God's house: how they miss such their fellow-worshippers, if by chance they are absent: how, if they meet them elsewhere, or do but hear their names mentioned, presently cheerful and edifying thoughts of this holy place and its services arise in their hearts. Indeed, there is no end to the ways, in which those who are used to walk to the house of God as friends help each other, knowingly or unknowingly, to obtain yet further blessings from God. No wonder then that the Apostles continued together "with one accord in one place;" and that place, the place of Holy Communion; while they were waiting for the Spirit. They did so, all of them, because as yet they all had leisure to do so. Many of us have little or no leisure so to come into God's house on week-days: but it would be well, if all who have health and leisure did come, according to some constant rule, as their own conscience tells them would be best. It would soon make a great difference on our Sundays and great days, if the Christian people would make up their minds to make more use of the Church on common days. Putting themselves more in the way of grace, they would be more likely to receive grace. Abiding together in the Upper-room, they would be where the Holy Spirit is most likely to descend: just as the Israelites in the old time, if they would fain see the Glory of God, knew that their best chance was to abide with God's priests in His Tabernacle or Temple.

No wonder, again, if we find it so particularly mentioned that the disciples continued, as with one another, so also with the rest of them who had been nearest our Lord in times past. "They" (the twelve) "continued in prayer and supplication with the women and Mary the Mother of Jesus, and His disciples:" to the number, all together, of one hundred and twenty. We see at once, what their rule and principle was: what one love it was, which ruled in all their hearts. It was the love of Jesus: *therefore* they abode together, because each helped the other to remember Jesus. And by whom could they remember Jesus so well and so entirely, as by Her, whom He had made nearest Him of all creatures—by His own blessed Mother? Surely, when they looked on her, it must have helped them greatly to remember Him. For His sake, they must have greatly loved and revered her, so long as she was permitted to remain on earth among them: even as He Himself had plainly directed one of them, and that one His own beloved, "^cBehold thy Mother." It was a great and high privilege to have her with them, and no doubt it helped them greatly, as she and they prayed together, in their mutual preparation for the coming of the Holy Ghost. And is she not also in a manner with us also? Yes, assuredly, by virtue of the

^c S. John xix. 27.

Communion of Saints, that may be said of all our solemn assemblies, which is said of the marriage of Cana. "The Mother of Jesus is there" with Him and His disciples. Christ our Head being here, all His glorified members are with Him in spirit and in truth, and therefore we may think of that same company, which waited so devoutly for the first Whitsunday, as waiting in some sense with us here, even the Apostles, and the women, and Mary the Mother of Jesus and His brethren. So far as we are members of Christ, we are in real communion and fellowship with them. When we are honoured, they rejoice with us: they cry unto the Lord on our behalf, "How long, O Lord, holy and true?" And we on earth praise the Lord in the words which they have left us. Very often, as you know, we use in the evening service the holy hymn of the Mother of Jesus, "My soul doth magnify the Lord." God gives us that help by her, as who knows but she may in the same words have helped the devotions of that congregation in the Upper-room on Mount Sion? It is not the less a token of communion with her and the other saints, because they are out of our sight, and we know not, perhaps, whether or no we are in their sight: we have their holy and comfortable words, we have their pure and devout example ; and with the thought of them we are permitted to strengthen and refresh ourselves in these our hours of waiting.

Further : it is said they continued in prayer and supplication; not only with the Mother and brethren of our Lord, with those who were nearest to Him after the flesh, but also with certain women. What women? The same, no doubt, who had so long waited on Him: following Him out of Galilee, ministering to Him of their substance, standing by His Cross, coming early to His Sepulchre. These weak and simple women, one of whom at least is believed to have been a very great sinner, were with the Apostles and our Lord's blessed Mother and brethren, both in the preparation for Whitsunday and in the great day itself. Are you then weak and simple? Is any of you a great sinner? See what blessed encouragement you have: you are not only permitted but earnestly invited to draw near and prepare yourselves to receive the gift of the Holy Ghost. The Holy Church, your mother, accounts herself imperfect without you: she longs to have you duly preparing yourself now, that she may present you next Sunday to be a worthy communicant: even as the Apostles and the Blessed Virgin, and the brethren of Jesus Christ, would have reckoned their assembly in the Upper-room imperfect, if the women from Galilee had not been present also.

All this care is taken of us: and shall we take no care of ourselves? Only imagine, good brethren and sisters, how it would have seemed, if any of that favoured company had turned his back on the gracious offers of our Lord. Our Lord said, "Stay in Jerusalem: stay but a short time: continue in the place which I have chosen, with My saints, in prayer and supplication: and you shall receive the gift of the Holy Ghost." Our Lord said it; they did it; and the Holy Ghost came down upon them, and they were most blessed. But suppose any of them had scorned our Lord's words. He said, "Stay in Jerusalem." What if one had gone straight out of the place, after his own worldly fancies? What if he had left the company of the Apostles? What if he had taken no care to remember his Lord's death? What if he had left off prayer? What if he had staid in the company, only to wrangle and disobey orders, and set up his own self-willed ways? You see how it would have been. Such a person would have forfeited the promise of his gracious Saviour, and he would not have received the gift of the Holy Ghost on Whitsunday. No more shall we, if we turn our back on the Church; if we refuse to remember our Lord in Holy Communion; if we neglect prayer, real prayer, and diligent self-examination. We know very well that to such as do so, Whitsunday will come and go without a blessing: and so it will to those who, although they may be diligent in these spiritual exercises, are not endeavouring to be truly humble in the practice of them. There is such a thing as going to Church, praying, considering, nay even communicating, and yet driving away God's Spirit. How? Because people worship, consider, communicate, in ways of their own, and not in Christ's true way. Their hearts are serious after a fashion, but they are not humble, lowly, penitent, obedient hearts. God preserve you and me from this!

SERMON XVII.

PATIENT WAITING FOR PROMISES.

WHITSUNTIDE.

Ps. xlviii. 8.

"We wait for Thy loving-kindness, O God, in the midst of Thy temple."

THESE words of the prophet and Psalmist seem to contain a short and plain account of the temper and behaviour of the friends and Apostles of our Lord, during those days of hope and patience, which came to an end on the morning of the first Whitsunday. Our Lord, on departing, told them, that as surely as John had baptized with water, they should be baptized with the Holy Ghost, not many days from that time. How many, He did not say; but He distinctly forbade their moving out of Jerusalem, or doing any thing in their great office of witnesses to Him, until they should be so endued with power from on high. They were to wait for the promise of the Father, which they had heard from Him. Accordingly, having solemnly worshipped Him on His departure, they "[a] returned to Jerusalem with fear and great joy; and were continually in the temple, praising and blessing God." Thus exactly did they fulfil the

[a] S. Luke xxiv. 52, 53.

description, which the Holy Spirit by the mouth of David had so long before given in the text, of the temper and behaviour which He approves of in His Church, and in every member of the same, concerning His great and precious promises. We are to "wait for His loving-kindness in the midst of His temple." "ᵇHe that believeth shall not make haste." There is "ᶜ need of patience, that after we have done the will of God, we might receive the promise."

We naturally think the time long, while we are expecting any blessing, more especially when the Word of God is pledged to us for the blessing itself. And the blessing, which the Apostles were now waiting for, was both in itself, and to them, infinitely beyond all others that could be desired. It was the return of Him Who had just departed from them, not leaving them comfortless, but coming to them again by His Spirit. But so perfect had their faith now become, that they endured His absence, not only patiently, but with a holy and reverential joy; in this, as in other things, offering an instructive contrast to the behaviour of God's elder Church, the Church of the Israelites in the wilderness, when their mediator had been out of sight in the mountain for several days. They began to complain, "As for this Moses, we wot not what is become of him;" and their complaining ended, as you know, in profane idolatry. But the spiritual Israel, those out of whom God was about to complete the foundation of His Church, they waited patiently for the Lord. They had taken it on His word, however unaccountable it might sound, that it was expedient for them, His

ᵇ Is. xxviii. 16.   ᶜ Heb. x. 36.

going away; and they were prepared to trust Him still further, and to abide in faith and quietness any length of time, during which the Comforter might delay His coming.

Further; observe the place where they waited. The prophecy had described God's people as waiting in the midst of His temple. Our Lord ordered His Apostles to tarry in the city of Jerusalem, and they were continually in the temple. And, as it is said in one of the oldest Prayer-books of the Church, it was "in an upper room of holy and glorious Sion," where they were assembled with one accord, when the windows of heaven were opened, and the unspeakable Gift poured forth; the same Upper-room, no doubt, which is mentioned in the first chapter of Acts, to which they had gone from Mount Olivet, immediately after our Lord's Ascension, where all the Apostles abode together, "with the women, and Mary the mother of Jesus, and with His brethren." There they continued, with one mind, in prayer and supplication: they were also continually, that is, at the services in the temple, praising and blessing God, until the great miracle of miracles happened, and the kingdom of heaven was opened to all believers.

Now, does not this teach us something as to the disposition and frame of mind, which God approves of and will bless in His Church, and in all to whom His promises are made? Does it not seem to shew, first of all, that patient waiting is the strength of God's people; that they greatly err if they pretend to fix His times, or to take His matters into their own hands; and, secondly, that they are to take things as they find them, and set out on God's work in their social callings from the present moment, and the present state of things, whenever and whatever it be? They are to make the best use they can of it, in doing or suffering their Maker's will: even as the Apostles did not separate themselves from the temple-worship, imperfect as they knew it to be, nor from the communion of the unbelieving Jews, though newly stained with their Master's Blood. They continued, as we have seen, in the temple; they solemnized the great day of Pentecost, which the Jews kept in remembrance of the giving of the Law, by assembling together with one accord at the third hour, which was one of the Jewish hours of prayer; an hour no where appointed in the Law, but ordained by the voluntary piety of God's ancient people, and so far approved by God's testimony, as that He several times answered the devotions of His people at that hour with great and signal blessings from Heaven.

In these and other instances, the holy Apostles shewed themselves the true followers of Him, Who came not to destroy the law but to fulfil; and they seem to set us an example, how we too should follow His steps. In other words, we are not to draw back, and let our time pass unimproved, or indulge in any sort of spiritual idleness, on the plea, that "really the state of things is so very bad, we would mend it if we could, but we cannot; and therefore we will just behave ourselves as the world does. If we had lived among the first Christians, or if our own families, or neighbourhood, or acquaintance, were more favourable to such efforts than they are, then the case would be different, we would try and do something; but, as it is, we are sure it would do no good; it is not for us to reform the world; we are not called to it; so we will even stay as we are for the present, and wait until God shall send us better opportunities."

This is no uncommon way of speaking, as might be shewn by many familiar instances. Did you never, for example, know a father or a mother of a family, who delayed to come to the Holy Communion, until their children had left off vexing them? Or a person who refused to come to Church, because he could not find a sitting exactly to his mind, or because he had something to say against the minister? Did you never know a person in service, or in some other situation in life, who avowedly put off serious thought and turning to Almighty God, with this sort of speech, "Bye and bye I shall get a quieter place, or more leisure, or a home nearer Church, or companions who will not laugh at me, and then I will be more serious; but, for the present, it is no use to ask me?"

Surely, whenever we hear or see such things, we hear and see what must forfeit the blessing and favour of that God, Who rewarded the devotion of His Apostles, while they had only the temple to worship in, and only Jews to worship with, by the gift of the indwelling Spirit. It is His will that people should set out from the spot whereon His providence has placed them, be it favourable or be it unfavourable, and ask the way to heaven with their faces thitherward; sure to find it, if they ask with obedient hearts. Let us depend on it, when we have said our worst against the times we live in, the Church or state we belong to, the companions among whom God has cast our lot, still our worst enemy and our most perilous struggle will be found at last within our own hearts. Let us patiently seek God's favour on our diligent use of all the means of grace which He has put within our reach, abiding in Jerusalem in the temple, and not seeking new ways for ourselves, and see (to use His own words by His Prophet), if He "[d] will not open the windows of heaven, and pour us out a blessing, that there will not be room enough" in this world " to receive it:" it will overflow into eternity.

Certainly, there can be no such encouragement besides to earnest repentance, to serious improvement, to patient continuance in well-doing, as the answer which God gave to those prayers, in which our Lord's disciples and His Mother continued during the ten days from His Ascension to Pentecost. The return of those prayers was, the Holy Ghost sent down from heaven, Jesus Christ coming by His Spirit, to save us, one by one, from the power of sin for the future; as He had before come in His own Person to offer Himself an all-sufficient Sacrifice for us, and so save us, one and all, from the punishment of sins past. As S. Paul speaks, in the Epistle to the Romans, "[e] If, when we were enemies, we were reconciled to God by the death of His Son, much more, being reconciled, we shall be saved by His life," by that heavenly life of His, which He communicates to us as Christians by His Holy indwelling Spirit.

[d] Mal. iii. 10.   [e] Rom. v. 10.

This should be very deeply considered; for it brings the mystery of Whitsunday much nearer home to us, than we are perhaps in general used to imagine it. Think of it in this way : that the most Holy and Divine Spirit, God the Holy Ghost, is come down, not only to enable the Apostles to preach the Gospel in all nations, whereby, as our Church thankfully confesses in the Communion Service for this day, " we have been brought out of darkness and error into the clear light and true knowledge of God and of His Son Jesus Christ:" not only is the light of Christ thus made to shine upon us by the coming of the Holy Spirit, but we are also made, inwardly and spiritually, partakers of the life which is in Christ. We now know that the Comforter is come to abide in the Church, so as that He dwells, personally and really, in every one whom He Himself by Baptism shall have first made a member of Christ.

This is the constant doctrine taught by the Holy Spirit Himself in the writings of the Apostles. "[f]Ye are all the children of God by faith in Christ Jesus. For as many of you as have been baptized into Christ have put on Christ:" "[g]And because ye are sons, God hath sent forth the Spirit of His Son into your hearts, crying, Abba, Father." And again, "[h]Ye are not in the flesh, but in the Spirit, if so be that the Spirit of God dwell in you. Now if any man have not the Spirit of Christ, he is none of His." S. Peter describes it as the very condition of Christians, that they are "[i]elect according to the foreknowledge of God the Father, through sanctification of the Spirit, unto obedience and sprinkling of the Blood

[f] Gal. iii. 26, 27.   [g] Ib. iv. 6.   [h] Rom. viii. 9,   [i] 1 S. Pet. i. 2.

of Jesus Christ." As much as to say, the Spirit was to sanctify them, that is, to renew the image of God in them, abiding in them, so as to make them "partakers of the Divine nature:" so might their obedience and good works be a sacrifice well-pleasing to God, being sprinkled with the Blood of Jesus Christ. Thus also S. John makes the presence of the Spirit the very token of the abiding of Christ among Christians, according to His own gracious promise, when about to depart from among them. "Hereby we know that He abideth in us, by His Spirit which He hath given us." The visible coming of the Holy Ghost, on the day of Pentecost, was the outward pledge of His invisible Presence, and Christ's invisible Presence by Him. Christians are thereby assured, to all generations, that their Lord has not left them comfortless, but is perpetually coming unto them; once for all in the Sacrament of Baptism, to make them members of Himself, and from time to time in the other blessed Sacrament, to nourish and perfect in them that sacred Communion.

Such was the loving-kindness, with which the Lord of old crowned His people, patiently waiting for it in the midst of His temple; and though that precious and unspeakable gift be no longer to be waited for, though it be come already, and we dwell in the midst of it, yet, even in this more perfect Temple, the Church and Household of the living God, we still have to wait for our perfection. "We walk by faith, not by sight." We cannot yet be fully like Christ, for we do not yet see Him as He is, but only through a glass, darkly. This very blessing, for which we are giving thanks, the indwelling of the Spirit, is altogether matter of faith ; there are no open miracles to assure us of it, no inward feelings on which we can positively rely: the Word of God sealing His Sacraments is our only warrant for quite depending on it.

This being so, the same graces which the disciples of our Lord were called on to exercise between the Ascension-day and Pentecost, must ever be part of our special trial as Christians; a trial, of which we shall be more sensible in proportion to our faith and seriousness. God keeps us waiting for His loving-kindness, for the full revelation of His glorious mercies, for the day when we shall know even as also we are known: and this our time of waiting will seem the longer to us, will practise us the more severely in patience and resignation, the more earnestly we are used to think of God, and to lay up our treasure in heaven.

Then, again, as to the other caution suggested by the words of the text: if the disciples were to wait for the Comforter in Jerusalem, in or near the visible temple, much more ought we to take care how we wander in any way, even in thought, beyond the bounds of the spiritual temple, "the Church of the Living God, the pillar and ground of the truth." As Christians, we hope and expect great mercies. God's Holy Scriptures are full of promise and encouragement to us, both as to blessings in store for the whole Church, and as to what we may look for ourselves, as individual souls, redeemed by Christ's Blood, and made members of Him by His Spirit. Let us so long and strive for these mercies, as never to forget the sort of persons to whom they are promised.

For example, with respect to those which concern the whole Church; every year shews more and more how great need there is of patience, since every year we seem to become better acquainted with the disorder and decay which so sadly prevail in Christ's kingdom; every year we may well fancy the saints' voices crying out more and more sorrowfully, "ʲ How long, O Lord, holy and true, dost Thou not avenge us of them that dwell on the earth?" And there are persons, and as it should seem, sincere ones, who are tempted by these appearances of disorder to take or encourage irregular ways of forwarding the good and holy cause.

Thus, whereas our Lord appointed that His Apostles only should send forth others to minister in His Church in His Name, many persons seem to think it wrong for this to be insisted on, in times and countries where there are many heathenish persons. They say, "Why, when the call is so urgent, may not any person, that feels sincere in heart, take on himself the work of the ministry?" If they were really as considerate, as I doubt not they are often well-meaning, it ought to be enough to answer them, that such means as they recommend do not answer to the inspired direction; that we must wait patiently for God to send His blessing, not expect to draw it down, like Saul or Balak, or other heathenish characters, by any enchantments or divinations of our own.

Other instances of like disorder might be given; to all which the saying of the father of the faithful may be applied: "My son, God will provide Himself a lamb for a burnt-offering." His hand is not

ʲ Rev. vi. 10.

waxed short; He has means enough to accomplish His purposes in His own time; He has no need of the irregular, disobedient, disorderly, any more than of the sinful man.

Pray then, and look, and long, and strive for the promised blessing and triumph of God's Holy Church; pray, and look, and long for the time, when "[k] the kingdoms of this world" shall "become the kingdoms of our Lord and of His Christ," and when "[l] the earth shall be full of the knowledge of the Lord, as the waters cover the sea;" when all the Church's "[m] children shall be taught of the Lord, and great shall be the peace of her children." But yet I say, do all that you do in the ways of the Church herself; for surely they are the ways of God, and to depart from His ways must be evil; and no appearance, nay, no seeming certainty of profiting ever so many of our brethren, should ever tempt us to break God's commandment, seeing how awful the censure is on those who say, "[n] Let us do evil, that good may come."

In conclusion, I may just say, that, as to particular individual blessings, which Christians, however unworthily, may venture to hope for, considering that God has made them partakers of this most unspeakable gift, His Spirit abiding in them: first of all, it would be well to consider seriously with ourselves, how little right we can have, knowing all the evil we do against ourselves, to look for any peculiar grace and comfort; next, that God's offers, how large and gracious soever, are all held out to those who shall

[k] Rev. xi. 15.   [l] Isa. xi. 9.
[m] Ib. liv. 13.   [n] Rom. iii. 8.

approach Him in His ordinances. Persevere in them, not so much caring whether they bring comfort at the time or no, and in time you will find your reward. The seed so thrown into the ground, though that ground might seem unkindly at first, will spring and grow up, you know not how, bringing forth "º first the blade, then the ear, after that, the full corn in the ear."

Persevere; in private and secret prayer, however little good you seem to yourself to feel by it. Do not leave it off for fear of becoming formal. If it be but accompanied with keeping of the commandments, it will do you good beyond the knowledge of man; just as a river, which seems to part with nothing of its waters, and makes no immediate difference in the look of the ground just about it, may yet, in a silent and gradual way, feed and cherish the whole country round.

The same may be said of going to Church, and even of receiving the Holy Communion. It is not in any wise necessary, that persons should be able distinctly to feel and point out a certain good effect on their minds and feelings, occasioned by such and such a service or Communion. Only let them attend decently and devoutly, and strive to be exact in all their conduct; and though they "ᵖnow go on their way weeping," yet "bearing forth such good seed, they will doubtless come again with joy, and bring their sheaves with them," in the last great harvest-day. Only look for one moment to the warnings of past experience. Seek in the Book of the Lord, or in the records of His Church, and see whether any

º S. Mark iv. 28. ᵖ Ps. cxxvi. 6.

one thing has done so much harm as impatience: in making people heretics, or dissenters, or heathenish churchmen. Has it not been generally so, that they wished to do good, but became impatient of waiting, and of the wholesome restraint of the temple? While Angels, on the contrary, stooping from heaven, are content to wait God's time; they desire to look into the secrets of our redemption, but they cheerfully put back the desire, and quiet it until it shall please God to fulfil it; and, in the mean time, they at once obey, and that for love's sake, whatever He would have done. May His will, by the might of His Spirit and for the love of His Son, be so done here on earth, as it is by them in heaven!

SERMON XVIII.

THE BREATH OF THE MOST HIGH GOD.

WHITSUNTIDE.

Ps. civ. 30.

"*Thou sendest forth Thy Spirit, they are created: and Thou renewest the face of the earth.*"

THESE words were apparently intended to put thoughtful readers in mind of the history of the creation of the world, as we find it in the book of Genesis. "The earth was without form, and void; and darkness was upon the face of the deep. And the Spirit of God moved upon the face of the waters. And God said, Let there be light: and there was light." The work of creation did not begin, things did not receive any order, nor had come into that condition which caused the Almighty, seeing them all, to pronounce them "very good," until the Holy Spirit of God had "brooded upon the face of the dark void deep," as one may imagine a bird brooding with outspread wings, according to the force of the original word. He brooded over it, and in some mysterious way made it apt to obey God's commands, and to bring forth out of its own bosom those marvellous works, which, one after another, God called into being out of the great deep, during those six days of creation.

In like manner, when all things were again become

in a manner empty and void and waste, by reason of the mischief which the wilful sin of Adam had caused; when it had become quite manifest, that men left to themselves must perish in their misery (they can but " die, and turn again to their dust "); then did God send forth His Holy Spirit, the Comforter promised by our Saviour, to unite them as true members to Jesus Christ, so to new-create them, and " renew the face of the earth." Since He came down on the day of Pentecost, a new heaven and a new earth has begun here among men; all things are changed, all put in a new light, all clothed with a kind of glory from above. So great is this change, that the New Testament mentions it repeatedly under the title of a "new creation," a "new birth," a "kingdom which cannot be moved," and the like: and the Church has always considered such Psalms as this hundred and fourth, which celebrates God's glory in the works of the first creation, to be in their Christian meaning, hymns of praise for the second creation also; for the regeneration of the world out of wickedness and confusion, as well as for its first birth out of disorder, and emptiness, and darkness.

The Breath of the Most High, then, mentioned in the text, is the Holy Spirit of the Father and the Son, the Third Person in the Blessed Inseparable Trinity, proceeding from the Father and the Son, to give life, and order, and harmony, to His creatures; especially to make His reasonable creatures, Angels and men, partakers of His unspeakable holiness. Therefore, the Psalm which so teaches concerning the Breath of the Lord, is appointed to be one of the proper Psalms for this great day; Almighty God having so ordered this world which we see, in reference to that better one which we do not see, that the one is throughout a kind of pattern or shadow of the other; and the hymns of praise for the first creation, which the book of Psalms has in many places, are suitable to be used when we are glorifying God for this His second and far more perfect creation, His spiritual and eternal world.

And as the Church on Christmas-day taught us to regard the light of the sun as a visible token of our Saviour, according to S. John's expression, "[a] That was the true Light, which lighteth every man that cometh into the world;" so at this season she teaches us to regard the Holy Spirit as being, in some wonderful sense, the Breath of God; as indeed the word "Spirit" would of itself imply, for in the first place it means "breath."

The Holy Spirit is called the Breath of God, as being breathed out in a mysterious and marvellous way over His whole creation, but especially into the souls of reasonable beings, to make all in their several measure partakers of God and of happiness. The Holy Spirit is God secretly present, encompassing us about, entering into us, piercing even to the very depths of our being, like the air we breathe, unseen, but known by its effects.

If this parable of Breath be well considered, it may seem to account for other like parables, so to call them, by which Holy Scripture teaches us how to think of This our most Holy Comforter. For instance, the Holy Spirit is sometimes compared to the wind, as in the discourse of our Saviour to Nicodemus: "[b] the

[a] S. John i. 9.   [b] Ib. iii. 8.

wind bloweth where it listeth, and thou hearest the sound thereof, but canst not tell whence it cometh, and whither it goeth : so is every one that is born of the Spirit." The wind, blowing so far and wide over the world, invisible, but possessed often of immense power, unknown as to where it begins and ends, and as to the rules by which it rises or falls, is set forth as an emblem of that Spirit, Whose coming was to-day made known to His chosen messengers by a sudden great "[c] sound from heaven, as of a rushing mighty wind," which "filled all the house where they were sitting." So the Holy Spirit came suddenly, not according to any rules which we could calculate upon, but according to God's good pleasure, when He saw the time was arrived for the kingdom of heaven to be set up. It was "a rushing mighty wind;" the whole world might perceive, that that there was a heavenly power in It, which had never yet made Itself known. "It filled all the house, where they were sitting:" the Spirit of God shewed Himself alike in all places of the Church at once. North, south, east, and west; it is the same Divine Presence and Power, accompanying the Sacraments of Jesus Christ, and answering the prayers of His people.

Thus the wind, when we hear or feel it, may remind us of the Breath of Almighty God; and the effects of the wind, the clouds which it brings over the earth, the moisture which the air takes up, the dews which descend, the rains which pour down, the springs which gush out, the waters which flow over the earth; all these are in Scripture tokens of the same Spirit, shewing Himself in gifts and sanctify-

[c] Acts ii. 2.

ing graces, and communicating spiritual life to His people.

Thus the cloud of Glory, in which, as well as in the Red Sea, the children of Israel were baptized, was the figure, as we learn from S. Paul, of the Holy Spirit by Whom Christians are regenerated in the waters of Baptism.

The dew which came down at the prayer of Gideon, first on the fleece alone, then on all the ground besides, leaving the fleece alone dry, betokened the gifts of the Holy Spirit in several degrees, for a long time given to the Jews only, then at the setting up of Christ's Kingdom made common to all nations, and that in an infinitely higher and more blessed way. The manna which came down all night, silently on every side of the camp, that too was a kind of dew from heaven, "[d] a gracious rain upon God's inheritance, refreshing it when it was weary," as another of the Psalms appointed for this season teaches, adding, that God's congregation was to dwell therein. The whole Church is to dwell in the Spirit of God, as in the air it breathes, as in the comfortable and refreshing dewy vapour, which makes this earth tolerable for her to abide in.

The water gushing from the smitten rock was the token and sign of the Holy Spirit, flowing forth from Jesus Christ crucified to every one of His members, even as He Himself declared: "[e] If any man thirst, let him come unto Me and drink: he that believeth on Me, as the Scripture hath said, out of his belly shall flow rivers of living water." "[f] This" (S. John adds) "spake He of the Spirit, which they that be-

[d] Ps. lxviii. 9.   [e] S. John vii. 37, 38.   [f] Ib. 39.

lieve on Him should receive." It is also compared to water generally, as in the Sacrament of Baptism; and in the vision wherein S. John saw living waters proceed from the Throne of God and the Lamb, and go out through the whole sacred city, "[g] a pure river of water of life."

Nay, and that well-known token also of a dove, by which the Holy Spirit manifested Himself to the Baptist, is not altogether of a different sort from these. For the hovering of the Holy Dove, we may suppose, was like a soft cloud, gently wafted from heaven to settle on the Son of God; and this may have been one reason why that figure in particular was fixed on.

You see, then, what a number of common things, the most common things in our sight, Almighty God has set down in His Word as emblems of His Holy and Blessed Spirit, the Teacher and Comforter of all faithful souls. If you do but see a cloud in the sky, you see what may remind you of Him, overshadowing the Church with blessed consolations and promises, coming to be the Tabernacle and Refuge, the Home and Shelter of all who are weary and heavy laden. The morning and evening dews are like His refreshing graces, ever new, never failing, given impartially to all, coming silently, but known by their purity and brightness, and by the holy hope and joy and strength, which they spread over the whole heart and life of man; not unlike the cheerful green, which follows on a timely shower in spring or summer.

Nay, even such an ordinary sight as a shower of rain is a sign of the same high Presence, if Christians

[g] Rev. xxii. 1.

will but have the heart to believe it. It tells us of Him Who is always ready, in answer to our true and faithful prayers, to "send a gracious rain on His inheritance, and refresh it" in its weariness.

And so, too, if we will follow the example of those who came nearest our Lord's own time, we shall not be ashamed to see continually, even in the wells by our doors, or in the brooks or watercourses that we meet with, something to remember Him by, Who has vouchsafed, once for all, to "sanctify the element of water to the mystical washing away of sin."

So many, and so common and cheap, are the lessons which the works of God all around will read to us, if we have ears to hear, concerning the ever-blessed Spirit; and how unspeakably deep and high, how infinitely important, is the truth which they join to teach! That He Who is the Finger, the Power of God, the Holy Ghost, One with the Father and the Son, as He is present in all His works, so is He ever in a peculiar manner abiding in those whom He has regenerated and made members of Jesus Christ: out of sight, out of hearing, beyond all feeling or any outward sense, yet infinitely nearer and closer to every one of us than any of the things we do see, hear, or feel, or can make out by reasoning; ready at hand to all His faithful ones, at every moment of their dangerous and trying pilgrimage, to guide and comfort, to purify and refresh them; so that, whatever difficulties arise, we may still say, "We are, by Baptism, partakers of God and of Christ; we have once renounced and overcome the Evil one, and by the same Power we may do so again, because 'greater is He that is in us, than he that is in the world.'"

More especially we are hereby taught to think of our own spiritual and hidden life, the life which we have, concealed and laid up for us with Christ in God, the life which is altogether of faith, not at all of sight. I say, whatever puts us in mind of the Holy Spirit, puts us in mind of that life; for He, as the Belief truly tells us, is "the Lord and Giver of life." Christ, we know, is our only life, as many as truly belong to the kingdom of heaven. Now the Holy Spirit joins us to Christ, makes us members of Him in Holy Baptism; keeps us so in the other Blessed Sacrament; and, therefore, especially is He called "the Lord, and Giver of Life" in the Creed. By Him "we live, and move, and have our being," as people of God.

Observe now, how well this agrees with the teaching both of the Old and New Testament, concerning the heavenly operation and providence of God's Spirit. First, the Spirit of God, moving on the face of the waters, prepared them mysteriously for the wonderful births, which God kept bringing out of them, till the six days' work was over. The waters cherished the still and dead elements, to bring forth life when Almighty God should command. Bye and bye, when mention is made of creating man, we read, "The Lord God formed man out of the dust of the earth, and breathed into his nostrils the breath of life, and man became a living soul." What was it, then, my brethren, that gave our first father life? It was the Breath of Life, the Spirit of God, breathed from above into his nostrils. The natural life, then, of the first Adam was a gift of the Spirit, a token of His Divine Presence; but much more so the spiritual life, which Christians have by union with the second Adam. To bring us, us I say, who are here present, unworthy sinners (for every one of us was then in His mind), to bring us to Almighty God, the Holy Ghost first performed this great wonder, He afterwards came down from heaven in the fulness of time, descended upon the ever-blessed Virgin Mary, and caused our Lord to be conceived in her womb, and to take our human nature upon Him, of her substance, she still continuing a most pure and holy virgin. Thus, that Christ's life might be communicated to us, did God's watchful love provide for Him to be first partaker of our life; and as our regeneration was to be the work of the Holy Ghost, so was Christ's Nativity ordered in like manner.

Again, at the Baptism of our Lord, when that water, and in it all water, was sanctified to be the outward means of that blessed union and communion with Christ, here also again the Holy Spirit came down from heaven to bless the water for the purpose. At Pentecost He came down as in cloven tongues of fire, to quicken the dead world and make it a living Church. In Baptism it is His gracious doing, that we put on Christ, Who is our Life. In the Holy Eucharist, He it is, He the most Holy Spirit, Who comes down in answer to the prayers of His Church, and works that unseen wonder, that the Bread and Wine become, to those who worthily receive them [h], the Body and Blood of Christ, verily taken and received. That is, in the Eucharist the Holy Spirit

[h] The author was speaking only of the benefits to the faithful receiver, without any reference to the case of the wicked. He held undoubtingly that the Holy Eucharist was, by virtue of the

comes down, to strengthen and refresh us in Christ, Who is our Life.

Lastly, the Holy Spirit is to us a Giver of life, because He plants even in our bodies a life-giving seed, Christ's Body received by faith; and it is a pledge that we really never die, but sleep; it is a token, in our very outward members, that we may look in hope for a glorious resurrection; as S. Paul reasons in the epistle to the Romans, "[i] If the Spirit of Him that raised up Jesus from the dead dwell in you, He that raised up Christ from the dead shall also quicken your mortal bodies by His Spirit which dwelleth in you."

Thus is Christ's Spirit to each one of us the Lord and Giver of Life from the beginning; thus is He near at hand, keeping us continually joined to Jesus Christ, our Head, if we have not thrown His grace quite away.

Surely, if we believe these things indeed, they will not pass away out of our minds; they must seem to us so great and wonderful, so near to our own selves, as to swallow up all other thoughts and cares in this one, how we may shew ourselves not unworthy of the miracles of God's mercy towards us, how we may

---

consecration, the Body and Blood of Christ to all; to the members of Christ, to unite them yet more to Christ; to those who profaned His Body, to their hurt. The words are equivalent to the prayer in the Roman Missal and other Eucharistic Liturgies, "that it may be *to us* the Body and Blood of Thy most dearly Beloved Son our Lord Jesus Christ." The writer was one who coöperated with Bishop Forbes in writing (what there was not time allowed, in which one person could write) "the theological defence for the Bishop of Brechin," in which Eucharistic doctrine was fully set forth. E. B. P.   [i] Rom. viii. 11.

avoid grieving that good Spirit, and forcing the Almighty Father to take Him from us. If we believe that, as baptized and justified Christians, we are really temples of the Holy Ghost, members of the Son, partakers of the Divine Nature, even as S. Paul and S. Peter plainly teach; which of us can say, that he has been or is behaving himself with that awefulness and fear, which becomes those, to whom God is so very nigh? Which of us is thankful, as he ought, to that gracious and merciful God, Who has given us not this or that blessing, but the Gift, the gracious and unspeakable Gift, even His Own Self, to dwell in our hearts and bodies, to cure us of all evil, and perfect us in every good? Surely our condition is now, since our Baptism, like that of God's Angels, before any of them fell; we are brought very near to Him, nearer than any of us can imagine or express: our blessings are heavenly blessings and privileges; our communion is with the inhabitants of heaven; we see "[j]the light of the knowledge of the glory of God in the face of Jesus Christ," in His Church, and in His Scriptures; and we know and feel all the while that we have as yet all our blessings, and the hope of infinitely greater ones, on trial; we have them to make sure of, or to lose, for ever, according as we try to keep God's commandments or no. This is, so far, like the condition of the high Angels in heaven before they fell; or like that of our first parents in Paradise.

Let us not, I beseech you, be so childish, as to put off serious thoughts of this our state with the ordinary saying, "God is merciful; and I hope I

j 2 Cor. iv. 6.

shall find pardon, though I have sinned, as many more have done." Was not He the same merciful God, was not His mercy over all His works, when the Angels sinned and when Adam fell, as truly as it is now? And yet His sentence came to pass in both cases; the one lost Heaven, and the other Paradise. Whatever else we do, then, or refrain from doing, let us at least endeavour to open our eyes, and contemplate our real condition. The outward world indeed is to us the same, as if we were no Christians; the breath of heaven is around us, the dew falls, the winds blow, the rain descends, the waters gush out, and all the other works of nature go on, as if we had never been taken out of this wicked world, and placed in the kingdom of God. But in reality, we know that there is a meaning and power in all these common things, which they can have to none but Christians. They are so many tokens of the Holy Ghost, the Comforter, the Breath of God, Which proceeded and yet proceeds from the Father and the Son, to new-create a ruined world, to renew each one of us in particular to a new life, the life of Jesus Christ. That good Spirit is around us on every side; He is within us; we are His temples; we do not leave Him behind us, when we go out of Church; only let us so live, that we force Him not to depart from us at last!

SERMON XIX.

CHRIST'S BAPTISM, A TOKEN OF PENTECOST.

WHITSUNTIDE.

S. LUKE iii. 21, 22.

"Jesus also being baptized, and praying, the heaven was opened, and the Holy Ghost descended in a bodily shape like a dove upon Him."

WITHOUT all question, there is a deep and mysterious connexion between the Baptism of our Saviour and the coming of the Holy Ghost upon the Apostles. They are, if we may so speak, parts of the same wonderful work of God, the saving Christian people by the kingdom of heaven. Christ's Baptism was the beginning, the coming down of the Holy Ghost on the day of Pentecost was the middle, the Baptism of each Christian is, in a certain sense, part of the end. First, the Holy Spirit came down on Jesus Christ, our Head and Surety; then on the whole body or assembly of the Apostles and other Christians at Jerusalem, to make them truly Christ's Body; thirdly, He descends upon each individual person, first in Baptism and afterwards in Confirmation, to make each one individually a member of that Body, a partaker of the blessing.

Accordingly, as the heaven was opened at the

Baptism of our Holy Lord Jesus, and the Spirit of God was seen descending, in a bodily shape, like a dove, and abiding upon Him, so was the heaven silently opened, as on this day, ten days after the Ascension, and the Holy Ghost was again seen and heard, coming down with a rushing mighty sound, with cloven tongues, like as of fire, which settled on each of the Apostles, and they began to speak with other tongues, as the Spirit gave each one power to do. That is, being filled with the Holy Ghost, they presently set about the great work, to which they were called, of preaching to all nations in their several languages; as our Lord, for His part, being filled with the same Spirit, went out straightway into the wilderness, to accomplish that great combat with the devil, wherewith His ministry was to begin.

Our Saviour was praying, after His Baptism, when the Holy Ghost came upon Him. So the Apostles, when they returned from witnessing His Ascension, continued with one accord in prayer and supplication, until He sent the Comforter according to His promise. As it was the same heavenly Person Who came down first upon the Head and afterwards upon the members, so there was, by God's providence, a great resemblance between the outward tokens given in the one case and in the other.

And one thing we shall do well to observe, for the better understanding of the great things which God has done for us; that it was not one or more special gifts of the Holy Ghost, but the Holy Ghost, the third Divine Person Himself, Who came down first on our Lord and afterwards on His Church. That Holy and Blessed Spirit has innumerable gifts and graces, which, both before and after the day of Pentecost, He divideth to every man severally as He will; but the greatest Gift of all, the Infinite, Unspeakable Gift, is His coming down in His own Person to dwell in the souls and bodies of men, join them as true members to Jesus Christ, and cause them to have from Christ a new and heavenly life.

It is the Holy Ghost Himself, not the gifts of the Holy Ghost only, for which to-day we give God thanks; and although many gifts and graces had been vouchsafed to favoured persons in all times before, the Holy Ghost Himself had not been given. S. John informs us, that He "[a] was not yet given, because that Jesus was not yet glorified."

Abraham, therefore, Isaac and Jacob, Joseph and Samuel, Moses and Joshua, Job and David, Elijah, Daniel, and the Prophets, great and holy and good as they were, and mightily blessed with the gifts of God's Spirit, yet that very Spirit Itself they had not yet, in the same sense as Christians have It after their Baptism: they were not yet regenerate, they were not yet members of Christ, they were not yet in the kingdom of heaven. This greatest blessing they have obtained or shall obtain, in some way unknown to us, after their departure out of this world; as S. Paul teaches in the epistle to the Hebrews: "[b] These all, having obtained a good report through faith, received not the promise: God having provided some better thing for us, that they without us should not be made perfect." But to the Church this astonishing change was wrought openly, as on this day; and ever since then, every little child who is made a member of Christ by Baptism, had thereupon the

[a] S. John vii. 39.   [b] Heb. xi. 39, 40.

Holy Ghost dwelling in him, in a nearer and more heavenly way than He dwelt in S. John the Baptist, who was the greatest saint before Christ came.

We have our Lord's own word for this: "[c]Verily I say unto you, Among them that are born of women there hath not risen a greater than John the Baptist; notwithstanding he that is least in the kingdom of heaven is greater than he."

So great and precious is the heavenly gift, the Holy Comforter entering into men's hearts; and it could not be before this time, because that until now "Jesus was not yet glorified." And of this, the promise of the Father to Christ's members, the Spirit descending on Christ Himself, was a Type, a Firstfruit, and a Beginning.

Now although the gifts of the Holy Ghost were not always accompanied with outward and sensible signs, yet the Holy Ghost Himself, descending as He did on our Lord and on the Church, has always, so far as appears from Scripture, seen fit to manifest Himself thus outwardly. When He came down on Jesus Himself, it was "in a bodily shape like a Dove," and with the voice of the Almighty Father, "This is My beloved Son, in Whom I am well pleased." When He came down on the Church, there was an appearance of fiery tongues, cloven tongues of fire, that sat upon each of the Apostles. When He comes to each one of us in Baptism, then also there is both a sight and a voice; the sight of the water wherein the person is baptized, the sound of the priest's voice saying the holy words, " I baptize thee in the Name of the Father, the Son, and the Holy Ghost."

[c] S. Matt. xi. 11.

So that we are no more to doubt whether an infant, rightly baptized, had received the Holy Spirit, than S. John the Baptist doubted of the Spirit's descending and remaining on our Lord, when he had seen the Dove and heard the voice; no more than we should have doubted, had we stood by on the Day of Pentecost, and heard the rushing mighty wind, and seen the cloven tongues like as of fire. Our own Church's direction to us is, " Doubt ye not therefore, but earnestly believe" these things.

But further, we may plainly see that those outward tokens of the Holy Comforter's Presence do not only make us sure of that Presence, but also instruct us not a little in the manner and in the greatness of the change He works in us. Water, for example, pure water, springing out of the earth, or dropping from heaven by the immediate gift of God; who sees not at once, that it represents the refreshing and cleansing power of that Divine grace, which, coming direct from God, purifies the stain of our hearts, and makes us strong and active to keep the commandments? Who is not reminded by it of the living water which the Lord hath promised to give us, not only to quench our thirst for the time, but to be in us "[d] a well of water springing up into everlasting life?"

Again, what signified the fiery tongues which settled upon each of the saints on this great Day of Pentecost? We perceive in a moment that the shape of tongues was intended to point out the gift of divers languages, which was suddenly communicated to all of them. But why was it in the sub-

[d] S. John iv. 14.

stance of fire? Surely, because of the searching power of Christ's Spirit, which in a wonderful manner tries every man's heart, of what sort it is, penetrating into all the dark corners of our souls, and where it is not resisted, enlightening, warming, melting all; spreading all ways, and transforming all into its own nature, sometimes not without grievous pain and suffering. Think of grace working in this manner, and you will presently see that it is like a refiner's fire, purifying the elect of God, and purging them as gold and silver, that they may stand the terrible trial of the Last Day.

Lastly and chiefly, consider well the wonderful appearance in the text. When the Lord of all had been baptized, and was praying, He went up straightway out of the water, "and the Holy Ghost descended in a bodily shape like a dove upon Him." It is probable that the appearance of fire, or of a bright cloud, which had taken in former times the shape of a pillar guiding the Israelites, and which afterwards took that of fiery tongues lighting on the Apostles, now hovered over the Blessed Jesus in somewhat of the form of a dove, with wings spreading over Him; and we may be certain that it came down with the gentle steady motion of a dove.

What are we to learn from this? For we may be sure it is not told us in vain. The second Person of the Blessed Trinity, partly because of His unspeakable patience, and lowliness, and innocency, is often, we know, called a Lamb; and doubtless we may discern the same kind of reason, why the Third Person vouchsafes to represent Himself as a Dove.

We may think, for instance, of the prayers, the

"dovelike moanings," which this blessed Comforter puts into the hearts of God's people. "ᵉ The Spirit," says S. Paul, "helpeth our infirmities: for we know not what we should pray for as we ought, but the Spirit Itself maketh intercession for us with groanings which cannot be uttered." That is a true saint's description of the sacred Spirit of God and of Christ, earnestly praying in the hearts of Christ's people, filling them with longing desires and earnest breathings after heavenly things, causing them to cry mightily unto God, to thirst and long after heavenly delights, as the hart after the rivers of waters. Herein the Holy Ghost is like a dove, because the dove goes on in such wistful, plaintive, longing tones, sometimes far into the night, very often in the early morning. They who lie awake, or who are about betimes, know the sound very well; and one can hardly listen to it without feeling as if it told us, what a restless thing this world is, and how we have need to set our hearts on an infinitely better treasure, which as yet is far away from us. And it goes on, like a person earnest in prayer, still repeating the same note, as if it could never be tired nor stop, until it had found the rest which its soul loveth. Such is the voice of the Holy Ghost in prayer, inwardly uttered in a Christian's heart; and because it is like the unwearied melancholy tones of the dove, that may be one reason, why the Blessed Comforter came down on our Lord in a bodily shape like a dove.

This reason is given us by a great and holy Bishop, S. Augustine; and he adds another, the simple harmless innocence of the dove; and yet another, its

ᵉ Rom. viii. 26.

gentle, peaceful, loving nature: whereby it becomes the token both of truth and charity. And whereas it is said, that the dove never forsakes its mate, this may serve to remind us of the Infinite unchangeable love of the Most High God, enduring for ever and ever upon them that fear Him. His promise is, "[f] I will never leave thee nor forsake thee." "[g] Can a woman forget her sucking child, that she should not have compassion on the son of her womb? Yea, they may forget; yet will not I forget thee."

In these and other ways the holy Dove is God's token to us of the Almighty and Blessed Comforter; and it is also His token of the grace which He bestows upon His Church. For such as He is, such He would have us to be. The very purpose and glory of our Christian calling is to bring us back to God's Image, from which we are so sadly fallen.

"[h] We know not yet what we shall be, but we know that, when He shall appear, we shall be like Him; for we shall see Him as He is." The Church, therefore, the sanctified, is called in Scripture a Dove, as well as the Holy Spirit Who comes to sanctify. The Church is called a Dove, as when it is said, "[i] My Dove, my undefiled, is but one; she is the only one of her mother, she is the choice one of her that bare her:" because there is but one Church, to which all the promises are made. Again, each obedient Christian soul too, in which Christ delights to dwell by His Spirit, is compared to this sacred bird, the Dove: because it is changed by the indwelling Spirit into His own likeness; to be gentle and loving, simple

[f] Heb. xiii. 5.   [g] Isa. xlix. 15.
[h] 1 S. John iii. 2.   [i] Cant. vi. 9.

and peaceful like Him. Thus David wishes that he had " wings like a dove," grace and help, such as is given to the saints, to flee away from the troubles of the world, and be at rest in holy meditation. Thus our Lord Himself is introduced, mercifully encouraging the devout soul to present herself before Him in prayer, and tell Him all her wants. "[k] O my Dove, that art in the clefts of the rock," (that is, whose thoughts are in the wounds of the Holy Jesus, as the wild pigeon makes her nest in the cliffs by the sea,) " let me see thy countenance, let me hear thy voice." Thus that ancient dove, which Noah sent out of the Ark, was a type of the true spiritual mind abiding with our Lord in His Church, and finding no rest any where else; and wherever her thoughts wander, even in this lower world, still finding tokens of peace and hope, and humbly acknowledging God's mercy in them, as Noah's dove returned to him and to the Ark, with an olive-leaf plucked off in her mouth.

We see, then, our calling, Christian brethren; we see what our Lord would have us be; we see what especial graces and virtues He sets before us, to be thought on, and prayed for, this high and holy day. We are to be simple and harmless as doves. It is His own Word; we are to be simple and harmless. We are to put far away from us the unchristian fancy, that it is good to be knowing about wickedness. Never again, as long as we live, are we to be ashamed of that happy ignorance, whereby God's fatherly care would keep us out of mischief. Never again are we to imagine, with Eve, that it becomes us to know something of evil as well as of good.

[k] Cant. ii. 14.

Remember this in particular, you that are preparing to be confirmed. The consecrated hands of the Bishop are, we hope, soon to be spread over you, in token of the presence and outstretched wings of that Dove which descended on our Saviour. See, He warns you, how you are to get yourselves ready for that awful yet blessed moment. Be "[1] harmless as doves." Be "[m] simple concerning evil." Make up your minds to that saying of a wise man of old: "[n] The knowledge of wickedness is not wisdom, neither at any time the counsel of sinners prudence." Care not to seem clever and knowing among foolish men; care not for their ridicule, when you know you are trying to please God.

Then, remember that Christ's Dove is undefiled; and think what a miserable thing it will be, should you come to kneel before God with any wilful impurity of heart and life, and bring a curse on you instead of a blessing. Remember that Christ's Dove is without gall, without bitterness, or malice, or spite, or envy. She is very gentle, and has good words, aye, and kind thoughts too, and prayers, for them " that despitefully use her and persecute her."

Remember lastly, that Christ's Dove is full of lowly and earnest moanings to Him; she prays and mourns continually, because, though contented with her condition in this world, she is ever longing to be in a better world. She thirsts for God, yea, even for the living God: her thought by day and by night is, "[o] When shall I come to appear before the presence of God?"

[1] S. Matt. x. 16.   [m] Rom. xvi. 19.
[n] Ecclus. xix. 22.   [o] Ps. xlii. 2.

My brethren, if we know in our secret hearts that these marks of the saintly character, these tokens of Christ's love, find as yet little in us to answer to them, let us not rest, let us be afraid; for it is probable that we are far worse than we know: let us be afraid, but never let us despair. We cannot indeed enter heaven, until we are greatly changed. But this Spirit is mighty to change us, as well as All-Holy to hate our sins. He can do great things in a short time, in making the proud lowly, the unkind gentle, the worldly full of penitential love; He came to us in Holy Baptism, and pledged Himself to do so, if we sincerely and with all our hearts call upon Him in good time. Call upon Him, and seek Him early, and you will find Him waiting at your doors. He will prepare you to meet your Saviour, and your Saviour will carry you into heaven.

SERMON XX.

FORGETFULNESS IN CHRISTIANS, NO EXCUSE.

WHITSUNDAY.

S. JOHN xiv. 26.

"The Comforter, which is the Holy Ghost, whom the Father will send in My Name, He shall teach you all things, and bring all things to your remembrance, whatsoever I have said unto you."

AMONG other ways which careless people have of getting rid of the matter easily, when they have committed sin, one shall sometimes hear them say, They are sorry they did wrong, but really, at the time, the temptation was strong upon them, and they did not recollect that it *was* wrong. Angry and passionate people, for one instance, very often employ this excuse. They seem to imagine that God cannot be very much displeased with them, if they can but say that what they did amiss was done in a hurry, and without thinking.

But it is worth their considering very seriously indeed, whether the very circumstance of their being in a hurry, and doing bad things without thinking, was not itself their own fault.

Not to give yourself time to think, whether what you do is right or wrong, this surely is a sort of conduct very unworthy a reasonable being, who knows that it is as much as his soul is worth, whether he use himself to do right or wrong.

And the fact is, that this excuse of doing things in a hurry, together with all others which sinful Christians are apt to plead for themselves, has been completely done away with by that great mercy of God in giving us His Holy Spirit, as on this Day, to be with us always, and help us to do good.

In particular, no Christian can fairly pretend to plead his having forgotten his duty, and therefore done wrong, after this most gracious promise of our Lord and Saviour in the text, that the Comforter, that is, the Holy Ghost, should not only teach His disciples their duty, if they did not know it before, but should also put them in mind of it, if at any time they had forgotten it.

The words indeed were first spoken to the Apostles, who, being to carry through the whole world the message with which Jesus Christ had entrusted them, might well fear, if left to themselves, lest they should forget it, or remember it wrong. It was therefore exceeding merciful and considerate, both for them and us, to tell them beforehand, that they would not be left to themselves: that the Holy Spirit of God, Who alone can give man knowledge at all, would be with them continually; so that they should be always able to speak or write down, without any material error, the words of Christ and the truths of His Gospel.

By this promise we know and are sure, that the things written in the four Gospels concerning our Lord Jesus Christ, are the very things which He said and did: and the lessons contained in the epistles, the very instructions of His Holy Spirit, telling us what we must do to be saved.

Because, however, by the frailty and weakness of our mortal nature, we are in danger of forgetting, either for a time or altogether, what we once knew perfectly; we also, in some measure, stand in need of a promise like this: though we be not sent out, as the Apostles were, to teach all nations. If they might forget what Christ said in their hearing, we also, especially those among us who cannot read, may forget what they have written for our instruction. We have reason, therefore, to think, that our Blessed Saviour in the text was speaking, not to the Apostles only, but to all who should at any time become disciples of His. He tells them, one and all, that it must be their own fault if they forget His will, any part of it that is necessary to salvation. For He, in compassion to their infirmities, gave them, when they were baptized, His Holy Spirit, to teach them their duty, and bring it to their remembrance.

But then, in order to be taught, they must be willing to learn. They must steadily make up their minds to do their duty, when they know it; and they must ask God to teach it them, with a sincere and hearty goodwill. Then they are sure, upon the word of an Apostle, not to be left in ignorance. For S. James has said, "[a] If any of you lack wisdom, let him ask of God, Who giveth unto all men liberally, and upbraideth not; and it shall be given him."

The true cause, then, of men's forgetting, or being ignorant of, their duty, is their not praying to God

[a] S. James i. 5.

as they ought. Perhaps they say over some prayers every day; but they do not in their hearts desire the thing they pray for. They say in the Lord's prayer, "Deliver us from evil;" but they do not seriously wish, while they say so, to be delivered from their bad desires and foolish fancies, their worldly hopes and expectations, their false pleasures and profits. Again, whenever they join in the Communion Service, they pray that God would incline their hearts to keep all His laws, one as much as another; and would write them in their hearts. But while they say those words, they are perhaps thinking of something else. For all such prayers as these, there may yet be some favourite sin, from which they do not even wish to be delivered. It is no wonder, if men go on in such devotion all their lives long, and are never at all the better for it. And yet, for all this, it may be, and is, quite true, that no man, who sincerely keeps asking of God to teach him his duty, will ever, in any thing of consequence, be left in ignorance or forgetfulness of it.

Not that Christians are to expect, in answer to their prayers, any thing like sudden illumination or inspiration from God Almighty. This is a fancy of some persons, who do not enough consider the difference between earth and heaven. If ever, by God's great mercy, we shall be so happy as to come there, God will speak to us, as it were, face to face, and we shall have no trouble to find out His will. But here, when our sins have put such a distance between us and Him, we must not expect such favours. We must humbly and patiently do our best, and leave every thing else to Him: remembering always, that our great business, the purpose for which we are to pray, and live, and do all things, is, not to be comfortable here, but safe hereafter.

Although, however, we are not to expect that the Holy Spirit should pour into our hearts any sudden, sensible comfort, in answer to our most earnest prayers; yet it is easy for us to see, in some measure, how our continually praying for grace should help to keep us continually from sin. We never pray to God in earnest, without seriously considering and bringing it to our minds, that He is with us. If we pray to Him on a journey, we must recollect that He is about our path; if in our chamber, that He is about our bed: in short, wherever we are, we cannot use thoughtful prayer without having it strong upon our minds, that God "spieth out all our ways." Now although the folly and misery of man is so great, that not even this recollection will always keep a person from private sins, yet no doubt it very often does so. If he still indulge bad thoughts, yet this remembrance of God's Presence makes them more uneasy to him, and gives him, so far, a fairer chance to repent of them and forsake them.

And hence the saying which I have often heard, that you cannot keep your prayers and your sins together. This would hardly be true, if it were spoken of such prayers, as the generality, it is to be feared, are content with. We see and know by sad experience, that men may keep up some sort of prayer, both in public and in private, along with many of the sins which God most hates. But that sort of prayer, which in earnest brings with it the remembrance of our Maker's Presence: this, indeed, it is hardly possible to continue for many years, and yet to go on carelessly in what we know will displease Him. One of the two, the habit of praying with thought, or the habit of sinning wilfully, must, one should think, wear out the other, in no very long time.

Prayer, therefore, as being a kind of holy meditation, and as bringing the Presence of Almighty God continually to our remembrance, is, of itself, likely to keep a man out of much mischief. But over and above what it is of itself, there is the promise of Jesus Christ added to it, that His Father will give the Holy Spirit to them that ask Him : that is, the Spirit of God, God Himself, will be always at hand, to keep those, who pray as they ought, from forgetting their duty.

For a Christian, then, to complain, that he cannot recollect his duty in the hour of temptation, is a sort of excuse which only makes bad, worse; for it is affronting God, in supposing that He is not at hand to fulfil His own promise. A poor man must not complain of being cruelly starved, when he knows he may have what he wants, upon merely asking for it : neither must a sinner plead that he has not grace to think of what he ought to do, now that he knows of the Holy Comforter, Who is come to bring all Christ's sayings to the remembrance of His people.

Besides, let us consider for a moment, what sort of things they are, in excuse for which we hear Christian people pleading this sort of forgetfulness. It is not in nice and hard points; but in such plain and necessary duties, as one would think no one could mistake; things, in which forgetting is itself a great sin, since it could not happen without a shameful carelessness about right and wrong.

Thus, men wrong and cheat their neighbours, and yet lie down at night with a quiet conscience, and think they have done nothing strange or shocking, because they forget that every Christian is a brother to them; and that, in robbing and cheating him, they are robbing and cheating a brother.

Now this is a thing which they cannot be excused for forgetting; any more than a mother could be excused, if she had cast off the care of her child, till she forgot that it was her's, and so came to use it unkindly.

Again, Christian men and women allow themselves to indulge wrong desires, and fall into sins, which are not fit to be named among us; because they forget what God has threatened to all such. They do not consider that, by pleasing themselves now with forbidden things, they wilfully give up their bodies hereafter to the worm that never dieth, and the fire that never shall be quenched. They do not call to mind what God's Spirit has plainly enough taught them; that it is madness to give themselves up to such things, unless they have made up their minds to dwell with the devouring fire, with everlasting burnings.

Now you see plainly, that such forgetfulness, being altogether their own fault, is itself a great sin, so far from being an excuse for other sins.

Suppose a father had warned his son very earnestly, not to steal, not to swear, not to tell lies, or anything else of that sort, which every child knows to be wrong. Would the father take it for a good excuse, if the son did the very thing forbidden, and said he forgot that his father had told him any thing about it?

But if, besides speaking to him earnestly himself, the father had left a friend to be with his son always, and keep his warnings fresh in his mind: then the excuse of forgetting, which would be foolish enough in any case, would be a much more wicked and undutiful mockery.

Now, this is just the case with Christians. They have not only the commandments of Jesus Christ, to let them know His will; but they have His Spirit also abiding with them, like a friend whom He has trusted, to put them in mind continually, when they are tempted to do amiss.

We may very well judge, then, what sort of an answer God Almighty will make at the last Day to those Christians who plead forgetfulness, when, if they would, they might have had grace to call upon Him in all temptation. And He is never far from those, who call on Him in good earnest.

In like manner, all the excuses, which ill-minded Christians employ, to keep themselves easy in their sins, are done away with, when it is once known, that the Holy Spirit is among us; as we are taught by His wonderful descent upon the Apostles, as on this Day.

We cannot now lay upon our corrupt nature the blame of what we do amiss; since, however bad that may be, God Himself is at hand to cure it, if we will apply to Him.

We cannot say, it was all bad example: since here we are assured of the assistance of the Holy Ghost, to turn our thoughts from the base and evil things we see around us, to the pure and blessed conversation of good men in times past, or of angels in heaven.

We cannot say, it was too much to expect from weak mortals, that they should resist the enticing customs of the world, when we consider what power and support it is, which we have given us to lean on; the power and support of the Spirit of God, God Himself.

In short, when once a man believes, after a Christian manner, in the Holy Ghost; believes that he, however poor and mean, is yet, *as a Christian*, the Temple of God, and has the Spirit of God dwelling in him, from that time all excuses for sin are taken away, and it becomes indeed, as S. Paul calls it[b], most "exceeding sinful." It becomes like the rebellion of those Jews, who cried out against God and Moses, while the cloud was overshadowing the tabernacle in their sight; or like the sin of Balaam, who went on in his covetousness, when he saw the Angel of the Lord with his sword drawn in his hand.

If people will disobey God wilfully under such circumstances, we have great reason to believe they would disobey Him in heaven itself, as the devil and his angels did; and therefore they can no more reasonably expect to come to heaven, than the fallen angels can expect to return thither.

Such is the aweful, but most true notion, which the Church to-day would teach to every Christian concerning wilful sin and forgetfulness of God, when found in any soul that has been baptized, and that has received, of course, the grace of the Holy Ghost.

It is no wonder, then, that the devil should always

[b] Rom. vii. 13.

have done his best to root this doctrine out of the minds of God's people; to make them forget, if possible, that the Spirit of God dwelleth in them. And sad experience shews, that it is but too possible, nay, easy for him, to keep such thoughts out of men's minds, that they may the more freely indulge themselves in their sins.

For can any one think, that such sort of Christians, as one commonly sees in the world, have really any serious consideration of God's Holy Spirit, as dwelling in them, and being in them? They could not be so easy in their secret sins, could not so composedly go about to defile themselves with all sorts of base pleasures, if they really laid this truth to heart; that they are doing all this, not only in sight of their God, but, while He is, as it were, speaking to them expressly, and coming close to them, to hinder them from such sins.

It is, therefore, the purpose of our adversary, the devil, to prevail upon us either to neglect this truth altogether, or to think of it amiss: as though the gift of the Spirit were partial, and as if (though He may have come to some Christians in this particular way) He had not come to us; in which case, we persuade ourselves, we have less to answer for.

This being the purpose of Satan, our purpose, of course, must be just the contrary, if we would save our souls. We must hold fast the doctrine of the catechism. We must "believe in God the Holy Ghost, Who sanctifies us and all the elect people of God," all Christians whatever; and believing, we must do all our best, that we receive not the grace of God, His last and greatest favour, in vain.

SERMON XXI.

BAPTISM WITH THE HOLY GHOST.

WHITSUNDAY.

Acts i. 5.

"John truly baptized with water; but ye shall be baptized with the Holy Ghost not many days hence."

OUR Saviour here makes a promise, which sank deep into the heart of the holy Apostles, and was understood by them to be very full of mysterious and gracious meaning. He was just on the point of departing out of their sight, and sitting down at His Father's Right Hand: and He turns their thoughts more and more to the great Promise which had always been the end of His preaching: the promise of the Holy Ghost to come down from the Father, and set up the kingdom of heaven. He renews this promise to them for the last time in such a way, as to signify that it was connected, in some mysterious way, with the former baptism of S. John, though that was by water only, this with the assured Presence and Power of the Blessed Spirit also. "John truly baptized with water; but ye shall be baptized with the Holy Ghost." It was the great point of our Lord's farewell blessing. No wonder that the blessed Apostles treasured it up in their minds, and applied it more than once as a prime law and rule of the kingdom of heaven. Thus S. Peter, when he was blamed for admitting Cornelius and other Gentiles into the Church as well as the Jews, told them how he had seen with his eyes the Holy Spirit come down upon them, and how that heavenly sight recalled to his mind our Lord's own words. "[a] As I began to speak," says the holy Apostle, "the Holy Ghost fell on them, as on us at the beginning. Then remembered I the word of the Lord, how that He said, John indeed baptized with water, but ye shall be baptized with the Holy Ghost." And so S. Paul long after, finding certain disciples at Ephesus who knew no baptism but that of John, spoke unto them as one who would have them think so seriously of the baptism of S. John, which had gone before, as to receive Christ, Who came after, the better and more truly for it. When they said, they had been baptized with John's baptism, S. Paul's answer was, "[b] John verily baptized with the baptism of repentance, saying unto the people, that they should believe on Him which should come after him, that is, on Christ Jesus." And in his last regular discourse to the Jews, which being rejected, he turned to the Gentiles: "[c] God, according to His promise, hath raised unto Israel a Saviour, Jesus: when John had first preached, before His coming, the baptism of repentance to all the people of Israel."

By all these places it is very evident, that there is some deep and heavenly connection between the beginning and the end of the Gospel: the baptism of S. John, and that of the Holy Ghost. Between

[a] Acts xi. 15, 16.   [b] Ib. xix. 4.   [c] Ib. xiii. 23, 24.

these two, I say, there is such a connection, as all would do well to take notice of: our Lord Himself recommending it to the very serious thoughts of all His people. So too at the beginning of the Gospel, we find, on the other hand, no less distinct reference to this, the designed crown and end of it. The very form and object of S. John the Baptist's ministry was, as we all know, by baptizing with water, to prepare the way for One Who should baptize with the Holy Ghost. Twice indeed, to a few chosen disciples he said, "Behold the Lamb of God:" but to the whole multitude his saying was (before he knew for certain that Jesus of Nazareth was the Person), "[d] I indeed baptize you with water unto repentance, but He that cometh after me is mightier than I, Whose shoes I am not worthy to bear: He shall baptize you with the Holy Ghost and with fire." And after he had come to know Jesus (by what occurred at His Baptism), still when he had to speak of Him to the multitude, it does not appear that he pointed out to them His very Person, or spoke of His being the Lamb of God, but he spoke generally, and described our Lord as before. "[e] There standeth One among you, Whom ye know not, of Whom I said, He cometh after me but is preferred before me: He shall baptize you with the Holy Ghost, and with fire." The Baptism with the Holy Ghost was that great thing, which they to whom Christ was preached were taught to look on to from the beginning: it was (if I may say so) the Sign of the Son of Man. So that when it actually took place, in that wonderful manner, as on this day, Christians and especially the Apostles,

[d] S. Matt. iii. 11.   [e] S. John i. 26. 27. S. Luke iii. 16.

looked back to the sayings of S. John, and said to themselves, "Now we know their meaning, now we see how God has been gradually preparing us for this His greatest work of all, the setting up of His kingdom by the coming of His Spirit to dwell in the souls and bodies of His people."

In particular, they would then seem to know, better than ever they had known before, concerning the astonishing Baptism of our Lord Himself. They would perceive that there was a sort of mysterious connection and correspondence between S. John's baptizing our Lord with water, and the whole Church being baptized by Christ Himself with the Holy Ghost. The Church, we know, is the Body of Christ. His natural Body is in many respects a kind of Type of that spiritual Body, of which His Person is the Head, and which has all its life from Him, made manifest in the flesh. The water therefore poured upon His visible Body by S. John was a token and type of the baptismal water, by which sinners were in all time to be born again and made members of Him. And the Holy Ghost, which descended in a bodily shape like a Dove and lighted upon Him, was a type and token of the same Holy Spirit descending, as in cloven tongues, like as of fire, with a hovering, perhaps, and dove-like motion, and settling on His Mother and His disciples, the first members of His mystical Body. Who knows too but the sound as of a rushing mighty wind, which came suddenly from heaven, and filled all the house where they were sitting, might answer in some wonderful way to the voice from heaven, which said, "Thou art My beloved Son; in Thee I am well-pleased?" seeing that those who then received the Spirit were truly made sons of God, adopted by Him as true members of Christ Jesus, and thenceforth, their eyes being enlightened, they discerned in all the house where they were sitting, in all the Church and the world around them, nothing but voices and tokens of His mysterious Presence. As many as receive Him, to them He gives the privilege thus to become the sons of God, even to them who believe on His Name. He gives them power, not only to be accounted, but really to become, His children, by true Sacramental union with Christ His Son.

Thus it may appear that our Lord's Baptism by S. John was the pledge and in a manner the beginning of His Church's Baptism by Himself. He then, as our Head, received the Holy Ghost for us. He was anointed with It; so S. Peter speaks, "anointed with the Holy Ghost and with power." And as the precious oil upon the High Priest's head "ran down unto the beard and went down to the skirts of his clothing," so the Holy Spirit, poured upon the Head of the Church, did on this day begin to flow over her members, one and all, and shall do so until the end of the world, when she shall have attained her full stature, and the number of those chosen to be grafted into her shall be complete. Behold here, as in all things, the merciful condescension of our Redeemer: how when He wanted nothing, He condescended to receive all, that we might receive it through Him. That He might baptize us, He consented to be baptized Himself: that He might confirm us, to be confirmed: that He might ordain some among us, to be ordained. For so the Holy Scriptures and the

Church represent the deep meanings of His Baptism by S. John. By His heavenly touch He sanctified the waters, not only of Jordan, but of all the earth, to the mystical washing away of sin: by receiving the Holy Ghost presently afterwards, He sealed to us not only the baptismal Gift, but also that further Gift of the Spirit, which the Church teaches us to call Confirmation. And since S. Paul affirms that the saying, "Thou art My Son, this day have I begotten Thee," was the Father's commission to glorify Christ as our High Priest[f], we have reason to think that His Baptism, so far, was a pledge of that holy gift also, which He gave His Apostles, when He made them priests in His Church. And in a word: for whatever holy and divine purposes God intended to give the Spirit, in due time, to the Church and her members; for all of them together we believe that He gave the same Spirit to the Divine and most merciful Head of the Church. Christ received the Holy Ghost without measure, that unto every one of us He might give grace, according to the measure which He saw to be proper for each.

Since it was for us only, not at all for Himself, that He received that good Spirit, we need not fear to say and believe the very highest things regarding the privileges, with which He has endowed His Church and kingdom, for which He hath obtained that unspeakable Gift. We may truly say, that as He was anointed to be Prophet, Priest and King, so His Holy Spirit has anointed His whole Church, and what is more, each particular Christian, to be in some sort prophet, priest and king in His stead. The Church, Christ's Body on earth, is a prophet in

[f] Heb. v. 5.

our Lord's absence, because the Spirit which dwells in her is a Spirit of prophecy, enabling her to foretel things to come, guiding her into all truth, opening her understanding, that she may understand the Scriptures. As Christ's prophet, and our teacher under Him, the Church has provided us with Creeds, declaring to us the true meaning of the Holy Bible, and which of all the truths which it teaches are particularly necessary to salvation. And not only in Creeds, but in Liturgies and in catechisms and in many other ways, the holy Church throughout all the world does the office of a prophet to God's people, warning them of their duty, calling their attention to God's written Word, giving them sure tokens when He is especially near them, shewing them how He will be praised and worshipped, what prayers and Sacraments they should offer Him. Nay, and all the Lord's people too are prophets, now that He hath put His Spirit within them: they all know Him, from the least to the greatest, so far as that He has made them aware of their duty: they know what great things He has done in coming into the world and dying for them, and how infinite the consequence of their hearing or refusing to hear. They are prophets, because they can look on into eternity. They are prophets, because they have in them the Holy Spirit of the Father and the Son, teaching them, in answer to their diligent prayer, what to do and what to avoid.

Again, Christians are priests likewise, and kings: "[g] a royal priesthood, a peculiar people." So speaks S. Peter: and S. John gives glory "[h] unto Him that

---

[g] 1 S. Pet. ii. 9.   [h] Rev. i. 5, 6.

loved us, and washed us from our sins in His own Blood, and hath made us kings and priests unto God and His Father." And the whole Church is, so far, made partaker of Christ's priestly office, as that she is entrusted by Him to offer up spiritual sacrifices, to do that in remembrance of Him, which He did the night before His death, in order to our being all made partakers of His most blessed Body and Blood. The Apostles indeed and their ordained successors only have commission to do it with their hands; but in virtue and effect it is the offering of all Christians, for themselves and for one another. So indeed are all her solemn prayers and intercessions. If it is a great thing to have one righteous man praying earnestly and fervently for us, much more to have the whole Church: because the Church is the Body of Christ, anointed with His Spirit, the Spirit of grace and supplication, and encouraged to intercede for His members by very special promises. And in that she sacrifices and intercedes, she is so far a Priest. The grace of His mediatorial office runs over, as it were, and is communicated, in a lower and ministerial sense, to His Church.

Now as to our Lord's third office, that of King on His throne: the sayings of Scripture are quite express, that we shall reign with Him for ever: that such as overcome shall sit with Him on His throne: that we are even now raised with Christ to sit with Him on God's right hand in the heavenly places. And it is the same, where either Prophets or Apostles make mention of the whole Church as one. She is called the bride of the Lamb, Who is King of kings, and Lord of lords. She is the queen; "the king's daughter, all glorious within," standing on the right hand of Him Who is most mighty. To her is given that kingdom and dominion, which all people nations and languages are to own and obey for ever: before which the kingdoms of the world are to become as dust, carried away by the whirlwind. Thus is the holy Catholic Church invested with her Lord's kingly office also, anointed to it with the Holy Ghost in mystery and type at His Baptism, and really on the Day of Pentecost, when the kingdom of heaven began.

What could the Lord have done more for His vineyard, that He hath not done in it? What if after all, when He looks that we should bring forth grapes, He finds us bringing forth no better than wild grapes? The same Scriptures, which instruct us so largely in the Church's privileges and our own, teach also no less plainly, what fruit He expects both of the Church and of us her members. The Spirit which rested first upon our Lord in Baptism, then upon His whole Church at the Day of Pentecost, thirdly, on each of us individually, when we were baptized and made members of Christ: this Holy Spirit the Lord declares by His prophet to be the Spirit of Wisdom and Understanding, the Spirit of Counsel and Might, the Spirit of Knowledge and of the Fear of the Lord. Wisdom first, and Understanding: that is, as it may seem, right thoughts concerning those things both in heaven and in earth, which Christian people ought to pursue and seek after. These are the first tokens of God's Spirit: a true judgement of things eternal, as compared with things temporal, and of things in this world, as they may or may not be made helps towards eternal blessings. We have reason then to hope, that we have not forfeited or thrown away the Blessed Spirit of God given us at our Baptism, if we find and feel that eternal things take up the chief place in our will and mind, and that we use to measure other things by the hurt or good they do to our immortal souls.

Again, Christ's Spirit is a Spirit of Counsel and Might. He shews people the right way to obtain what they seek after, and gives them the heart, the courage, the good will, to set at once about that way, however disagreeable to flesh and blood. It is a good sign as to our having the Spirit, when we are ready at once to do those things which our conscience tells us ought to be done, without asking questions, without making excuses or difficulties. When we are bold to say at once to foolish irreligious friends and companions, "I *will* not go with you in sin, and there is an end of it:" when we make ourselves good rules, or what is still better, observe the good rules of the Church, and keep resolutely to them; when we mind the laughter of idle people less and less, and the secret whisperings of our conscience more and more: when, having considered beforehand and made up our minds what is right to be done, and strengthened ourselves with prayer and Holy Communion, we steadily deny ourselves in order to perform our good intentions, not listening to our own indolent scruples nor to the frivolous objections of men: all these are good marks of our still being possessed with the Spirit of Counsel and Might, Who was given us at our Baptism.

But most especially He is the Spirit of Knowledge

and of the Fear of the Lord. Those who have not in any degree made void His gracious influences have a sort of inward light within them; an instinct, such as that by which children know their parents, which tells them at once what ought to be done, without long calculation and reasoning. And most especially He causes the Fear of the Lord to be present with us. He brings it home to our hearts, that God is looking on; that whatever we do, must not be done at random, seeing an account is surely taken of all; an account, the result of which will no less surely be made known to men and Angels, when Jesus Christ comes to judge us. When we have this thought entirely rooted in our minds, and the dreadful picture of the last Day filling our hearts and imaginations, so that we are really afraid to sin, and ashamed to be cold and lukewarm in serving God: then may we hope that the sacred Spirit, of Whom we were born again unto righteousness, has in no wise departed from us: then may we trust the Lord Almighty, that we have still the portion which He freely gave us in His Son: then may we, in all humility and thankfulness, endeavour to go on unto perfection, without such restless, devouring anxiety, as if we had still the first foundations to lay.

This is what Christ would have us be, whom He hath Himself baptized with the Holy Ghost: and what we might all be at this moment, had we duly kept, according to our power, the covenant we then made with God in Him. This is what we might be, and what He gave us power to be. What we are, is another question: a most painful one for very many of us to answer, yet one which must be laid to heart and sincerely answered, as in the Presence and hearing of Him Whom we cannot deceive: else we shall but go on from bad to worse; and any peace and calm of mind we may now seem to enjoy will prove no better than a deceitful soul-destroying dream, from which we shall awake before long to everlasting incurable shame and anguish. Let us not shrink from asking ourselves, again and again, every day of our lives, the serious question, "Am I living as one who has been baptized with the Holy Ghost, made one with Christ, endowed with grace to be in some true sense a king, a priest, a prophet under Him? Am I wise to love heaven, really, better than earth; strong to keep my good resolutions; full of humility and fear, as constantly remembering the last dreadful day?" Let every man's own heart make him the true answer to these most aweful questions: let him compare what he is with what he might be: and then although, blessed be God, there is no ground for despair in any, yet surely there will be found in most of us deep reason for humiliation and penitence through the whole time of our life: too happy, if even so we may be forgiven and saved at last!

SERMON XXII.

THE FREE GIFTS OF GOD.

WHITSUNDAY.

1 Cor. ii. 12.

"We have received, not the spirit of the world, but the Spirit which is of God, that we might know the things which are freely given us of God."

The Church's collect for Whitsunday mentions two gifts of the Holy Ghost, and instructs us to pray for them together. Those two gifts are Wisdom and Joy, " to have a right judgement in all things, " and " evermore to rejoice in His holy comfort." We, the Christians who are now living, when we say that collect, put our Lord in mind of what He did for the first Christians on the first Whitsunday. He "taught the hearts of His faithful people, by sending upon them the light of His Holy Spirit." Such sayings represent to us the condition of Christians, here in this present world, as being, in some respects, like that of children in a school. Christ our Teacher; His Creed our lesson; our hearts the tablet on which that lesson is written; His Spirit, that by which it is written: as S. Paul says of his own instructions, that they were written "[a]not with ink, but with the

[a] 2 Cor. iii. 3.

Spirit of the Living God; not in tables of stone, but in fleshy tables of the heart." So it is now, and so it has been from the beginning. Men think that they learn Christian knowledge at school, by reading such and such lessons, getting by heart the answers to such and such questions. And it is very true that such things, rightly used, are helps to knowledge; but they are not the same as Christian knowledge by a great deal; they are but words, in which a child, yea or a man, may be perfect, and yet not know anything really of Jesus Christ and Him crucified. To learn certain words and sayings, and the history, how certain things happened, is what any may do for himself, if he will take the trouble. The spirit of the world, that is, men's natural skill knowledge and understanding, what they are born with, or what they obtain by experience, will enable them to say the right words; but it will never help them to have the right thoughts. The Apostles, they might have known in other ways, as Pilate and the chief priests knew, the things which happened about the Death and Passion of our Lord; but to know the power and virtue of that Death, to enter into the true spirit and meaning of it, that is what the whole world and all its wisdom could never have taught anyone. That kind of knowledge must be God's special teaching: the Apostles, to have that knowledge, received, not the spirit of the world, but the Spirit which is of God. The Third Person in the Blessed Trinity, Whom Christ our Lord sent down as on this day to dwell in men's hearts, uniting them to Himself, He only could teach us really to know, what we may easily enough teach ourselves to answer and talk about, the things which are freely given us of God, the great matters which He has done for us, for no merit of ours, but entirely of His free gift. We can neither judge of these things rightly, nor rejoice in them holily, without Him.

What a great and wonderful thought is here! That, whenever a person thinks worthily on the secrets of God as made known to us in the Bible by the Church, that person is under the immediate teaching of God's Spirit: he is partaker, in some slight measure, of that which is called inspiration: the Breath of God is breathed into him, more or less, in the same sort of way as it was breathed of old into the Apostles and Prophets. What a fearful thing, then, must it be, for any one to deal carelessly and irreverently with Christian instruction; which, so far as it is anything real and good in any wise, is the very teaching of the Most High and Holy God, the Wisdom from above conversing with us, not face to face, nor word to word, but, as a holy Bishop once said, "thought to thought." Truly we know not what we do, when we turn away from such good and holy meditations. Still less, when, having been favoured with them, we depart to our old ways, our old sins. And even when men fall short of such extreme impiety, it is no small guilt and danger which they bring on themselves, by talking and thinking of the ways of God and Christ without deep and due humility, as in God's presence. So our Lord warned the Jews, when they received disrespectfully His sayings concerning the Bread which came down from Heaven. "[b]Murmur not among yourselves: no man can come

---

[b] S. John vi. 43, 44.

purpose, but with sincere purpose, that our Father's Name should be honoured and His Will done? How frequently have we ventured on what we know to be right, not minding the foolish wonder and unkind sayings, which we might bring on ourselves, so long as we could but obtain approbation from our Father out of sight?

But God freely gave us also to be "inheritors of the kingdom of heaven." When, of ourselves we were but dust and under sentence to return to dust, for our own and our father's sins, He breathed into us by His Spirit the breath of everlasting life; He gave us the hope of reigning for ever with Christ. Look back, my brethren: remember your own ways of thought. How much of your daily time and care is taken up with recollection of this great thing? How near have you come as yet to the good advice of the wise man, "[d]Whatsoever thou takest in hand, remember the end." Remember the great end of all things: remember death and judgement: remember eternity: remember that what you now do will make a difference to you for ever. Have these been your sayings to yourself to-day? or yesterday? or the day before that? Have you ever made it a rule to have such thoughts?

These are some of the good gifts, which Christ gave us when He made us Christians: and He gave them quite freely. We had not done, we could not do anything, to win for ourselves so great blessings. We were but little infants in our nurses' arms, unable to have any thoughts of our own at all: and as full of natural corruption, as much by our own nature

[d] Ecclus. vii. 36.

inclined to evil, as any of the millions born in heathen lands, or before the coming of Christ, whom God never called to Himself in this world, at all. This is our election: and we ought to think more of it than we do. We ought to be more thankful than we are, for not having been born or left among those, who never had the chance of being made members of Christ. They are by very far the greater part of mankind. Even at this present time there are supposed to be in the world, by hundreds of millions, more unbelievers than believers. Who elected and chose us out; us, I say, who are here present, that we should be here in Christ's portion, rather than far away in the portion of the enemy? Surely this also is much to be thought upon, that every one of these great things is freely given to us of God. They are all of grace, not of debt. They came not of our works or deservings; they were a mere and pure gift, as much as our life and being was so.

God's gifts to us in Holy Baptism were freely given; yet when we think of them under the guidance of His Spirit, we shall remember that they are not yet absolutely ours: we may forfeit them, if we choose to do so. We never could have won them for ourselves, but we may lose them for ourselves. This also is a point to be much borne in mind. If you think of the privileges of Christianity as being yours for certain, you have great reason to fear that your thoughts are breathed into you by the spirit of the world, not by the Spirit of God. For the Spirit of God ever whispers, " ᵉ Be not high-minded, but fear. Remember that you are running a race ᶠ ";

ᵉ Rom. xi. 20.   ᶠ 1 Cor. ix. 24—27.

and the prize is not yet won. Keep yourself under, both body and soul: bring yourself into subjection, lest after all you be a cast-away." So speaks the Spirit of God to the souls of Christians, even the most saintly, while they are yet in this world.

Thus He teaches us to " have a right judgement in all things:" but for the other part of the Church's Whitsuntide prayer, that " we may evermore rejoice in His holy comfort," for that He rather bids us look on to the other world. For our comfort He reveals to us, what "[g] eye hath not seen nor ear heard, neither have entered into the heart of man: the things which God hath prepared for them that love Him." He so far reveals heaven to His faithful and obedient ones, that they may have a sure and certain hope of it, and a dim and mysterious delight in meditating on it, and considering what it may be. As those who are to be introduced to some wise and kind person, who has done great things for them, but whom they have never yet seen, naturally spend much time beforehand in conjecturing how he will look, who will attend him, under what circumstances they shall be admitted to so great an honour: so those who have the Spirit of Christ may be expected to turn their thoughts, in humble hope and joy, towards that moment of glory and perfection, when they shall see Him face to face, see Him as He is, and be made like unto Him.

And even in this world, they may take to themselves this great comfort, that they look at things, in some measure, as Jesus Christ does: they have the mind of Christ; a fellow-feeling and sympathy with

[g] 1 Cor. ii. 9.

Him. Although they know themselves to be full of sin and error, and never for a moment imagine that they are quite right in any one thing, yet Almighty God mercifully allows them, on the whole, the witness of a good conscience: they go on, from day to day and from hour to hour, in a reasonable hope, that they are on Christ's side, and not on the side of His enemy: that their sentences and thoughts about things are, on the whole, such as He approves: that He is with them and not against them, guiding them upwards, not suffering them to fall more and more away from Him.

Such is the good and comfortable hope of those who practise indeed in Christ's school, keeping the commandments as well as learning them by rote. They must not be disheartened, if others misunderstand them. "[h] The natural man receiveth not the things of the Spirit of God: neither can he know them, because they are spiritually discerned." And many persons, by sin and unbelief, have brought themselves more or less back into this their natural condition; they, of course, find fault with holiness when they see it, just as a heathen person would have done. We must deal calmly and charitably with them, but we must not be disheartened by what they say or think of us.

Neither again let it daunt us too much, if we feel, as surely almost every one of us must feel, that we are but beginners and babes in Christ; requiring, as the Apostle speaks afterwards, to be fed with milk and not with meat. We may well indeed be humbled and ashamed, that we so long continue in that

[h] 1 Cor. ii. 14.

unto Me, except the Father, which hath sent Me, draw him." "[c]No man can come unto Me, except it be given him of My Father." As if He had said, "you think, the truths of the Gospel, the meaning of the Scriptures, the lessons of the Church, are matters on which you may use your judgement, just as on things of this world, relying on your own skill and sense. Be not deceived: it is not so. Left to your own skill and sense, you will surely go wrong in these things. If you are right in them, it is only because the Father is drawing you to Him by His Spirit." Think earnestly on this, and let it make you very humble, very full of fear and reverential awe, like persons who, being present at some aweful religious ceremony, scarce dare lift up their eyes or draw their breath: like Moses, when he hid his face and was afraid to look upon God: like our Lord's disciples, when at various times they were afraid to ask Him questions, knowing, as S. John says, that He was the Lord. So ought we all to tremble and restrain ourselves, when divine matters are spoken or thought of, those matters, which we know the Holy Ghost has kept for His own especial teaching.

S. Paul in the text speaks especially of "the things which are freely given us of God." "The Spirit which is of God," he says, helps us to know about those things: the spirit of the world, mere human skill or learning, never could have obtained us that knowledge. Consider for a moment what these things are," freely given us of God,"the knowledge of which is so divine and aweful. Some of them are already bestowed on us in this world: for some we must wait

[c] S. John vi. 65.

until it please Him to bring us to a better world. Now already, even in this world, we are, by the special working of the good Spirit, born again; already in this world we are made "members of Christ, children of God, inheritors of the kingdom of heaven." We have learned to say this long ago: we have said it over and over, as often as we have said our catechism: but are we used, really and in earnest, to meditate upon it? How often do we try to withdraw our thoughts from the company and concerns of this present world, and to fix them on this great truth, that we are members of Christ; really and truly united to Him Who was made Man and died for us on the Cross? How often have we said to ourselves, when temptation came near, and we were in danger of evil thoughts, "Do we not know that our bodies are members of Christ? Shall I then bear the thought of taking the members of Christ and making them the members of an harlot?" Do we, or do we not, force ourselves to respect and love all Christians that come in our way, considering that they, as well as we, are members of Him Who died on the Cross; of His Body, of His flesh and of His bones?

Again, God has freely given us to be His own children. We may say to Him, "Abba, Father." We may kneel before Him as often as we please, saying, "Our Father, which art in heaven." What have we done, what are we doing, in the way of earnest meditation on this great gift? How many troubles have we borne patiently, from a deep conviction and feeling, "It is our Father; He knows best; He doth not afflict willingly?" How many good works have we set about, not for any present or worldly imperfect state, when, for the time, perhaps, we ought to be teachers. Well may it humble and shame, but it must not discourage us. If we are sorry to be but children in understanding, let us strive at least to be children, i. e. inexperienced, in malice and mischief; and He will help us, by degrees, to a more manly way of understanding things also. Put off carnal thoughts, thoughts of pleasing yourself. Be ready to take the lowest place, without inwardly praising yourself for doing so. Pray, strive, watch, against envying and strife and divisions. Be content to learn in Christ's school, which is the Church, instead of making out ways of your own. Try to fix your thoughts very often on the Presence and teaching of the good Spirit: learn more and more to fear and reverence Him, as actually abiding in your heart, and to think tremblingly of holy things, as pertaining especially to Him. These are safe and sure ways to have the Holy Ghost for our teacher through life, and our Comforter in the last great Day.

SERMON XXIII.

FLESH AND SPIRIT.

WHITSUNDAY.

S. JOHN iii. 6.

" That which is born of the flesh is flesh, and that which is born of the Spirit is spirit."

THE great work of God the Holy Ghost, which He came down to do as on this day, is our new birth and our new life. We were naturally lost and dead in sin: but He descended, in order to join us to Jesus Christ our Lord, and so to make us partakers of a new, a heavenly and Eternal Being. Our minds are naturally therefore turned at this time to the sayings of our Divine Master concerning our new birth and our new life, and concerning that good Spirit, Who is the Almighty worker of so great a change in men. And as, after the accomplishment of any great undertaking, people look back with a special kind of interest to its first rude and tender beginnings, to the time when it was first thought and talked of; so Christians in all times, since first the kingdom of heaven was set up on the day of Pentecost, have ever thought very much of the obscurer and more private hints and sayings of our Lord, when He first began to give notice of that kingdom. Their minds have turned back in earnest consideration to that solemn discourse which our Lord held by night with Nicodemus, when they two alone discoursed of the way, in which He was to save us. Nicodemus did not then understand Him; but he treasured up all His words, and bye and bye he came to understand Him. At the time, it was too strange and hard a saying for him, that a man must be born again of water and the Spirit, or ever he can enter into the kingdom of God. But when our Lord had died, and was risen again, and had gone up into heaven, and when, as on this good Day, He sent down His Holy Spirit to make men partakers of a new life through and in Him, Jesus Christ: and when Nicodemus saw that this unspeakable gift was bestowed upon believers not without water; for so the Apostles told them in Christ's Name, "[a] Repent and be baptized every one of you: and ye shall receive the Gift of the Holy Ghost:" then he understood what at first had been too hard for him; then he remembered the remarkable words which our Lord had spoken to him by night, and no doubt gave special thanks to Him Who was so gloriously accomplishing those words in sight of the whole world. And when he saw, what a new life that converted and regenerate people presently began to lead, how they walked with God all day long, how they "[b] continued stedfastly in the Apostles' doctrine and fellowship and in breaking of bread and in prayer:" how they were all of one accord and of one mind, and what fervent charity they practised among themselves, as if what they had was only lent them for the help of their brethren who needed it:

[a] Acts ii. 38.   [b] Ib. 42.

I say, when Nicodemus beheld all this in lives of the first believers, he might well remember and understand the next saying of our Saviour, "That which is born of the flesh is flesh, and that which is born of the Spirit is spirit." He might say to himself, "Now I see and know what those words meant; and how truly they prophesied of the difference between the natural and spiritual man."

For as children are partakers of the same nature as their parents, and are commonly more or less like them in their bodily shape and features, so Christian persons, children of God, are partakers through Christ of a heavenly and divine nature, and ought to shew their high parentage by their actual resemblance to Him Who so begat them. "That which is born of the flesh is flesh;" i. e. Adam's posterity, all of them, children as they are of a frail and sinful parent, inherit from him frailty and sin. You may know them by their likeness to their fallen and corrupt father. And no less surely on the other hand, "that which is born of the Spirit is spirit." Those who by the power of the Holy Ghost have been made parts of the family and household of our only Lord and Saviour, children as they now are of Him that is perfect, inherit from Him holiness and righteousness: wisdom to know what is good, a good will to choose it, and strength to bring that good will in very deed to good effect. All this they have from their heavenly Father, Who has adopted them to be His sons, because of their union with Him, Who is His true and only Son, Jesus Christ. As the natural man, man left to himself, has all bad tokens from fallen Adam; so the spiritual man, man regenerate and born again in Jesus Christ, has or may have all good tokens from Him, our risen and ascended Lord and Saviour. Let us endeavour to set the two side by side, and see how the one differs from the other, in respect of all the chiefest things, on which our good and evil depend, both in time and in eternity.

And first, as concerning faith: He that is born of the flesh only is mere flesh in this respect, that he minds, quite or almost entirely, the things of the flesh, bodily and earthly things, the things of this present world. He is all taken up with meat and drink, company and diversion, work and play, gain and pleasure and praise. If he is well off, he says to his soul, "[c] Soul, thou hast much goods laid up for many years; take thine ease, eat, drink and be merry:" "[d] to-morrow shall be as this day, and much more abundant." If he is poor, he says, "I have my bread to get: *that* is care enough for me: why should I trouble myself about things in another world, so far off, and out of sight? why may I not divert and indulge myself in what little leisure I have?" Thus, every way, the children of this world, they which are born of the flesh, live by sight only and not by faith: as Adam and Eve, when they ate of the deadly fruit, thought only of what they saw, and would not at all turn their minds to what God had told them.

But that which is born of the Spirit is spirit, and tends upward to the place from whence it came. That is to say, those souls, which by God's special grace are made partakers of the new and divine birth in Holy Baptism, have that in them (if they

[c] S. Luke xii. 19.   [d] Is. lvi. 12.

quench it not by their sins) which will hinder them from being quite satisfied with any thing that they find here on earth. Our Saviour Himself said, "[a] I am come to send fire on the earth:" the sacred fire of His good Spirit, which should spread over all nations, kindling one heart after another, and causing all to mount upward, as flames might from an altar, with earnest desire to be where He is, Who is their Fountain, from Whom they have all their light and heat. This holy fire laid hold of us; it kindled upon us, as it were, at our Baptism. Is it now alive within us or no? The question is a very serious one, a mournful one, alas! for too many of us; yet let us not shrink, let us not be afraid to ask it of our own consciences, now on the great Day, in which we celebrate the first lighting-up of that fire on earth. Are our thoughts, and desires, and wishes, turned towards heavenly things, regularly, as a matter of course? Do we think within ourselves very often, when we set about anything, "Will it hurt or help me in the next world?" Do we try, when we can, to consider seriously, that the Eye of the invisible God is looking down upon us? Do we look backward to the Cross of Christ, and forward to the Day of Judgement? If not, it is a sad confession, but surely we dare not deny it,—though we were once born of the Spirit, we are so far in the flesh again: we are driving away the heavenly Guest, after He has come to dwell within us: we are quenching the fire which God Himself has kindled in our hearts.

Try yourselves again, my brethren, by your prayers. The natural man, he who is either yet unre-

[a] S. Luke xii. 49.

generate, or who by his sins has cast himself back into a heathenish and unregenerate mind; such an one has no love for his prayers; no constant love, I mean; no such mind towards them, as that he will say them regularly and try to think of them, though it be ever so much trouble and inconvenience to him. He readily puts up with excuses for being careless about prayer, saying to himself, "God knows my meaning and my wants, without my trying to express them to Him; He knows my sins, without my particularly confessing them; He knows, whom I mean to pray for, without my pausing to remember them. He can hear me, as well sitting as on my knees; any where else as in Church; half asleep or broad awake." And so persons go on, till they have excused themselves in all sorts of hurry and irreverence: the fact being, that all the while they have no real love for their prayers, no real faith in God as in Him Who heareth prayer. But he that is born of the Spirit, and is not in the way to quench that Spirit, to him prayer is a great and real work. He knows and considers that no one thing which can happen to him in the whole day is of so much consequence to him as his prayers, well or ill performed: that no company that he goes into can be worthy of such careful preparation as the Presence of the great King of heaven and earth, with Whom, would he but lay it to heart, he is alone as often as he prays. This is the mind concerning prayer, which the good Spirit puts into the hearts of those Christians who are willing to obey His godly motions: and *their* prayers do them good indeed: for they are not so much their own, as the prayers of the Holy Ghost within them. I do not say that they always pray *comfortably*, that they *feel* as if God were answering them in mercy: on the other hand, I suppose that they are for the most part troubled and ashamed to think, how very ill they pray: how their thoughts wander, how soon they grow weary, how hard they find it to set God always before them. But after all, praying as they try to do in earnest, and with a full purpose of heart to live accordingly, their devotions are devotions indeed, and they are counted before God as "f continuing instant in prayer."

Another difference between the partakers of the spiritual and only of the carnal birth, is this: that the one use the creatures of God only for their own present maintenance or enjoyment, the other lift up their minds from them continually to the great things out of sight. It is this which our Saviour noticed when He said, "g Labour not for the meat which perisheth, but for that meat which endureth unto everlasting life, which the Son of Man shall give unto you." Thus He taught us in His Sermon on the Mount, to consider the flowers of the field. All persons, even the most carnal and earthly, consider the flowers, so far as to admire their beauty when they see them. "But you Christians," says Jesus Christ, "ought to learn something heavenly from them: how to trust in God and His fatherly Providence." So in regard of such a common matter as the weather, and the changes in it: the world's family consider it only as it affects them, their health and wealth: but God's family learn always to see His

---

f Rom. xii. 12.   g S. John vi. 27.

Hand in it, and to think of Him ordering it all for His own wise purposes, secret to us.

But of all created things, those which most bring out the difference between the carnal and spiritual mind are perhaps the holy Sacraments. The water of Holy Baptism, the Bread and Wine of Holy Communion, are nothing to an irreligious man: but to a true believer they are in a sense every thing: and so, in proportion, it is with respect to all other things which God vouchsafes to use in His solemn service. Unbelief scorns them, as Naaman did the waters of Jordan; but faith uses them as so many steps prepared by our Almighty Friend to bring us nearer and nearer to heaven.

We are employed, as you know, all the week long, each in his own line of life; some in building, some in trade, some in service, the most part in tilling the ground; some in other ways which we cannot now reckon up. Now a person may look at these several works merely *as* works, merely as ways of procuring employment, of spending time, of getting their bread or of maintaining the state of the world. Or each one may look upon his own worldly employment as being, what we know it is, God's special way of dealing with him especially: God's especial trial of each one, whether or no he will remember Christ, pray to Him at all times, and for Christ's sake do always to others, as he would have others do to him. To a person who really tries to look on things in this way, whatever happens in his own work and trade is one token more of God's aweful and gracious Presence; one call more to remember the great unspeakable things which have been done for us; one remembrancer more of eternity.

How differently again do men behave in regard of the pain and sickness, from which so many of us are at all times suffering! How differently do we ourselves feel tempted to behave at different times! That within us, which is born of the flesh, and is flesh, is led away sometimes into murmuring and complaining, sometimes into anxious inordinate care about the future; sometimes it merely strives, as well as it can, after some ease and refreshment; but that which is born of the Spirit, and is spirit, makes it all an occasion of high Christian virtues. The more the body suffers, the more steadily will he that is spiritual submit himself to God, deny himself, provide as he may for the comfort of his afflicted brethren: and so he will turn the present bitterness into a blessing which will last for ever.

Thus anyone who will just look around him, may perceive something of the opposite fruits of the spirit of the world and of the Spirit which is of God. But to know their difference perfectly, we must wait and see their end. We must wait until Christ returns to Judgement, and then we shall not only see but feel the deep the infinite importance of our doings here. God grant us so to live, so to believe, to pray and to use all His good creatures, that the good Spirit Who descended even now to prepare us for that day, may be our Comforter when it comes!

SERMON XXIV.

CONFESSION AND SELF-DENIAL, TOKENS OF THE WORK OF THE HOLY GHOST.

WHITSUNDAY.

Acts xix. 20.

" So mightily grew the Word of God, and prevailed."

THE Word of God is the doctrine of the Gospel, the religion of Jesus Christ, which His Apostles began to preach as on this Day with the Holy Spirit sent down from heaven. They had preached it before. So far they were commissioned, as a message from Jesus Christ. But now the whole of it was made known to them; and the blessed Comforter, God the Holy Ghost, came down according to Christ's promise, to teach them, and guide them into all truth. Then they began to speak with all authority, and to declare to men in Christ's Name the whole Counsel of God, all His wonderful works wrought for the salvation of mankind: not only as before, that men should repent, and that the kingdom of heaven was at hand; but the whole of what is contained in the Apostles' Creed: the whole of what Christians must believe, in order to be Christians. This the Apostles taught, and they taught it in Christ's Name, i. e. as persons who had Christ dwelling within them by His Holy

Spirit, and opening their mouths to say and to teach these things. The epistle to-day has told us of the beginning of that teaching, on the great Day of Pentecost. The second morning-lesson has told us how it went on, no long time afterwards, to be made known among the Gentiles: how, after a sermon by S. Peter, the Holy Ghost fell upon the good centurion Cornelius, and upon all who, with him, heard and believed the word. And bye and bye we shall hear in the second evening-lesson, how after many years this good work was going on and prospering in the rich and learned city of Ephesus. S. Paul was there, preaching and teaching for two whole years: and God wrought special miracles by his hands: "so that from his body were brought unto the sick handkerchiefs and aprons, and the diseases departed from them, and the evil spirits went out of them."

Now in this city of Ephesus there were many of those whom the Scripture calls wizards and soothsayers, whose way was, to have dealings with evil spirits, or to pretend that they had so: and some of them, seeing S. Paul's miracles, made believe to do the same, using our Blessed Lord's Name: "We adjure you by Jesus, Whom Paul preacheth." But though they took in their mouths the Name of Christ, they were in reality about the devil's work: they were trying to do that, which our Saviour Himself had long ago declared to be impossible: i. e. to cast out devils by Beelzebub: and it happened as might be expected: "the man in whom the evil spirit was, cried out" as that spirit taught him, "Jesus I know, and Paul I know, but who are ye? and he leaped on them, and overcame them, and prevailed against them, so that they fled out of that house naked and wounded." Thus the people of that place were plainly taught that there was an inward Power in the Church and Body of Christ, far above all those evil powers which they depended on and made idols of: and all feared, and many believed. They felt, as S. John writes [a], "These Christians are of God, and have overcome the world: for greater is He that is in them, than he that is in the world."

In that time then, and in that place, the kingdom of God was clearly coming on, and the great work, which had begun at Pentecost, was advancing towards perfection. And our Church has appointed this history to be read as the last lesson for Whitsunday, in order perhaps, that we might have before us a sort of token or sample of what has been and is even now going on, and will go on unto the world's end more or less openly, in the spreading and prevailing of the Church and Gospel of Jesus Christ.

Now, thoughtful people are apt to be continually asking for signs and tokens of the progress of Christianity, both outwardly in the world, and inwardly in their own hearts. They would like to know, whether or no there are from time to time more and better Christians than there used to be: and also they would like to know whether they themselves and those belonging to them, are really and in earnest going forward or backward. Now if we will attend to this history, we shall find that Almighty God has here given us two sure and clear signs, whereby we may know both for ourselves, and for others committed to our charge, whether or no things

[a] 1 S. John iv. 4.

are going well with us in the great matter of saving our souls: whether or no we are growing in grace and in the knowledge of our Lord Jesus Christ : whether we are carrying on or hindering the work of the Spirit, begun on the first Whitsunday.

These two signs are, first, sincere confession of sin, and next, giving up for Christ's sake what people would be glad to keep. For so it was in Ephesus at that time. "The Name of the Lord Jesus was magnified." And how might men know that it was truly magnified, and not in word only ? " Many of them that had believed came, and confessed, and shewed their deeds." *That* was one sign of real conversion : the sincere confession of their sins. The other is described as follows : " Many of them also which used curious arts, brought their books together, and burned them before all men : and they counted the price of them, and found it fifty thousand pieces of silver." What is the meaning, when it is said, "They used curious arts ?" It means that they are magicians, sorcerers; what we call conjurors. It means that they had, or imagined themselves to have, secret dealings with the evil spirits. They were, then, idolaters of a very bad sort, depending upon the devil for that help, which men ought to seek of God only. Now the secrets of this their hateful and accursed knowledge were written in certain books : rare books and very costly : i. e. foolish persons, who wanted to prosper in the world and thought they might do so by such help as this, were willing to give a great deal for it. For the owners therefore of these books, to part with them and throw them into the fire, was making a real sacrifice, parting with something that cost them a good deal : it was making themselves so much the poorer for Christ's sake : and in this case we read how they counted the price of the books which they burned, and found it fifty thousand pieces of silver ; i. e. more than sixteen hundred pounds of our money : a very large sum indeed at that time. All this money they gave up, and likewise all the credit and profit and consequence which they might enjoy by their skill in such matters : all, at once, they cast into the fire; they gave it up with all joy and eagerness, to take Christ's part against the devil, to please their God and to save their souls.

Thus, you see, those Ephesian Christians gave two remarkable signs of the work of the Spirit going on within them. They had believed, it appears, some time before, and had received God's grace in Baptism; but the wonderful things which they now saw moved them to a deeper fear of God, and a more entire repentance : and they proved it in these two ways : they confessed their sins, and they burned their bad books. And we know that those two things were very pleasing in God's sight, and were accepted by Him as real helps to His kingdom : for the Scripture, after relating them, adds, "So mightily grew the word of God, and prevailed."

Now that great and Holy Spirit Who began His work to-day at Jerusalem, and Who, as you have just now heard, afterwards did so great things at Ephesus : He is the same Spirit now that He was then, and His work is the same; to turn men from Satan to God, and to set up His heavenly kingdom in all our hearts, by making and keeping us members of Jesus Christ. The signs then, whereby Christian people may know whether that gracious Spirit is still abiding in their hearts, are the same now, as they were then. There was not one manner of conversion for the Christians of Ephesus in S. Paul's time, and another for us in these days: but as we believe in the same Father, and worship the same Saviour, and are sanctified by the same Comforter, so the fruits and tokens of His Divine Presence must be the same now as they were then. If it was well for those Ephesian Christians to come and confess and shew their deeds, it is also well for us. If it was necessary for them to burn their bad books, it must be also necessary for us to cast away sinful studies and amusements, whatever it may seem to cost us.

As to confession, it is most properly a work of the Spirit, a work of this holy time of Pentecost. For the Holy Spirit, Who graciously offers Himself at this season to dwell more and more in our hearts, He will not, He cannot abide in the same lodging with an impure spirit, nor dwell in the body which is subject to sin[b]: and therefore, where He is invited to come, the bad spirit must be turned out: and we know that one of the most effectual ways of driving the Evil one out of our hearts, when he has got himself a place there by our unhappy sinful ways, is to confess the sin, truly and humbly: to make, as the saying is, a clean breast of it. We know: at least all who have been used to care at all for their souls know, what a great relief such confession is, how it seems, almost immediately, to take off a part of our burthen, and to make room in the heart for better things. "Now I have told, I feel much easier:" is not this a

[b] Wisd. i. 4, 5.

thought, which even young children can understand? And if it is a relief to them to pour out their shame and grief, when they have done amiss, into their mother's bosom, how much more, when God's sinful children humbly acknowledge their sins to Him! If the one drives away the sullen and impenitent spirit, how much more the other! If the parent's very heart yearns over his son or daughter, drawing near to own transgression and ask pardon: how unspeakably sweet will be the consolations of God, when we have knelt before Him in earnest, and tried to tell Him all our faults! So we are told by one, who had deep experience, first alas! of sin, and then of confession and pardon. Holy David tells us, "[c] I said, I will confess my sins unto the Lord, and so Thou forgavest the wickedness of my sin." "[d] Thou art a place to hide *me* in; Thou shalt preserve me from trouble; Thou shalt compass me about with songs of deliverance."

But let us well understand, what that confession is, to which so great things are promised. Of course it is not merely owning in general, that you are a sinner, as other men are. It is not merely going to Church, and kneeling down with the rest and joining in the General Confession: for this all men may do, light and serious, sincere and hypocritical alike. But true and devout confession, such as Holy Scripture approves of, is first of all, humbly considering in your heart your own particular sins, whatever they are, and however long ago committed; as Joseph's brethren were stricken to the heart, when God's Providence caused them to remember, so many years

---

[c] Ps. xxxii. 6.   [d] Ib. 8.

afterwards, how guilty they were concerning Joseph. True confession, that confession of the heart, which is really the work of God's Spirit, recollects the miserable past, one bad thing after another, all those particulars of our sin, which tend to made us hate and abhor it. True confession cannot be, where people suffer themselves to dwell with satisfaction on the praise, which in the bottom of their hearts they know they cannot really deserve. Again, observe this very particularly : that you cannot make a true confession to God, if, in order to hide your sin, you wilfully use deceit and lying towards man. How common is it, how completely a matter of course, for persons, when they have done amiss, to deny it as nearly as they dare, on being asked about it! How readily do they find excuses, to make themselves out less blameable than they know they are! Many, I fear, go on doing this in little ordinary matters, for a great part of their lives, and hardly ever repent of it in earnest: and yet they think themselves decent people, good enough to obtain God's mercy through Christ without any special repentance. O that they would consider it in time, and pray God to shew them, whether they are in a safe way! For observe, how unlike such doings are to the fruits of the Spirit as described in God's Word! When S. Peter preached at Jerusalem, on the first Whitsunday, those who heard him were pricked to the heart, and instead of making light of their sins, came to the Apostles in great distress, saying, "ᵉ Men and brethren, what shall we do?" And you have heard how S. Paul's miracles caused Christians, hitherto imperfect, to re-

ᵉ Acts ii. 37.

member their old sins: to come and confess them, and shew their deeds: their *own* deeds, one by one. They did not merely own that they were sinners like all others: they openly and willingly took shame for what they had done. At least then let sinners now meekly submit to the shame, if it please God to make their sin known; let them not hide it deceitfully, nor be angry when told of it. Let them freely and thoughtfully confess their sin to those whom it may concern: to God always, all their sins: to the Priest, if they conveniently may, those sins which perplex their souls, and cause them to desire further comfort or counsel: also to any of their brethren whom they have wronged, if so be that, by confession, they may set matters more nearly right; restoring unlawful gains, unsaying false or unkind words, or asking pardon for offences. All these are so many works of true Christian confession, fruits of the Holy and Blessed Spirit, tokens that the Word of God is growing mightily and prevailing in the souls which are so moved, and in the congregations where many such souls are found.

Confess your sins thus heartily and entirely, and He will not only, for His Son's sake, forgive the wickedness of your sin, but will also "'inform you and teach you in the way wherein you should go." He will give you more and more of His Spirit, and help you to avoid, more and more entirely, the evils which you so earnestly repent of.

And as part of your reward, you may hope that He will enable you to deny yourself more and more for His sake. For this is that other true token of the

f Ps. xxxii. 9.

Holy Comforter abiding within you, which, being joined to real and humble confession, will cause you to keep a blessed and joyful Whitsuntide. Do not, I beseech you, think this a hard saying. It is our Lord's own word, "[g] If any man will come after Me, let him deny himself." If the Ephesians would turn in earnest to God, they must give up their curious arts, and throw their learned and enticing books into the fire. If we English Christians would keep the grace given unto us in holy Baptism, we must beware of the many corrupt books and papers, which in our times are constantly thrown in the way of almost all persons who can read, tempting them to all kinds of evil fancies, discontented, covetous, impure, unkind. We must turn away from the pleasantest companions, when we perceive that they are likely to lead us into sin. We must be willingly ignorant of many things, which the world and the flesh would tell us we ought to know. We must watch ourselves, eye, ear, and heart, that we do not wander after forbidden imaginations. This will be very troublesome, especially after the first strong effort is over, and before the habit of denying ourselves is formed. But will you not endure a little trouble, for the sake of saving your souls, and doing your humble part in the work of God's kingdom? Remember our first mother, Eve: what a great thing it would have been for her and for us, had she taken that little trouble of turning away her eyes, and checking her desire to know, what God in mercy would have kept from her. The Holy Spirit Who came down this day is a kind and loving Spirit: He watches night and

[g] S. Matt. xvi. 24.

day for every little token we may give of a dutiful and devout mind: nothing that we try to do right is suffered by Him to fall to the ground. He watches, to do you good.; do you also watch, to receive good from Him. Every night, confess to Him: every day deny yourself something for His sake. So shall you find bye and bye, that, without your knowing it, the Word of God has been growing mightily and prevailing within you. May the good God bestow on us this favour, through His Son Jesus Christ our Lord!

SERMON XXV.

THE ABIDING PRESENCE OF THE HOLY GHOST, OUR STAY AND OUR COMFORT.

WHITSUNDAY.

HAGGAI ii. 5.

"According to the word that I covenanted with you when ye came out of Egypt, so My Spirit remaineth among you: fear ye not."

WHEN we look around us, and see how very unlike the appearance of things is to what we read of in Holy Scripture, and in the histories of the first and best times of the Church, it is but natural, according to our human infirmity, that our hearts should at times feel as if they would utterly die down within us; we are tempted to say to ourselves, "[a] Hath God forgotten to be gracious?" Hath He quite "[b] cast away His people?" For instance; what a blessed sight was that which was seen at Jerusalem on the evening of the first Whitsunday, eighteen hundred and thirty years ago! [c] when three thousand were converted by one sermon of the blessed S. Peter, and being converted, so continued together, so stedfast in the Apostles' doctrine and communion, and in breaking of Bread and prayer, that all men might plainly see they were of one heart and one soul. There was such

[a] Ps. lxxvii. 9. [b] Rom. xi. 1. [c] Acts ii. 41, 42.

love of one another among them, that it seemed as if each one counted his property just as much his brethren's as his own. There was such love of God, as brought them *daily* to the blessed Feast of His Body and Blood: and a very great many of those who were before unbelieving, seeing how those Christians loved God and one another, were moved to come in and give their names to Christ: and so our Lord's directions in the Sermon on the Mount began to be most gloriously and happily fulfilled. His Church's light so shone before men, that they, seeing what good works were wrought therein, gave glory to the heavenly Father and King of the Church by true repentance, conversion and perseverance.

Such was the fair and bright appearance of the city of God, the holy city, new Jerusalem, the mother of us all, on this the first day of her earthly existence, when, by the coming of the Holy Ghost the Comforter, she did, as it were, come down from God out of heaven. And now we are keeping this our mother's birthday after so many hundred years, and it may be with us in some measure, as it is when persons who knew one another in the prime of life meet again in old age; so great is the change and decay that they hardly seem to one another the same persons. So the Christian Body, Christ's mystical Body, the Church on earth, seems in every part so full of spots, wrinkles, and blemishes, that it is hard for us to discover therein the true tokens of His "dove," His "undefiled," "[d]fair as the moon, and terrible as an army with banners," of whom such glorious things are spoken everywhere in God's book.

[d] Song of Solomon vi. 9, 10.

When thoughts such as these come over us, like a cloud over the heavenly sunshine of this good and great Day, the first thing we should say to ourselves is, "Let things be ever so bad, sure I am that it is not God's doing, but mine own. The decays and corruptions and divisions of the Church are my fault, and the fault of such as I am, our fault, our own fault, our own most grievous fault." Try always to consider such things with a meek and humble spirit. In no wise let them make you fretful and unbelieving. "[c] Let God be true, but every man a liar." He has told us beforehand that iniquity would abound, and the love of the greater part wax cold, but He has also told us, that no one soul will be lost, except by its own fault: for "[d] he that shall endure unto the end, the same shall be saved." Let us pray that the sad falling off, which it is impossible not to see, on comparing things as they are now with the first beginnings of the Church, may make us each one watchful and humble for himself and for those committed to his charge: afraid for himself and for them: compassionate to all, earnestly clinging, by prayer and humble obedience, to the Creed and commandments as he was sworn to them in Baptism: receiving them and all God's will as it really stands in the Word of God, not as the fallen and corrupting world interprets them.

Having so made up our minds, we may go on humbly to take to ourselves the special comfort which Holy Scripture provides for Christians, trying to be faithful in evil times. We are not to doubt, but earnestly to believe, that the backslidings of God's

[c] Rom. iii. 4.   [d] S. Mark xiii. 13.

people can never make void His Truth. As He is the same in Himself, Blessed, and Holy, for all our sin and misery, so is He the same to His Church, the faithful God, keeping His covenant of mercy. His promises in the Old and New Testament are not at all blotted out; Holy Baptism and Holy Communion are still His true tokens; in a word, His Spirit is still among us and within us, as on the evening of that great Day of Pentecost, although we, His new Israel, His own elect people, have so often and so long grieved Him by our many transgressions. It is of great consequence that we should be aware of this; otherwise we shall neither be duly thankful to our long-suffering God, nor careful, as we ought, to make the most of His grace.

We are to believe, I say, that God's Spirit continues with us, however fallen and corrupt the times may be. And in this faith we may be greatly encouraged, by opening our Bibles, and looking at the many promises which God gave to His people by His later prophets; I mean, by those whom He sent to instruct them when they had just returned from their captivity and were about building the second temple: such as Haggai, Zechariah and Malachi. Very great and grievous had been the sins of Israel: fearfully and sadly had the nation provoked God, profaning the holiest things and practising the most abominable ways, and heavily had the wrath of God fallen upon them; the city and temple desolate, the daily sacrifice taken away, and the chief of the people carried away captive. Compare this with the word which the same people Israel had heard from the Almighty at the beginning, " ᵉ I will dwell among

ᵉ Exod. xxix. 45, 46.

the children of Israel, and will be their God. And they shall know that I am the Lord their God that brought them forth out of the land of Egypt, that I may dwell among them; I am the Lord their God." Well might it seem, at the time of the captivity, that this promise had utterly failed: but when they began to repent in earnest, God graciously shewed them that He was their God as much as ever: His promise to dwell among them, had not failed; only the tokens of His Presence were obscured for a time. So He assures them distinctly by one of His prophets, at the time when after much discouragement they were beginning to build again the House of the Lord. They had got on some way with their work, and they had a melancholy feeling upon them, that after all it would not be half so beautiful as the old temple which Solomon had builded, and which had been of late destroyed for their sins. "Whosoever was left among them that saw this house in its first glory, when he looked at it now, it was in his eyes in comparison as nothing." *That* was a sad and discouraging thought: but hear how the Merciful One met it with good words and comfortable words. "'Yet now be strong, O Zerubbabel, saith the Lord; and be strong, O Joshua, son of Josedech the high priest: and be strong all ye people of the land, saith the Lord, and work: for I am with you, saith the the Lord of Hosts: according to the word that I covenanted with you when ye came out of Egypt, so My Spirit remaineth among you: fear ye not." This, you see, was just what they wanted. God had promised His good Spirit, His peculiar Presence, to

f Haggai ii. 4, 5.

be with their fathers in the beginning, and He, as a pillar of fire and cloud of glory had led them on though they rebelled and vexed Him, and had caused them to rest in the land of promise, and had dwelt with them continually; and now when they had begun to fear lest they should have finally driven Him away by their sins, it was everything to them to be told that He still remained among them, as in former times.

Now compare with this, my brethren, our own condition, and God's dealings with us. God's good word to His people at the first was, "I will dwell among them, and will be their God." Our Lord's new word to His own new people was, "g I will not leave you comfortless; I will come to you." "h I am with you always, even unto the end of the world." But this not in His own Person, but by His own and His Father's Spirit. "i I will pray the Father, and He shall give you another Comforter, that He may abide with you for ever: even the Spirit of Truth:" "k He dwelleth with you, and shall be in you:" and so, "l if a man keep My words, My Father will love Him, and We will come unto him, and make Our abode with him." This indwelling of the Father and the Son by the Spirit is the promise of the Father, concerning which the disciples heard so much from their Lord. It is the Gift, the free Gift, "m the Gift of God," the Gift by Grace, of which our Lord spake to the Samaritan woman, comparing it to living water; and S. Paul to the Romans, shewing how more than complete it is as a cure for all our sin and misery. It is That by

g S. John xiv. 18.   h S. Matt. xxviii. 20.   i S. John xiv. 16.
k Ib. 17.   l Ib. 23.   m Ib. iv. 10.

which we are members of Christ, children of God, inheritors of the kingdom of heaven. It is Christ in us, "[n]the hope of glory." It is therefore our all in all; our guide in life, and the pledge of our eternal bliss. What a favour, to be chosen out of the world to inherit such a promise! What a shame, what a loss, what an unspeakable misery, being chosen, to forfeit it by our unworthiness!

But now, however it may be with the several sinners who continue impenitent within the enclosure of God's Church; of whom, alas! there are too, too many; certain it is that Christ has promised never to forsake His Church itself, but to continue with those who stand in the place of His Apostles even to the end of the world. And again He saith to the same Church, "[o]As for Me, this is My covenant with them, saith the Lord; My Spirit that is upon thee, and My words which I have put in thy mouth, shall not depart out of thy mouth, nor out of the mouth of thy seed, nor out of the mouth of thy seed's seed, saith the Lord, from henceforth, and for ever." The tokens of this covenant are, the Bishops of the Church, the Holy Bible, the Creeds of the Church, the Holy Sacraments. Where these are, there is the Gift, there is the Holy Spirit of God, the Spirit inwardly and the Church outwardly, and there the blessed word in the book of Revelation is accomplished: "[p]The Spirit and the Bride say, Come:—and let him that is athirst come: and whosoever will, let him take of the water of life freely."

All these heavenly promises are as fresh now as they were at the beginning, would we but so take

[n] Col. i. 27.   [o] Isa. lix. 21.   [p] Rev. xxii. 17.

it. We, Christians who are now living, are the same people, the same family, with those who heard S. Peter preach, and were converted and baptized on the Day of Pentecost. We are Christ's family, for whom so great things have been done. We have been spiritually born as they were, of water and of the Holy Ghost; bred, as they were, in the one true Faith, taught evermore by the Church out of Holy Scripture. We have the same privileges as they had, if only we had the heart to claim them. Those children, when they stand up to say the catechism, say in effect the same words as Timothy said to S. Paul, when he was catechised by him in his young days. All of us in rehearsing our Creed, are but echoing the same sounds, the same form of sound words, which our forefathers in Christ have been rehearsing, ever since the Apostles were on earth. We have the same dangers and temptations as they had; and, thanks be to God for it, we have the same Saviour to plead for us, the same Holy Spirit to help us, the same hope of everlasting life to encourage and uphold us, the same rules of holy penitence to revive and recover us when we fall. In all these things we are one and the same with the Apostles and their companions, even as we must come to the same death, judgement, and eternity.

Wherefore, as it was said to the Jews returning from Babylon, "My Spirit abideth in you, according to My covenant, fear not:" so it is said to us. We Christians of these latter days are in one sense encouraged not to fear, while yet in another sense we are bidden to fear exceedingly. We are not to fear, as though Christ's Spirit were withdrawn, as though His heavenly mercies and judgements were not surrounding us on every side, far more wonderfully than they encompassed the Jews in the wilderness. We need not fear as though we were out of the Church, but we have the very greatest need to fear lest we prove unworthy of the Church. Observe, my brethren, how it was with those Israelites of the Captivity, to whom it was said, "My Spirit remaineth among you, fear not." They were not living at random, nor taking things easily: they did not say to themselves, "Why should we fear? we are leading as religious lives as our parents did before us, as strict as any of our neighbours." But they were continually about a great work of penitence, repairing the city and temple of the Lord, which lay in ruins on account of their sins. So must we, my brethren, each in his place and station, if we are to be partakers of the comfort given to them. We, each one in his providential place and station, must be working the work of the Lord, His penitential work; building up His spiritual city and temple within us, too nearly, alas! ruined by our many wilful imperfections and sins. We must be busy, really busy, in amending ourselves, our daily and hourly thoughts, words, and actions; and then we need not be too much cast down with fear, lest our old bad ways, or present frailties, should drive the Holy Ghost from us. We may say to ourselves, "It is too true: I have sadly broken my vows, and have sinned wilfully against the Lord. If He were extreme to mark what is done amiss, His Spirit would long ago have departed from me. But He is giving me daily all these signs, that

I am still in the Church, that my day of grace is not over. As He bore with Israel of old, as He bore with the murderers of His Son, as in times past He hath borne with me most unworthy, so as yet He is bearing with me: I will not despair, it is not His will that I should perish; He still bids me pray, and encourages me to do my best: and by God's grace I *will* do my best." By meditations such as these, continually accompanying our prayers, at home and in Church, we shall be encouraged in our daily task of penitence : we shall learn to love God more and more, as we obey Him more and more exactly, and the good Spirit Who came down to be the Comforter of His elect while our Saviour is away, will not forsake us, when He, the same Saviour, shall come again to be our Judge. He will hear on our behalf the prayer of His Church at this season: such a measure of His grace, that we, running the way of His commandments, may obtain His gracious promises and be made partakers of His heavenly treasure. So be it, O Lord, through the same Jesus Christ: To Whom be glory &c.

SERMON XXVI.

CHRIST IN ALL.

WHITSUNDAY.

Col. iii. 11.

"Christ is All and in all."

Is not this a short confession of a Christian's faith? Six little words, and easy to be learned by any child, and yet we have much reason to fear that a very large proportion even among thoughtful Christians, do not thoroughly receive more than the half of this confession. That "Christ is All" they allow, but they cannot comprehend how it should be true to say that He is *"in all."* Let us consider how this is.

When the Apostle in this place tells the Colossians that Christ is all, he means, first, all those things of which he had just before been speaking. What were those things? The outward advantages, which made so great a difference between one man and another before they were Christians, whether they were Jews or Greeks, circumcised or uncircumcised, Barbarian, Scythian, bond or free. These things made a great deal of difference in them while they were in their natural unconverted state; but after they had become members of Christ, these things were of no consequence to them whatever. Christ is to every Christian instead of all these outward advantages. They may have been by birth Greeks or Gentiles; but now, through Christ in Whom they are, they are become Israelites, a portion of the Lord's true people. They have never received outward circumcision, but through Christ they are all circumcised in heart. Their native tongue was that of Barbarians, foreigners, or even Scythians, the wildest of all; but now, in the hearing of the Angels they all speak the language of the kingdom of heaven. They have been some bond, some free, but now they have been all made children of the Freewoman, Christ's Church: they have been released, one by one, and admitted into the glorious liberty of His kingdom. Christ hath become all this to each one of them; their calling, their circumcision, their adoption, their freedom: Christ is become to each one of us all this and much more, for ª Jesus Christ, the Wisdom of God, is made unto us wisdom from God, even righteousness, sanctification, and redemption: righteousness to cure our sins; sanctification to make us holy, and prepare us to be happy with Him, redemption to pay all our debts and undo all our chains. Christ is our All. This, I suppose, we are quite ready to believe, as many as bestow one serious thought on their souls. Christ is our All. But how? In what manner, in what special way does He become All to each one of us in particular? For we know that by nature, and from the moment of our birth, He is none of all this to any one of us: rather we are in a way to give ourselves up entirely to another being, who is the very contrary of all these good things. By nature then,

ª 1 Cor. i. 30.

and by birth, Christ is not our All: how and when does He come to be so? This is what we are told in the latter half of S. Paul's short creed in the text: Christ is not only All, but in all. Then He becomes our All, when He enters in and dwells in us: when He unites us to His mystical Body, and makes us members of Himself: and when by virtue of that union we have power to do good works pleasing and acceptable in His sight. And of this happy and saving union God the Holy Ghost is the Author. His descent on the Apostles was the beginning of it to the whole Church, (as the Baptism of each Christian was the beginning to that particular Christian) and therefore the great feast of Whitsunday is appointed to be kept for ever in humble and thankful remembrance of it. Whitsunday is the birthday of the Church, as Christmas day is the Birthday of Christ. If we compare the three great and holy times one with another, Christmas tells us of God in Christ; Easter with Good Friday, of Christ becoming our All, dying, rising, ascending for us; Pentecost or Whitsunday, of Christ *in* us. Or to put it in another form, Christmas sets before us Christ as He is in Himself; Easter, Christ as our redemption; Whitsuntide, Christ as our sanctification.

And perhaps, if we will set our minds to it, we may come from hence to perceive the reason why Whitsunday is less thought of among us, than either of the other two great days. That it is so, no one I imagine will deny. We have only to count our communicants at this season year after year, and compare the number with that at Christmas and at Easter, and we shall find such a difference as to make it quite plain that this is by a good deal less thought of than either of the other holy seasons. But why? Some part of the disrespect is owing, we may well fear, to the greater abundance of ordinary feastings and diversions, which are so apt to take up a great deal of many people's minds and thoughts at this time of the year. Young persons especially permit themselves to be so carried away with the mere diversions, innocent perhaps in themselves, which come in their way at Whitsuntide, that they feel as if their hearts and imaginations were out of tune for the awful things of God. They think so much of Whitsuntide as a time of pleasure, that they almost, or altogether forget that it is a time of devotion. A sad thing, when you come to think of it, and quite enough to put those who feel it very especially on their guard, lest they come in time to be like that unhappy man, who sold his birthright for a mess of pottage, and "^b found no place of repentance."

But, if I do not mistake, there is another cause, besides the more than usual amount of diversion at this time, to make many of us less devout in comparison than we were at Christmas and Easter. Men do not understand so much of the mystery of this time, what God did for them, as they understand about Christmas, and Easter: and they accordingly care less for it. The Evil one, no doubt, takes pains to hide it from them; and his contrivances are often but too successful. Satan does not so much mind men's believing that Jesus Christ is God and Man, that He died and rose again and went up to heaven

^b Heb. xii. 17.

for us: Satan, I say, does not so much mind our believing this, if he can but make us doubt or disbelieve or forget our being members of that Christ: so united to Him by His good Spirit, that it is in our power to obey and please Him, if we will. The great deceiver has no objection to our thinking much of our Lord's Cradle and Cross, His mercy in taking our nature and dying for us, if he can but get us to stop there, and not to go on and lay it to heart what manner of persons we ought to be, who by the Holy Ghost are made members of this Holy Saviour, and able, through Him, to work out our own salvation. Satan will be willing enough to let you believe that Christ is All, yea, and to rejoice in that belief, if only he can effectually stay you from believing that He is in us all, by virtue of His own holy Sacrament of Baptism, and therefore, that all our excuses for not being holy are nothing worth. I will shew you this, or rather, S. Paul will shew it you, in a few plain instances mentioned by him just before the words of the text.

First, Satan is the king of pride and the author of envy, and he would fain have us as envious and as proud as himself. He would have us think very much of the ordinary differences among men here on earth; rich and poor, learned and unlearned, sickly and healthy, high and low in the world. Satan would have us think very much of these, in order that he may, if he can, make the one sort envious, and the other proud. Those who are worse off, he tempts to envy others. Who does not know it too well? The moment we see any one richer, healthier, cleverer, more admired than ourselves, there is generally something in our hearts which rises against them, a secret disposition to put them down and lift ourselves up. And on the other hand, the more favoured person is used to look down on the other, to scorn him, and congratulate himself like the Pharisee in the parable, that he is not such an one as *he* is. In either case the tempter has his own way with us; with the rich, if he can get him to despise the poor; with the poor, if he can get him to envy the rich: and to both temptations we have an answer, if we will but believe and earnestly recollect, that Christ is in us all: in our brethren whom we might scorn or envy, as well as in ourselves; "we are all one in Christ Jesus." This S. Paul teaches in saying, "Ye have put off the old man with his deeds, and have put on the new man, which after God is created in righteousness and true holiness, where there is neither Jew nor Greek, circumcision nor uncircumcision, Barbarian, Scythian, bond nor free, but Christ is all and in all." Why should you mind these earthly and temporal differences? They will presently pass away and be as nothing, nay there is nothing in them already as among Christians. Christians are all alike in this great thing, unutterably great— that Christ is everything to them, and is in every one of them. What can it signify to them, really, if one be born in a higher, another in a lower place, if one be richer and another poorer, or anything else of that kind? In good truth it does not signify at all, only to our weak and frail hearts it is very hard to think so. But we must *try* and bring ourselves to that good mind; the good Spirit will help us to it, if we try in earnest.

And there is another kind of differences among men; by occasion of which in all times the devil has endeavoured to pervert and ruin Christ's people; such differences, I mean, as those between Jew and Gentile, circumcised and uncircumcised, bond or free. It was a great thing for him if he could get people to fancy that the Gospel was only for the Jews, only for the circumcised; for so the Jews would be proud, the others would be careless, saying it was all nothing to them. So in our times it greatly serves his bad purpose, if he can possess any one with an imagination that Christian privileges and Christian duties are only for a few chosen ones, instead of being meant for the whole elect people of God, i. e. for all who are called to be Christians. He whispers to unstable souls, one after another, "If Christ were in you, you might indeed do God's will; but as it is, you cannot do it: Christ is not yet in you, and therefore God does not expect you to be so very particular in your conduct." These are the whisperings of the Evil one: but thou, O well-advised Christian, wilt know how to silence him at once, by simply trying to set thy mind and heart upon the certain fact, that Christ is in all; and if in all, then in thee also.

The Apostle mentions by name yet one more work of the devil, which would pass away from among Christians, if they all really believed and recollected that Christ is in them all. That evil work is *lying*. "Lie not," says S. Paul, "one to another, seeing ye have put off the old man and have put on the new." Or as it is in the Epistle to the Ephesians. "[c] Putting away lying, speak every man truth with his

[c] Eph. iv. 25.

neighbour: for we are members one of another." Of course, being all in Christ, we *are* all members one of another: through Him we are all united; the many corns to make up one loaf, the many drops to make one holy cup of salvation. "ᵈ We being many are one body in Christ, and every one members one of another." Over and over, you see, the saying is repeated: Christ is in us all, therefore we are all in each other: and consequently among other duties, we are earnestly forbidden on any account to lie one to another. Lying, more plainly than almost any other sin, is the work of the devil, one of the very first lessons which he taught our first parents, setting them an example in that he said (contradicting God, Whose words he well knew), "ᵉ Ye shall not surely die." And it is certain, that the more entirely the peoples and families of the world are left to themselves, the more false do they generally prove. Savages, no man can trust. And on the other hand, truth, exact truth, in word and in deed, we know to be a certain sign of the new man. Good and true words; words of praise to God, words of charitable truth to men, were the first-fruits of the Day of Pentecost. As soon as the Holy Comforter, according to Christ's promise, had come down upon them, to unite them to Christ, they began all of them to speak with new and Christian tongues ᶠ. And what did they first speak of? "ᵍ The wonderful works of God." What next? Peter standing up with the eleven, lifted up his voice, and preached to them the true Gospel of Christ's Resurrection. "Speaking the exact truth" was the first, the very first fruit of the Spirit: and

ᵈ Rom. xii. 5. ᵉ Gen. iii. 4. ᶠ Acts ii. 4. ᵍ Ib. 11.

so it has been ever since. For as Christians cannot lie to God, Whom they know to be always in every place, and to read every secret of their hearts, so neither can they lie one to another, for that is still lying to God, since each one of them has Christ i. e. God abiding in him. How should they lie in wait to deceive, since each one, knowing that Christ is in both alike, knoweth also that such craftiness would be trying to make Christ deceive Himself? Each one seeks not his own only but his brother's good, why should one ever wish to deceive another?

And yet, it is indeed a sad thought, a very sad one, how very, very easily, do most people, I fear, allow themselves to lie. For what a mere nothing, what a trifle, what a dream of a shadow, such as to avoid a little scolding, to obtain some small indulgence, to gratify some dislike or partiality, to win a moment's praise and admiration; any of these things, any slighter reason even than these, would be an excuse in the mind of too many for telling any number of lies. It could not be so, if Christians generally had not learned to despise their calling, to think little of their union with God through the Holy Ghost, even though they do really think much, in their fashion, of Christ dying for them on the Cross. They could not be so free in lying, if they understood and believed, what Whitsunday means. O that they would be wise enough to consider this in time! Here is the God of Truth watching you: He has given you a tongue to speak the Truth: He has given you sense to know what will come of not speaking it: "[h]all liars shall have their part in the lake which burneth with

[h] Rev. xxi. 8.

fire and brimstone: which is the second death." He has given you, above all, His Holy and blessed Spirit, to overcome temptation, and force your tongue to speak true, when that unruly member is inclined to go beyond bounds. These are God's unspeakable gifts, to one as much as to another among you, since Christ is in you all. Truth or falsehood, which will you speak? Eternal life or death, which will you have? How weak must your faith be, if, being warned as you are, you still go on in any kind of falseness! What will it come to? And how will you be able to bear it?

Think on the other hand of the bright and glorious hour, when He, Who is the Truth, shall reveal Himself finally, and for ever, to all who have loved the Truth here on earth. It is written, "[i] God giveth not the Spirit by measure." He is no niggard of His gifts; they are poured out fully according as His servants are able and willing to receive them. If His Holy Ghost, descending to-day, was like a mighty rushing wind, coming on all sides at once, filling *all* the house where they were sitting: if the Tongues of Fire, softly gliding from heaven, left out none of the faithful worshippers, but sat upon each of them, lighting them up with such fire as that all generations should be kindled at it: what, think you, will be the outpouring of His glory, how will He give Himself without measure to those whom He shall find in His Church waiting for Him, when His last day is fully come! May it please Him, that you and I may be of that blessed company! But in order to be so, we must constantly speak the truth; for He is the Spirit of Truth, and He came to guide us into all Truth.

[i] S. John iii. 34.

SERMON XXVII.

THE WITNESS OF THE SPIRIT.

WHITSUNDAY.

Rom. viii. 16.

" The Spirit itself beareth witness with our spirit, that we are the children of God."

THE *Comforter!* That you know is the special Name by which it has pleased the Holy Spirit of God to make Himself known to His people, and come among them, as on this great Day. He came also to be our Guide, by leading us into all Truth: our Advocate, by prompting us inwardly in our hearts, how to pray to the Father and plead with Him, in union with the prayers and pleading of our Intercessor Jesus Christ: and most of all He came to be our Sanctifier, by changing our hearts, giving us a new nature, making us holy by uniting us to the Incarnate Saviour. The Holy Spirit came to be all this and more to us, more than we could ask or think. But the Name by which in His good Providence He vouchsafed to be especially known to us was the gracious and condescending Name, Comforter. By that Name our Saviour promised Him: "[a] I will pray the Father, and He shall give you another Comforter,

[a] S. John xiv. 16.

that He may abide with you for ever;" and again, "[b] The Comforter which is the Holy Ghost, Whom the Father will send in My Name;" and again, "[c] If I go not away, the Comforter will not come unto you; but if I depart, I will send Him unto you." By that Name we own Him in our hymns; "Also the Holy Ghost the Comforter;" and,

> "Thou art the very Comforter
> In grief and all distress."

And for His coming as Comforter we are taught to pray especially during the time that we commemorate our Lord's Ascension: "We beseech Thee, leave us not comfortless: but send to us Thine Holy Ghost to comfort us."

Now a Comforter, we know, is one who strengthens and refreshes another; cheers him up and supports him, and soothes and heals the wounds of his heart, in any distress or pain or loss or sorrow with which it may please God to visit him; and no doubt when the Blessed Spirit teaches us to call Him the Comforter, we are to understand that by Him more immediately the Holy Trinity visits all poor and needy creatures with all merciful and loving gifts. The Holy Spirit is the Gift and the Promise and the Consolation, in which all other gifts, promises, and consolations are contained. Nevertheless there is a special meaning, no doubt, in the word Comforter, by which He first made Himself known to the Apostles, and now continues to make Himself known to each of us. There was a special sorrow which at that time hung heavy upon them, and He came to comfort them under it. What was that special

---

[b] S. John xiv. 26.   [c] Ib. xvi. 7.

sorrow? It may be put in one word: they were orphans. He Who was their Father and more than Father, was departing from them, and leaving them, outwardly, alone and helpless in the world. That was the sorrow which filled their heart. They were on the point of being bereaved of Him Whom their soul loved, their Friend and Father and Saviour, Jesus Christ. Therefore our Lord expressly promises them, "[d] I will not leave you comfortless" (the word in the original Greek is the very word *orphans*) " I will not leave you orphans, I will come to you." See how the Blessed Lord, reading their hearts, touched the very string which He knew was moving them so deeply. They feared they should lose Him their Father and so be left orphans. He promises them, in the first place, that He would not leave them orphans; they should not be without a Father: and in the next place, because He had said, " I will pray the Father, and He shall give you another Comforter;" and the word " another " might make them jealous, as if they were going to lose Him, and they might say in their hearts: " If Jesus goeth, it matters not who cometh; we cannot be happy without Jesus," lest they should go on so troubling themselves, He adds, "*I* will come to you; I Who am now departing in Body will come to you again in Spirit: that other Comforter will work so marvellously with you and with Me, that in Him I shall be nearer to you, unspeakably nearer, than I am at present while you see Me; and that, never to depart more, for He will abide with you for ever, and by Him I shall abide also." Thus the second Adam, the Father of all Chris-

[d] S. John xiv. 18.

tian souls, promised the Holy Ghost to comfort His Apostles, His eldest children in the Faith, under the sorrow of losing Him.

But was the comfort for the Apostles only, and for those who had known our Lord's Face in the flesh? No, surely: it was intended for us all: for by nature and birth we are all spiritually orphans, all without God our Father in the dangerous, forlorn, cruel world: all and every one, as surely as we are of Adam's seed, are in the condition of that poor helpless prodigal, who wandered as far as he could from his father's house, and made haste to spend all his substance in riotous living. And as the great thing to that poor wanderer, when he came to himself, was, to be received back again, on any terms, into his father's house, and the offended father, still loving him most dearly, and knowing all that was in his heart, not only received him, but received him as a son; running to meet him, and falling on his neck, and kissing him, and ordering out the fatted calf, the shoes and the ring and the best robe, and so adopting him again into all the privileges which he had forfeited, and not suffering him to doubt, that he was his son as much as ever: such is the work of the Comforter for us sinners, bringing us one by one into our Father's house again, first by Baptism, afterwards, if need be, by a harder but no less sure way, by repentance. He gives us this sure comfort, that whereas we were outcasts from our Father and our home, now we are admitted to a place in the family again, not as servants but as sons; by virtue of our union with Him, Who is the True, natural, Eternal Son. So long as men are out of God's family, they

are, as our Lord saith, of their father the devil; but
when He adopts us for His own in His beloved Son,
then God is our Father, Christ our elder brother,
heaven our inheritance, Angels our ministers, the
Bread of heaven our nourishment. This, our adoption to be children of God, is the great Whitsun
Gift: for this, most especially, the Holy Ghost came
down from heaven as at this time with all those
mighty signs and wonders. He came down, to work
in each one of us that change, which our Lord calls
being born again, and S. Peter, a partaking of the
Divine Nature[e]. The Spirit came down, I say, to
work this change in each one of us; and He signified His coming by the cloven tongues like as of
fire, the rushing mighty wind, and the rest, that
dutiful persons might have the comfort of knowing
His blessed Presence, and their share in it. Thus
He was their Comforter, sealing to them their adoption. The wonders which they saw and heard confirmed the deep inward conviction, which the Spirit
itself, at the same time entering into them, wrought
in their hearts, that they were now really taken into
a new and heavenly state, adopted into God's family,
endowed with a new and heavenly life. We, my
brethren, as Christians, have our portion in the same
blessings, sealed to us by the same Spirit; only, instead of the fiery tongues and the rushing mighty
wind and the other miracles connected with that
first outpouring, we have His Presence sealed to us
by His sure promises to be with His Church and in
His Sacraments to the end of the world. E. g. little children are brought here, Sunday after Sunday,

[e] 2 S. Pet. i. 4.

and are baptized, as He ordered, with water, "in the Name of the Father, and of the Son, and of the Holy Ghost." And the Spirit itself is there; for so our Lord promised, both making and declaring each one of those little ones to be verily a child of God. This the Spirit itself testifieth, before the child can have any will or knowledge. Bye and bye, as time goes on, God Almighty blessing the work of His Church, parents, godfathers, teachers, Pastors, not altogether neglecting their duty, and the children themselves not wilfully breaking away from His loving Hand, that which S. Paul calls "the witness of our spirit" comes to be added to the witness of God's Spirit. As long as we are too young to think on the matter, the Holy Ghost bears His witness *alone*, that we are children of God. He beareth witness *with* our spirit, when we come to have serious thoughts; thoughts of God, thoughts of eternity, thoughts of our Lord and His Cross; and more especially, the Apostle here teaches, doth He, the Holy Comforter, bear His proper witness in our hearts, when we try in earnest to pray. Mark the holy and comfortable words: "Ye have received the Spirit of adoption, whereby we cry, Abba, Father." As if He should say, "Here you are, so many Christians of different ages, men and women, youths and maidens; for one and all Christ died: to one and all He gave His good Spirit in Baptism, and if you had died that moment, you would have surely died children of God. Now, would you not wish for the comfort of a reasonable hope that you are still in His family, that, whatever your backslidings may have been, you have not quite cut yourselves off from Him, but are still His sons and daughters, however erring and imperfect? Well, the Apostle seems to say, here is a sign, a token which God points out to you by me, whether you are yet His children or no. Do you really try to pray in earnest? Do you really wish, and endeavour to speak to God as your Father, because it is your duty, because you know in your heart, that you belong to Him, and cannot be happy without Him? Do you feel vexed, really vexed and grieved and ashamed in heart, that your prayers have been and are so very imperfect and irregular? that you know not, what you should pray for as you ought? And do you in your secret heart call upon your good Lord, and wish that by His help you may pray better? Like the disciple who so earnestly said, "[f] Lord, teach us to pray," and so helped to win for himself and us that great gift of the Lord's Prayer. If these are your thoughts, and you encourage them when they come, and try to make much of them, it is a good and hopeful sign for you: the Spirit of God is so far testifying with your spirit that you are the child of God; the Ear that heareth all things will distinguish even in your faint unsteady tones the call which you have learned of your Saviour, 'Abba, Father,' even as parents know the meaning of the imperfect sounds their infants make long before they can speak plain. Thus even in the humblest beginnings of sincere prayer that gracious and wonderful saying may have an accomplishment, "[g] We know not what we should pray for, as we ought: but the Spirit itself maketh intercession for us with groanings which cannot be uttered. And He that

[f] S. Luke xi. 1.   [g] Rom. viii. 26, 27.

searcheth the hearts knoweth what is the mind of the Spirit, because He maketh intercession for the saints according to the Will of God."

It is of the greatest consequence, brethren, that we fall into no mistake in this matter. Consider: would it not be sad indeed, exceeding dangerous, if a person, because he has occasional good feelings, and so far thinks himself in earnest, should therefore say in his heart, "The Spirit itself bears me witness; I feel in myself that I am a child of God?" And yet perhaps all the while that man may be going on in some great and deadly sin: lying, or cheating, or thieving, or uncleanness, or evil-speaking, or selfish unkindness. O, is it not dismal to think of the words which will too likely be spoken to such a man bye and bye, when he with the foolish virgins shall stand without and knock at the door, and the answer will come from within, "I know you not:" and the self-deceiving heart perhaps would say, "I felt the witness within me, I had great comfort in my religion:" but still there would be but one reply, "[h] I know you not;" "depart from Me, all ye workers of iniquity." As you would escape this worst of miseries, observe, I pray you, my brethren, that it will never do to trust our own feelings simply. The Holy Spirit is not given to make us comfortable but to help us to heaven. If you want to know whether His witness agrees with that of your own heart, the only safe way is to examine yourself strictly; how you pray, and how you live. If you come to God constantly in prayer, in Church and out of Church, as a child to a parent, wishing you could pray better, and

[h] S. Matt. xxv. 12. S. Luke xiii. 27.

really trying to do so: if the eye of your soul look singly and in faith towards that unseen inheritance which is promised, where we read, "If we are children, then heirs: heirs of God, and joint-heirs with Christ: if so be that we suffer with Him, that we may be also glorified together;" if the love of Christ, growing in us more and more, lead us to think more and more of seeing Him in that world (for you see the Christian's hope is not only to be an heir of God, but still more to be joint-heir with Christ;) and lastly if, devoting ourselves to Him, we make up our minds to suffer with Him: all these are happy signs indeed; and where they are, the humble heart may reasonably, and assuredly say within itself, "I trust it is not my fancy alone, but that I really have the comfortable witness of the Spirit: God give me grace never to grieve, never to tempt, never to vex that good Spirit: God keep me from ever so relying on His consolations, as to become less careful of my ways!"

These, my brethren, are some of the great Whitsuntide thoughts: very deep and serious thoughts indeed: thoughts, which we cannot put away from us, without great risk and hazard of losing our souls. Encourage them, I beseech you, by all means in your power. Set your heart to meditate deeply on that which occurred at Jerusalem to-day; not only, nor chiefly, for the greatness of the miracles, but because it was the beginning of His deep mercies in converting men's hearts, joining them to Christ, leading them in His steps, and so preparing them for heaven. Think also much of your own Baptism: that day, whenever it happened, was a sort of Whitsunday to you, the Holy Spirit coming down for the first time upon you individually, to seal to you your portion in Christ. Remember your Baptism, and the vows that are upon your soul ever since; and as the Apostles, after the first Whitsunday, went out and preached everywhere, so do you lose no time in setting about your special duties. Do all to Him, for Him, by Him; as knowing, that you can do nothing at all without Him. "[i] And may the very God of Peace sanctify you wholly, and I pray God your whole spirit and soul and body be preserved blameless unto the coming of our Lord Jesus Christ!"

[i] 1 Thess. v. 23.

SERMON XXVIII.

THE UNIVERSALITY OF THE PENTECOSTAL GIFT.

WHITSUNDAY.

Acts ii. 4.

" And they were all filled with the Holy Ghost."

LET no man imagine that this great miracle, of which we keep the remembrance to-day, is a thing gone and passed away from us, so that we who now live have nothing more to do with it, than to believe it, and thank God for it. It is not so at all, my brethren. We are as much concerned in the work which God wrought on Whitsunday, as in what was done on the other great days which all Christians think so much of. Why do we honour Christmas Day? Not merely because it was the Birthday of our best friend and only Saviour, but because it was the very way to our spiritual new-birth. He was made Man, our Head, that we might become members of Him, and through Him children of God. Why is Good Friday so very solemn and precious? Because it is the day not only of the greatest martyrdom, but also of the only meritorious Sacrifice. He died for our sins: for one as much as for another. We, blessed be His Name, have each one of us as great an interest in His Passion as the very thief who hung at His side, and to whom He promised, "ᵃ To-day shalt thou be with Me in paradise." Why is Easter so joyful a day? Because we are risen with Him: "in Christ we are all made alive." And why is Ascension Day, in one sense, even more triumphant than Easter? Because we are not only risen, but in spirit and mystery we are even ascended and taken up into heaven with Him: as it is written, "ᵇ He hath raised us up with Him, and made us sit with Him in heavenly places in Christ Jesus." Just in like manner, this day of Pentecost was meant to be the great day of comfort to us, quite as much as to the Apostles and the rest, on whom He came down on the first Whitsunday in the Upper-room on God's holy hill of Zion. We have as much need to be filled with the Holy Ghost as they: and the same encouragement from God's glorious and merciful promises; and that at this very time. Let us consider these things a little more particularly, as in the Presence of the Holy Spirit, even now waiting to come down upon us, and fill us every one with Himself, and in humble fear lest by some unworthiness we forfeit that unspeakable Gift.

First then, I say, that we have as much need to be filled with the Holy Ghost as ever the Apostles had: for they, as one of themselves said, were "ᶜ men of like passions with" us, and we are Christians of like privileges and calling with them. The Blessed Virgin Mary, and the holy S. Peter and S. John, and the rest of the hundred and twenty, who were together keeping their Pentecost more than eighteen hundred years ago, were born, as we are, of the fallen race of Adam; they needed a Redeemer as we do, and as they

ᵃ S. Luke xxiii. 43.   ᵇ Eph. ii. 6.   ᶜ Acts xiv. 15.

could not wash away their own sins, so neither could they by their own power graft themselves into Jesus Christ, so as spiritually to rise from the grave, and ascend to heaven with Him. They could no more do this, than they could mount bodily from earth to heaven, and go up through the air, as our Lord did, by the Virtue that abode in Himself. In all these great things, upon which their salvation depended no less than ours, they by nature were as helpless as we are: they needed the Holy Ghost, the Lord and Giver of Life, to enter into them one by one, and make them partakers of Christ, Who is our Life. They wanted Him as we do, to be their Regeneration and Renewal, their Justifier and Sanctifier: their case, in that respect, was all one with our case, and with that of all the elect people of God, of every one, who is chosen out of the world to be a Christian.

But you will say, perhaps, "The Apostles, and the others in that first generation of Christians stood in more need of the Holy Spirit than we do, in respect of their special calling, which was to be the beginners of the Gospel, by the miracles which they wrought, by their preaching in all languages, by the heavenly wisdom which guided them into all truth without possibility of error, and by the boldness and fervent zeal which enabled them to stand before rulers and kings, and to endure all manner of torments, and joyfully to die for Christ. They" (some persons may think) "having this high calling, which is not your calling and mine, needed the Holy Ghost more than we do: and therefore we have no such immediate part in the miracle of Pentecost as they had." I have met, before now, with persons who spoke in this way; but surely, my brethren, it is a great and dangerous mistake. As the Apostles' nature was like yours and mine, and they needed the Holy Ghost as we do, to turn and renew them day by day, making them, from children of Adam, perfect children of God; so your calling and mine is so far like that of the Apostles, that we have first to save each one his own soul, and then to take each one his part in the great work of the Church for the salvation of all souls, to the glory of God. And who is sufficient for these things? Which of us all can either save his own soul, or help to glorify God by saving others, without His special grace? Doubt it not, my brethren: the simplest and most ordinary Christian needs to be filled with the Holy Ghost for the work of his own calling, and for his own part in the Church, quite as much as the Apostles needed it to speak with tongues, to write the Scriptures, to set up and govern the Church. From the Holy Ghost alone such marvellous grace can proceed: and accordingly, we find that good Spirit promised, at His first coming, to all converts, quite as much as to the blessed Apostles. For thus it was said to all the multitudes, men, women, and children, out of every nation under heaven, who stood by at the Day of Pentecost, "[d] The promise is unto you, and to your children and to all that are afar off, even as many as the Lord our God shall call." What promise? The gift of the Holy Ghost which he had spoken of just before "[e] Repent, and be baptized every one of you in the Name of Jesus Christ for the remission of sins, and ye shall receive the gift of the Holy Ghost."

[d] Acts ii. 39.   [e] Ib. 38.

Neither is that heavenly Gift spoken of as belonging to Holy Baptism only, but, every where in the New Testament, you will find the Holy Ghost promised, in sundry ways and divers measures, to all Christians in all times of their warfare and pilgrimage here on earth. For thus saith the Lord, "[f] Whosoever drinketh of the water that I shall give him shall never thirst; but the water that I shall give him shall be in him a well of water springing up unto everlasting life;" and, "[g] If any man thirst, let him come unto Me, and drink. He that believeth on Me, as the Scripture hath said, out of his belly shall flow rivers of living water. But this spake He of the Spirit, which they that believe on Him should receive." It was to be not a sudden flood, coming down and doing its work at once; but a living stream from a perpetual fountain, from a spiritual Rock following them, and always at hand for them to drink of and wash in. It was to be all things to all men: grace given to every man "according to the measure of the gift of Christ." It was never to be at one stay, but always to flow and flow more abundantly; so that to such as are endowed with it might be said at all seasons, "Grow in grace; abound more and more, from Baptism to Confirmation, from Confirmation to Holy Communion, from one Communion to another: so that your whole life shall be as the patriarch's ladder reaching from earth to heaven, and not the Angels only ascending and descending, but the Holy Comforter in Person always present, to help you up the successive stairs, till you come to the Lord Jesus Himself, standing visibly above it."

[f] S. John iv. 14.   [g] Ib. vii. 37-39.

We are then to make no question, that, whatever other differences inward or outward there may be between us and that first generation of Christians who with the Apostles were assembled in the Upper-room on the first Whit-Sunday, in this respect we are on a level with them, that we, coming together in the Church, shall be filled with the Holy Ghost as they were, provided only we come prepared as they did: and that when we have received the Gift, It will make Itself known in us by tokens of the same kind, as those whereby It was discerned in them at the beginning.

Consider then, my brethren, with all seriousness of heart, how you have come prepared here to-day. Consider: for indeed it is no small matter, whether we be at this time, according to Christ's offer, filled with the Holy Ghost, or no. There is too much reason to fear, that such as at this holy season allow the Blessed Comforter to come so near, without any earnest endeavour to grow in grace, will find themselves in a condition too like that of Saul: of whom we read, "[h] The Spirit of the Lord departed from him, and an evil spirit," by the Lord's permission, "troubled him." For you may be quite sure of this, that a man's inward house cannot remain empty; and if Christ be not dwelling there by His Spirit, we know who is on the watch to enter in. A fearful thought, that the very time when the great God of heaven and earth had appointed to come and visit you, should be the time for you to open your doors to the foul, intemperate, unclean, profane spirit! And yet who can help fearing it, when he

[h] 1 Sam. xvi. 14.

considers the way in which too many spend this glorious Whitsun-week: yea, how they look on to it beforehand, for weeks, may be, or even for months: contriving how they may most enjoy themselves, without any scruple or fear lest they should be forgetting God, and serving only the lusts of their own hearts. God preserve you from every thing like this! God grant that we, and all who are near and dear to us, may so spend this accepted time, that we may be all filled with the Holy Ghost, and not with the unclean spirit!

And it will be so, my brethren, if we come prepared, as that congregation of saints came prepared to their Whit-Sunday. They, when they came down from the mountain where they had seen our Lord ascend, did not make haste to forget Him, did not hurry back to the world as persons glad to escape from a painful duty, but did their very best to keep their hearts fixed upon Him. They returned from Mount Olivet to Jerusalem, not in order to be busy in the streets and markets, the assemblies and diversions and ordinary ways of the world, but to abide, as continually as duty to their neighbour permitted, in the Upper-room, that place of most heavenly remembrances: where our Lord had given them His own Body and Blood, and where He had given them the gracious promise of the Comforter. Well for those who, at this time, bearing in mind that they hope soon to be filled with the Holy Ghost, try to make much of the great spiritual mercies with which that bountiful Spirit has already favoured them: who have not yet forgotten their Christmas and Easter, who have not (with too many, alas!) suffered the great Day of our Lord's Ascension to pass away unobserved and unthought of. Well for those who have *continued* with one accord in prayer and supplication: neither in Church nor at home permitting themselves to follow their own fancies and humours in so serious a matter: but forcing themselves to keep their rules of prayer as well as they could, whether, at the time, they felt inclined for prayer or no. Well for those who have charitably and discreetly prayed for and with one another; seeking out, as far as they had a choice, those companions who would most help them to keep near to our Saviour: as the Apostles continued with the holy women, and Mary the mother of Jesus, and His brethren. Well for those who are here to-day, not by chance, nor because they had a fancy to come, nor because decency and custom seemed to require of them that they should come now and then; but because they dare not on any Lord's Day forsake the assembling of themselves together; because they are happy to keep and obey the loving laws of their loving Saviour, Who has twice marked the First Day of the week for His own: once, as all of you know, by His Resurrection from the dead on Easter Day: and again, (what some of you perhaps may not have observed) by sending the Promise of His Father as on this day. Well, I say, for those, who are now here, because they know from the Word of God, that the way to be ready for His Spirit is, to be "all with one accord in one place," all of one faith, and hope, and love, in one Holy Catholic Church.

Blessed are they who have come so prepared: but not without a blessing, be sure, have those come also, who in any degree may be moved to wish themselves sincerely better Christians than they are: who, listening on such a great Day as this to the gracious promise of our Lord and the wonderful history of its fulfilment, and joining as they may in the devout praises and prayers of His Church, may feel, as the by-standers did on the first Whit-Sunday, pricked in their hearts, ashamed and sorry for the past, and ready to cry out to those whom Christ hath sent to help them, "[i] Men and brethren, what shall we do?" Would to God, there were many such: and to such, every one of them, our answer must be the same which S. Peter made at this time, "[k] Repent, and be converted, that your sins may be blotted out:" not now in Baptism, but in true penitence; and ye too shall receive the free gift of the Holy Ghost. And thus, if so be, there need not be one in this or any other congregation of Christian people, who shall depart this day to his house without the great Pentecostal Gift, without being filled with the Holy Ghost.

Alas! that it should almost seem idle to utter such a hope! And yet we are bound to hope it, because we are bound to pray for it. But of this at least we are quite certain: that it is in the power of each one of us, if he will, to receive this Gift for himself, if only he seek it with a true heart.

And now I will just point out to you in conclusion, some of the principal signs and tokens, whereby each one of us may judge himself, whether he have been this day partaker of the benefit or no. And I will mention those only, which the history of the Day sets before us.

[i] Acts ii. 37.   [k] Ib. iii. 19.

The Apostles and their companions were known to have received the Holy Ghost by their speaking with new tongues: and whether or no we Christians have received the same good Spirit on this His own Day, will be known (as one principal sign) by our setting or not setting a stricter watch over our tongue, than we have done hitherto. "[1] By thy words," saith our Lord, "thou shalt be justified, and by thy words thou shalt be condemned;" and by our words will men and Angels, and the Almighty God Himself, judge us, every one of us, whether we have this day been partakers of the Holy Ghost. Let this, then, brethren, be one of our main cares, when we leave this place of holy silence, and are at liberty to speak, and converse with one another again. Let no lie, no corrupt communication, no unclean, no bitter, no angry word, proceed any more out of any of our mouths; "but that which is good to the use of edifying:" kind, sober, serious, cheerful, contented words: words of exact and careful truth: words that will leave no sting, no stain behind them, even in our neighbour's conscience or in our own. That will be an excellent token that we have received the Holy Ghost, when we cease to grieve Him by our words.

Another fruit of the Spirit in the Apostles was their Christian courage: their boldness and fervent zeal, to declare Christ's Name before kings and governors, not counting their life dear unto themselves, so that they might finish their course with joy, and perform, like good soldiers, the work ordained for them of God. We too, each in his place, have need of Christian courage. We are in danger, not

[1] S. Matt. xii. 37.

so much from sword or spear threatening our lives, as from the mockery and evil report and worldly disadvantages, which constant profession of Christ's truth, and keeping His commandments, is, in a manner, sure to bring after it. Have we fortitude to stand this? If we were weak and wavering before, are we now, by God's blessing, stronger and more steady? Is there in any degree the same sort of difference in us, as there was in the holy S. Peter before and after Pentecost? Can we stand being laughed at, when we know we are doing God's will? This is another good sure sign.

Have you, moreover, a brave and steady purpose, come what may, to enter upon immediately, and to continue stedfastly, the wholesome and religious rules of the Church, such as the Apostles and their converts from the beginning observed? Especially, that necessary rule of receiving Christ's Body and Blood in Holy Communion, at least so many times in a year. If you have not so resolved, you are still, so far, resisting and grieving the Holy Ghost.

One more mark I will set down. That first Church in Jerusalem had none among them that lacked: "[m]for as many as were possessors of lands or houses sold them, and brought the prices of the things that were sold, and laid them down at the Apostles' feet: and distribution was made unto every man according as he had need." By this we may perceive that an open hand is an excellent sign of the Holy Ghost dwelling in a Christian. Freely to give, to be a cheerful giver, is what *they* cannot help, who have freely received of that Unspeakable Gift. The

[m] Acts iv. 34, 35.

vessels that are so blessedly filled must needs overflow for the benefit of the souls and bodies of all around them. Which of you, if he pleases, will not be able to try himself by this token?

In one word, my brethren, love, Christian love, heavenly charity towards God and our neighbour, *that* is what God the Father purposes, for His Son's sake, to "[n] shed abroad in our hearts by the Holy Ghost which is given unto us." The Holy Ghost is sometimes called the Eternal Love of the Father and the Son: His Day is very especially the Day of Love: if we are filled with Him, we are filled with love: love, ever occupied in doing good, and in keeping the commandments of the Beloved. Pray we, strive we, above all for this; it is all fruits of the Spirit in one: it is very heaven begun on earth: it was the last best gift of our departing Saviour. For thus He made an end of His final prayer to His Father: "[o] These have known that Thou hast sent Me. And I have declared unto them Thy Name, and will declare it, that the Love wherewith Thou hast loved Me, (i.e. the Holy Ghost) may be in them, and I in them." My brethren, He was praying for *us*. Should not our great care be, so to love, so to obey Him, that we may not cast away the fruit of so loving, so awful a prayer!

[n] Rom. v. 5.   [o] S. John xvii. 25, 26.

SERMON XXIX.

ONE SPIRIT, MANY GIFTS.

WHIT-MONDAY.

1 Cor. xii. 11.

"*But all these worketh that one and the self-same Spirit, dividing to every man severally as He will.*"

On the first Whit-Sunday, that is, above one thousand eight hundred years ago, that great wonder of God's mercy began to take place, of which the Apostle in these words, as every where else in his writings, declares the continuance. The twelve Apostles, with the holy and blessed Virgin Mother, and with the other devout women from Galilee, in short, all the followers of our Lord, being "with one accord in one place," in the Upper-room, no doubt, where they had ever since His Ascension continued to meet in prayer and supplication, "suddenly there came a sound from heaven, as of a rushing mighty wind, and it filled all the house where they were sitting." It seemed to be on all sides of them at once: "and there appeared unto them cloven tongues, like as of fire, and it sat upon each of them, and they were all filled with the Holy Ghost."

One and the same Spirit filled them all, and all

began to speak with other languages; not all alike, but as the Spirit gave them power to speak. Thus was fulfilled for the first time, to the very eye and ear, that, of which the Apostle in the text speaks, as a law of God's kingdom to be continued for ever. There were "diversities of gifts, but the same Spirit." It was one fire, but separated into many tongues: one sound, as of a rushing mighty wind, but different in tone, when they spake, according to each man's voice. One man spake one language, another another, but it was the same Holy Ghost that put words in the mouths of all. And all spake the same thing, "the wonderful works of God;" His marvellous mercies by Jesus Christ, His Son, made Man, crucified, risen, and glorified, for the salvation of the world.

. As it was thus in the beginning of the Church, so it continued to be afterwards. The Holy Comforter came down, as Christ had promised, upon one Christian after another, uniting every one to Jesus Christ, and giving every one such gifts as He knew to be best for him: as it is said in a verse a little before the text, "The manifestation of the Spirit is given to every man to profit withal."

But now these best gifts of God, as well as all His other gifts, are in danger of being profaned by men. And it seems that the Corinthians did profane them. They employed the power of speaking new languages, as well as other spiritual gifts, to their own glory, and not to God's glory alone. Those who had the higher and more abundant gifts, were tempted to think lightly of those who had less; and these again to be discontented and slothful, and think they had no occasion to try their best for God's sake. Just as rich men are in danger of permitting themselves to look down upon the poor, and poor men to envy the rich. To correct this, S. Paul would have all Christians remember these two things: first, that all Christians are one in Christ; secondly, that each one has his own work, his own place, his own character. Much in the same way "as the body" of a man "is one, and hath many members:" it "is not one member, but many;" "and all those members, being many, are but one body: so also," he saith, ": is Christ." His mystical Body, the Church, is like His natural Body, or any of our bodies, in respect that, although it is made up of many members, each having its own office, yet it is truly, strictly, mysteriously One.

What makes it one, and binds it together, is the Holy Spirit of God dwelling in each person's soul and body, to unite him truly to Jesus Christ: just as what unites the hands, feet, and other limbs, into one living and moving body, is the life which was breathed into them by Almighty God. "By one Spirit," the Apostle tells us, "we are all baptized into one Body, whether we be Jew or Gentile, whether we be bond or free; and have been all made to drink into one Spirit."

Thus are Christians put in mind of the one Church, to which all alike belong; and they are also put in mind of the diversity of gifts, whereby each member is made different from another. As in the epistle to the Ephesians, "[a] There is one Body and one Spirit, even as ye are called in one hope of your calling;" "[b] but to every one of us is given grace according to

[a] Eph. iv. 4. [b] Ib. 7.

the measure of the Gift of Christ." The eye, the ear, the hand, the foot, have their several offices in the body; so have different Christians in the Church. Each is to be pleased and content with his own, yet without looking down upon any other. Each is to do his own work, without either despising or coveting the other's work. This is what S. Paul goes on to teach at large.

First, to the weaker and less honourable members he says, "You are not to be cast down nor discontented, as if no one cared for you, because others have higher places than you. 'If the foot shall say, Because I am not the hand, I am not of the body, is it therefore not of the body? And if the ear shall say, Because I am not the eye, I am not of the body, is it therefore not of the body?'" The meaning of which is, Suppose you are a poor person, of little understanding or instruction, and altogether in a low place among Christians; you will be apt sometimes to say to yourself, " What signifies what the like of me says or does? Who minds me? If I were a scholar, and had abundance of leisure to acquaint myself with it all; if I were a rich person, and had many others depending upon me; then it would be of more consequence how I went on: but what difference can it make now?" In this way, or something like it, I imagine, people are not seldom tempted to make themselves easy, neglecting divine worship, the Church and the Scriptures, the thought of God and another world, because they are poor and needy, and much taken up with some hard work. This is just what S. Paul describes. For the poor or the ignorant person to give himself up, as though it were useless for him to try to serve God, is as if the foot should say, "Because I am not the hand, I am not of the body;" or as if the ear should say, "Because I am not the eye, I am not of the body."

"Nay," it might be said, "you surely have in you the same life, the same blood, that any other limbs of the body have. The pulse which beats in you comes from the heart, the power and will which guides you, from the head; you are as much a member of the man, as any of the limbs which are most precious. If you hear instead of speaking, if you move instead of ruling, if you act instead of ordering, you are not therefore the less parts of the body."

So, should any weaker Christian, giving way to discontent, become careless about his duty, because he has but a low place in the Church, and imagines himself to be thought little of, the Scripture seems to say to such an one, "Know yourself better; think more worthily of God's great mercies towards you. Remember the very first lesson you learned in your catechism, that you were made in your christening a member of Christ, a partaker, by His Spirit, of the heavenly life; do not for a moment believe that He can despise or neglect any of His members." We feel it all over, if any the smallest portion of our bodies is, but for a little while, in sharp pain: and can it be that He Who came down from heaven to find and save us when we were lost, He Who has joined us to His very heart; has become bone of our bone, and flesh of our flesh; can it be that He should not feel what happens to any one of His members? "Can a woman forget her sucking child, that she should not have compassion on the son of her womb? yea, they may forget, yet cannot I forget thee." These are the promises with which Christians should console themselves, when they feel low and desolate; when in their affliction it almost seems to them as if both God and man had forsaken them.

And much more should we quiet with the same gracious words all discontented and envious thoughts. Are you not a member of Christ, a child of God, an inheritor of the kingdom of heaven? and what is it, in comparison of so great mercies, if another man is more learned, more respected, richer, or healthier than you are? God hath set us with other members in the body, every one as it pleased Him. Enough for our happiness, and infinitely more than we deserve, that we are, any of us, there at all.

The weak then are not to envy the strong, and the strong on the other hand are not to despise the weak. "The eye is not to say to the hand, I have no need of thee; neither again the head to the feet, I have no need of you." Those who are above others, either in learning or in dignity, are of course in some danger of becoming proud and contemptuous. Therefore the Gospel so distinctly says to us all, " blessed are they that mourn: blessed are the poor: blessed are ye when men shall revile you, and persecute you, and cast out your name as evil." Christ says that the Gospel was especially preached to the poor; and that not the wisest and most honoured, but the humblest, shall be great in the kingdom of heaven. And again, since all Christians make one body, which is Christ, and the members of the same body feel of course one for another, it never will do for any Christian to deal scornfully with any other Christian. We know that in the natural body, "if one member suffer, all the members suffer with it; and if one member be honoured, all the members rejoice with it." Violent pain in any one limb hinders the whole body from being at ease: if the foot or the hand be throbbing with anguish, the eye cannot take rest; and, on the other hand, if the aching eye, or any other member, be relieved, it will give soothing and relief to the whole body in every part. Thus does Almighty God instruct us by our own constant feelings, how near every Christian is to every other Christian: how we should sympathize all in one another's welfare, should rejoice and sorrow with our neighbour, how far soever he may seem beneath us in any respect. Be he who he may, Christ died for him, and as a Christian he is partaker of Christ's Spirit. We cannot say, we have no need of him: we need his prayers as much as he ours. Our Lord and Saviour had need of him, for He came down from heaven to save him, and gave him His Spirit to make him a child of God; and if we think we can do without our brother, if we permit ourselves to scorn him, how have we the mind of Christ?

Let this then, Christian brethren, be the lesson settled in our hearts at this great and holy time; to believe that we are Christian brethren indeed, and to cherish in our hearts true brotherly feeling one towards another. The coming of God the Holy Ghost from heaven, to dwell in our hearts and bodies, and unite us to Jesus Christ, is so great, so vast an event, that it may well overwhelm and confound our minds, if we try to think of it all at once, and to feel all we might and ought from it: it is well that we should select some one point of what it teaches, and meditate on it with all our hearts: and let this our subject to-day be, the One Holy Spirit, with His differing gifts, abiding alike in every member of Christ.

Consider, what a fearful notion this gives us of our condition. To know that we are in God's sight, that He looks on our heart, is exceedingly aweful: to know that He looks on us as persons whom He has called to be His own, whom He bought with His own Blood, and for whom, therefore, He cares with especial care, this makes our case still more serious: but to be aware that the Most High and Holy Spirit, by the covenant of our Baptism, is really abiding within us: that we are, as S. Paul said, "the temple of God, and that the Spirit of God dwelleth in us:" this, indeed, is awful beyond all awefulness. How can we be idle, thoughtless, negligent of our souls; how can we deal lightly with any duty; above all, how can we pollute our souls and bodies with any kind of wilful sin? we, to whom Christ has said, "I will pray the Father, and He shall give you another Comforter, and He shall abide with you for ever."

Now, then, with this deep faith in Christ's Holy Spirit, as having really been given to dwell in our hearts, let us think on any other person, whomsoever we will, as being also partaker of the same Spirit. Consider; if he were partaker of the same blood with us, if it were our brother or sister after the flesh, should we not be full of love for him? Should we not look on all he did with indulgence, judge him as favourably as we could, pray for a blessing on him heartily, and seek his good always? How much more, when the very same Spirit, which is our life, is his life also; binding us to him by the same kind of unity, by which the Son of God is One with the Father: for so He Himself prayed: "[d] that they," that is all Christians, "may be one, even as We are one."

Again, because this Spirit deals not with all exactly alike, but divides "[e] to every man severally as He will," how should the remembrance of Him fail to make us content in our places, orderly and diligent in our duties? Since wherever we are in God's work, He assigned us our place: whatever we have to do, He set us our task; if we seem to have to do nothing, but only to suffer, still it was He Who laid the burthen upon us.

Are you then a rich and prosperous person? Do not trust in your own riches; beware of thinking that you can do without the poor, that you need them not. You cannot do without them: you have the greatest need of them: you need their prayers and blessings in return for your alms, to guard you against the deadly snare of setting your heart upon this world, or any thing in it. If your alms obtain you the prayers of the poor, this will, very likely, by God's mercy through Christ, be a means of delivering your soul from death.

Are you on the contrary, a poor man? Then beware how you allow yourself to think sadly on the rich, as being better off than you are. Such thoughts are too likely to end in repining and envy: and therefore we should never use ourselves to meditate much

---

[d] S. John xvii. 22.   [e] 1 Cor. xii. 11.

on men's being above us, on their having more grace, for example, on their being enabled to do greater things for God, without deeply meditating also on the mysterious ever-present Spirit by Whom such differences were made. When it comes into your mind, "How far such an one is from the wants and doubts and troubles which annoy me," do not stop there, lest you begin to grudge him his tranquillity; but go on saying to yourself, "God, Who knows and loves us all better than we do ourselves, He saw fit to make this difference between my brother and myself, in just judgement perhaps, for my sins; it is His doing: I dare not dispute or complain of it."

Again, are you in comparison learned? are you able to read the Scriptures? yet do not trust in your reading: do not think that you can make out your duty, and save yourself well enough: you still need the prayers of Christ's afflicted and poor, you still need communion with His saints, both living and dead. Seek that blessing in all charity.

Are you, on the other hand, an ignorant person, and does it mortify you to see and feel that you know much less than most others? Care not for it, but turn your thoughts to the infinite and wonderful truth, which, as we all know, belongs to us and to the very wisest alike: turn your thoughts to the Holy Ghost abiding in you: it will be a wonder if you still go on envying and repining.

Are you so far blameless, as to have kept, by God's mercy, your soul and body from wilful deadly sin? You know it is altogether the work of God's Spirit: believe and think of this; it will keep you from pride and self-righteousness.

And last, and most mournful of all, are you a guilty person, your conscience laden with grievous sins, perhaps many sins, after Baptism? Then, indeed, the thought of the Presence of God's Spirit must be precious in your heart, for it tells you of your only hope; but that, please God, a sure and certain hope; namely, that He, unseen within you, has still the power and will to enable you to repent: and if you truly repent, He is faithful and just to forgive you, for His dear Son's sake.

God keep us ever one, by His Holy Spirit in our hearts; and dispose us to be contented where we fall short, and humble with what He gives us!

SERMON XXX.

GRACE WELL-USED ATTRACTS MORE GRACE.

MONDAY IN WHITSUN WEEK.

Ps. cxix. 55. 56.

" I have thought upon Thy Name, O Lord, in the night season, and have kept Thy law: this I had because I kept Thy commandments."

WE know, by more than one expression of our Divine Lord and Master, that there is a sort of character, which, though it cannot entitle men to receive the Gospel, yet prepares and fits them for it. No man can possibly deserve so great a mercy: but some, by God's grace, are worthier to have it than others are.

So Jesus Christ Himself teaches, where He says, that "[a] no man, having put his hand to the plough, and looking back, is fit for the kingdom of God." As much as to say, that the temper of mind which disposes men to be content with mere beginnings and good intentions, will never agree with the resolute self-denying spirit, which they had need have in them, who mean in earnest to take up their cross and follow Christ. Upon which it would seem to follow that the opposite disposition, the mind which urges men to be constant, steady, persevering, does on the

[a] S. Luke ix. 62.

contrary tend to make a man fit for the kingdom of God.

To the same purpose is the well-known and most gracious declaration concerning little children, "[b] of such is the kingdom of heaven." It is prepared especially for trusting, affectionate minds: for those who cling fondly to their friends and parents, and love in every thing to resign themselves up to them, instead of pretending to choose in all things for themselves: to such the Gospel of Christ is especially suited, and they in a manner are suited to it.

By these two instances (to mention no more at present), we learn this lesson concerning the heavenly gift, in acknowledgment whereof this holy season is appointed, the indwelling of the Holy Comforter in the souls and bodies of believers, which is sometimes called the kingdom of God: concerning this best Gift, I say, we learn from such sayings as have been now mentioned, that although the grace and mercy of the Holy Ghost is indeed free, all-powerful, sovereign; blowing, as our Lord said, "[c] where it listeth," there is yet a certain frame and temper, certain habits of conduct and behaviour, a certain disposition and preparation of heart and mind, which is likely, if not sure, wherever it is found, to draw down God's further blessing on him who has it. It is itself the good gift of God; and it prepares the way for other and better gifts.

There are sundry examples of God's dealing with His people of old, which tend to confirm this account of our Lord's meaning. Abraham pleased God, by following at once the voice which called him to leave

[b] S. Matt. xix. 14.   [c] S. John iii. 8.

his own country; and God rewarded him, by giving him grace to be willing, if need were, to sacrifice his son in obedience to the same voice.

Moses shewed a loyal and devout spirit, refusing to be called the son of Pharaoh's daughter, and boldly interfering when he saw God's people oppressed: and God rewarded him by making him their great prophet and leader out of Egypt.

Samuel shewed himself a considerate and dutiful child, and God called him to bear the burthen and the strife of the people of Israel, in very trying times.

David, as a youth, was remarkable for courageous trust in the Most High, for kindness and generosity towards men, for boldness and fervent zeal in doing the duty of his calling; and he came to an exceeding height of thankful devotion, so that his Psalms are the Church's treasure of praise, and he is himself known constantly by the name [d], the man after God's own heart.

And perhaps it might be truly said, that the verse which I just now read to you out of the hundred and nineteenth Psalm, contains in it the rule or principle (as one should call it, speaking as a man) whereby God vouchsafes to order, as it were, His own doings, in encouraging generally the faint beginnings of goodness. "I have thought upon Thy Name, O Lord, in the night season, and have kept Thy law. This I had, because I kept Thy commandments." Keeping the commandments, as has been well said by a wise and pious Bishop of our Church, is rewarded by keeping the commandments. Because the Psalmist had so much piety in him, as in a general way, all day long,

[d] Acts xiii. 22. 1 Sam. xiii. 14.

to do what he knew was God's will: therefore God gave him, as Job says, "songs in the night." He poured into his heart grace to think on His Name, to be full of holy meditations, in the night season, when few can any how serve Him. He enabled him to keep His law, during the hours which seemed most unlikely to have allowed a chance of such a sacrifice. Thus the Psalmist went from strength to strength: and thus in all the saints of God, a lower degree of grace and obedience, faithfully improved, is constantly rewarded by a higher one.

Now this rule and law of God's working is wonderfully illustrated by the manner in which the Gospel was first made known to the Gentiles, and the door of the kingdom of heaven thrown open, by the extension of the gift of the Holy Ghost to them also. This we read in the history of Cornelius, part of which is the epistle for this day. No one, with ever so little thought, can help perceiving what great encouragement that history gives to all endeavours to be good, be they but sincere, however faint and imperfect. With this view one may gather, as it were, into one, the several particulars related of him: the many disadvantages under which he served God; the sort of service which he rendered; how he was employed at the very time the gracious offer was first made him; how he improved that offer; with what special favours, one after another, it pleased God to crown more and more his faith and devotion. I will say a few words on each of these heads more particularly.

First: we see the sort of person whom the Lord delights to honour. When we look at Cornelius's condition, and observe under how many drawbacks and difficulties, the like of which are too commonly found enough to discourage almost any one, he contrived (if I may so speak) to be an acceptable worshipper. He was not a Jew, but a Gentile; not one of God's people, but a heathen. Who can express the amount of this disadvantage? It may be comprehended, in some degree, by considering, how much we think is said in excuse of any particular sin a man falls into, if it can be truly stated of him, that his friends and parents were little better than heathens, and he was brought up such altogether. When this can be said, it is generally thought to go a good way towards apologizing for the errors and vices of any one. How much more in the case of a real heathen, brought up altogether as such, and only thrown among Jews, by God's Providence, as a soldier serving in their country, and at a time when they were so very degenerate, full of hypocrisy and iniquity!

Again, Cornelius was a soldier; a pursuit and way of life, not thought in general particularly favourable to the exercise of true devotion. He was a soldier in the Roman army, a set of persons remarkable for pride, and for contempt of all but their own will and pleasure.

Yet even this person, being stationed by the will of God among His own nation, the Jews, within reach of the Holy Scriptures and of the temple worship, was so impressed with the truth and goodness of the law and service of the Eternal God, that although it does not seem as if he had become a regular proselyte, he yet devoted himself to the worship of the Most High; he became a devout man, and used himself to serve God with all his house; giving much alms to the people, that is, to the Jews, (whom most Romans so greatly despised,) and praying to God always.

This leads us to say something, secondly, of the sort of service which Almighty God is likely to bless and approve, in persons unfavourably situated, as Cornelius was.

First, he was a devout man; that is, one who cherished in himself the holy and reverential thoughts, which came from time to time into his mind; and which, though he could not as yet know or dream of such a thing, were the godly motions of that good Spirit, which was preparing to come down and regenerate him, dwelling within that heart which shewed itself so ready to obey His calls from a distance. Cornelius was a devout man, and lived in a sense of God's Presence.

The next thing told of him is, that he served God, with all his house. He did not, as some do, think it enough to have pious wishes in his mind; according to the expression which I have heard more than once, when people were called to account for their open neglect of religion: I have heard them say, "Ah, nobody knows what good thoughts I have secretly in my heart." Cornelius did not so: he felt that merely wishing is nothing, and therefore he took care to serve God openly in his house: he strove to make his servants also religious. No doubt he brought on himself the wonder, and sometimes the laughter, of his associates in the Roman army; but still he went on praying himself, and teaching and encouraging his servants to pray.

Does not this teach us something, as many as live in a Christian country, and yet suffer any slight excuse to hinder them either in their own regular prayers, or in seeing that their families pray, morning and evening? And is it not the greatest encouragement to those, who put up with some little inconvenience, for the sake of securing a few minutes, for the daily sacrifice of prayer and praise to the Most High, in their own households, if they cannot attend His Church?

Observe, I say, the daily and regular sacrifice; for this, in particular, is noted of Cornelius, that he prayed to God, not by fits and starts, but always. He was glad when they said unto him, "Let us go into the house of the Lord: let us worship and fall down, and kneel before the Lord our Maker." He was not, as we too often are, glad to have been to Church in the morning, because we think ourselves thereby excused from going in the afternoon. But, as it is recorded of a good and holy man of our own Church, and not far from this very neighbourhood, two hundred years ago, "he would have rejoiced to spend his life in that place, where the honour of his Master, Jesus, dwelleth." "He prayed to God alway;" that is, he never missed, if he could help it, the occasions and opportunities of solemnly worshipping Him.

And he added to his prayers both alms and fasting; the two wings, as they are called, of prayer. "He gave much alms to the people," preferring in his bounty those whom he had caused to think God preferred: according to the rule of S. Paul: "[e]Do

[e] Gal. vi. 10.

good unto all men, especially to them who are of the household of faith."

This was the general course of his life, under all his disadvantages. And to mark especially God's approbation of it, observe how he was employed at the very time the Angel came to him. He was keeping a solemn fast on a certain day, having taken nothing until the ninth hour, that is, until three in the afternoon; at which time he set himself to pray the appointed service, which God's people used at that hour in his house: for the ninth hour, that is, three in the afternoon, was one of the regular hours of prayer, constantly observed among the Jews, and afterwards also among the Christians.

Such was Cornelius's employment, when an Angel of God stood before him; called him by his name; assured him (O unspeakable reward for a whole life of self-denial!) that his prayers and his alms had gone up for a memorial before God; and told him where and to whom he should send, to receive instruction as to God's purpose of grace; and not only instruction, but admittance into the kingdom of heaven, the Holy Spirit coming down to dwell in his heart. And these blessings he was to receive, not for himself only, but, as the first of believing Gentiles, for all who from all quarters of the world should come in, and give their names to be servants of Christ. And to make the favour still more signal, the Holy Spirit at the same time instructed S. Peter, by a wonderful vision, that it was His will to break through, in the person of Cornelius, the partition wall which had so long separated the Gentiles from the people of God. And besides all this, when the

Apostle had come and had spoken to Cornelius and his family, and they, (as they had no other thought) were listening with humble and obedient and believing hearts, the Holy Spirit Himself, in His visible signs, fell on them that heard the word; they began to speak with tongues, and to magnify God: and thereby S. Peter felt quite sure, that the Divine Spirit had chosen them for His inhabitation, as entirely as those who had before been called to be Christians from among the Jews: and no time was lost in baptizing them, that they might be regenerate, and have the Spirit, not only prophesying by them, but dwelling in their hearts, and uniting them to Jesus Christ.

Such is the rich, the unspeakable, inconceivable encouragement, which this history of the calling of Cornelius offers, to all who humbly endeavour to serve God under great worldly discouragements: setting out (as one may speak) from the spot whereon they now stand; favourable or unfavourable; and trying to keep themselves, by prayer, by fasting, and by works of kindness to their brethren, alive and open to the influences of the Holy Spirit.

It is a part of Scripture particularly meant for those, who for various reasons think religion nearly out of the question for *them* ; for those who are very destitute and ignorant, living perhaps on the charity of others; for those whose whole time seems engrossed by hard work or by troublesome trade; who are made anxious by their families, or by the state of their health: to all such the word is gone forth, if they will but have the heart to receive it: "'God is

^f Acts x. 34, 35.

no respecter of persons, but in every nation," every condition, under every sort of disadvantage, "he that feareth Him, and worketh righteousness," will surely be accepted of Him.

And when He says, "accepted of Him," it is no ordinary blessing that He speaks of, but it is the crown and sum of all blessings, the justification of a Christian man. It is that which our Lord promised when He said, "[g] If a man love Me, he will keep My words, and My Father will love him, and We" *i. e.* the Father and the Son, by the Spirit, "will come unto him, and make Our abode with him."

[g] S. John xiv. 23.

SERMON XXXI.

THE UNIVERSAL LANGUAGE. I.

MONDAY IN WHITSUN-WEEK.

ZEPH. iii. 9.

"*For then will I turn to the people a pure language, that they may call upon the Name of the Lord, to serve Him with one consent.*"

It is very clear from the book of Genesis, that language was the especial gift of Almighty God to our first parents. God brought all things to Adam, "[a]to see what he would call them: and whatsoever Adam called every living creature, that was the name thereof." And it should seem that notwithstanding the confusion and violence which brought on the flood, yet this original gift continued until many generations after Noah. When the whole earth had filled with inhabitants again, it continued, as the first lesson to-day declares, "of one language and of one speech." This unity of language was a token that it came from God, Who is One; as all the other perfections in which man was at first created, reason, understanding, memory, foresight, dominion over the creatures, immortality, were so many shadows and images of His perfections.

[a] Gen. ii. 19.

But when man had lost holiness, that perfection which was in a manner the grace and life of all the rest, then these gifts all became dangerous, too often fatal and deadly : they were but as weapons in the hand of a strong bad man, to do the more mischief with to himself and others : and it was therefore of God's mercy that He took them away or lessened them.

Life He first made subject to death, and then very much shortened its duration, partly in punishment, partly also, as it may seem, that the evil-disposed may have less time to fall away wholly and irreconcileably from God. The understanding He made dim, the body feeble and subject to disease; the earth was accursed, to bring forth no fruit without labour; the animals, the wilder part of them, seemed to be withdrawn from man's dominion.

And even to our apprehension there appears but too good reason for all this, in the sad abuse which men, left to themselves, continually make of these precious gifts. Their understanding they abuse, to find excuses for sin and unbelief; their bodies, to corrupt themselves and others; the gifts of the earth, to luxury and indolence; their command over the animals, to pride and cruelty. God was even forced, by our ill use of His gifts, to withdraw from us more or less of them : and so it was with the gift of language too, that gift, which is especially brought before our consideration by the history of this time of Pentecost.

The whole earth being of one language was a great advantage to any one who could manage men and get them all to act together in anything that they set about. Now it seems, that in a certain number of generations after the flood, they had again so far revolted from the only true God, as to set about building a city and a tower, in defiance of His Majesty: as if to prevent His ever again destroying the earth with a flood. "[b] They said, Go to, let us build us a city and a tower, whose top may reach unto heaven; and let us make us a name, lest we be scattered abroad upon the face of the whole earth."

This was their foolishness: it was a proud earthly dream, like the projects of great kings and conquerors among men: and the Almighty confounded them, as He ever will confound all profane projects and endeavours, that set out without His blessing. As He had made us mortal, shortened our lives, clouded our understanding, enfeebled our bodily strength; so now He took away the unity of our language. "[c] The Lord came down to see the city and the tower, which the children of men builded. And the Lord said, Behold, the people is one, and they have all one language; and this they begin to do: and now nothing will be restrained from them, which they have imagined to do. Go to, let us go down, and there confound their language, that they may not understand one another's speech. So the Lord scattered them abroad from thence upon the face of all the earth: and they left off to build the city. Therefore is the name of it called Babel," (i. e. confusion;) " because the Lord did there confound the language of all the earth: and from thence did the Lord scatter them abroad, upon the face of all the earth."

[b] Gen. xi. 4.   [c] Ib. 5-9.

Thus we see, that as the other good gifts of the Most High, so this great gift of one and the same language to all, being greatly abused, was in process of time taken away. And now, as you know, every country has its own peculiar language: strangers cannot understand us, nor we them; and it takes a very long time for one, nurtured and brought up in one language, to be able to understand, much more to speak, another.

But the kingdom of heaven, when in due time it should be set up by the Incarnation, Death, Resurrection and Ascension of the Eternal Son of God, and the coming of the Holy Ghost: this kingdom was to bring with it a cure for the confusion of tongues, as for all the other evil consequences of sin. So the prophet tells us in the text: "Then" (i. e. in the times of the Gospel) "I will turn unto the people a pure language, that they may all call upon the Name of the Lord, to serve Him with one consent." And the prophecy of Isaiah concerning Egypt points to the same thing: "[d] In that day shall five cities in the land of Egypt speak the language of Canaan." And in another prophet: "[e] In that day there shall be One Lord, and His Name One:" as all shall worship one and the same God, so all shall call Him by one and the same Name. There shall be unity, both of inward faith and of outward worship.

Such being the great and merciful purpose of Almighty God concerning His Church: when that Church was really set up in the world, a great sign was presently given of the doing away with the difference of languages, and joining all nations in the

[d] Is. xix. 18.   [e] Zech. xiv. 9.

one service of God. The very first consequence of the coming down of the Holy Ghost was their all beginning to speak with divers languages, which they had never learned: and also, as it seems, their mutually understanding each other: that as sin had separated men, so on their turning to God in Christ, they might again be perfectly joined together. This outward sign or gift of tongues seems to have lasted but for one generation: but no doubt it was a sign of that union of heart and tongue, inward and outward, which ought to be among all the members of Jesus Christ. For what if we still speak different languages, and so, without particular instruction, know not the meaning of one another's voices, and are so far foreigners, or as S. Paul says, Barbarians, to one another: still if we all knew that we served the same Lord, with the same prayers and Sacraments, repeating the same Creeds, and reading the same Scriptures; if we prayed heartily for one another, and gave and received the outward signs of communion, as often as we had opportunity; the difference of language would make no difference to us as Churchmen: God's Name would still be One over all the earth in reality, though it sounded differently in one country from what it did in another.

And this was the case for many generations and ages, from the first publication of the Gospel at Jerusalem. There was unity of doctrine all over the world; it was one Lord and one Faith: the Lord Whom we honour and the Faith which we profess in the Creeds of the Holy Church. All who professed and called themselves Christians were then of one mind and one mouth in these great things: or if any one presumptuously differed, he was presently cast out of the Body. There was also unity of Sacraments: it was one Baptism, as well as one Lord and one Faith. And the soul of Christian religion being thus exactly the same in every part of the Christian world, no wonder that the body and outward form of it was also in a great measure one: not superstitiously and exactly, to every jot and tittle, but in substance and in all great matters. For example, the solemn prayers and method of offering and consecrating the Holy Communion were undoubtedly for many ages the same every where in all material points. They remembered each other in their public prayers; not generally only, but particularly and by name, when great need was, though at ever so great a distance. And if a Christian had occasion to travel in foreign parts, he had but to bring letters from his Bishop and Pastor, to certify that he was a communicant at home, and he was presently admitted, all the world over, to all the privileges of Christian brotherhood.

Thus did the coming of the Holy Ghost in a great measure undo the curse which fell on the world at Babel: and though men still spake on worldly matters with different languages, yet in the Faith and Worship of God they might be truly said to speak the same language, and to understand one another, all the world over. And thus the Almighty, for six hundred years, restored unto His people what they had lost in Paradise: "a pure language," pure from profaneness and falsehood, "that they might all call upon the Name of the Lord, to serve Him with one consent."

How this great blessing has been in a great measure lost among us, and what our duty is, whom God has called to be His servants in times so unlike those first, we may well consider another time: one thing however is very plain, that we cannot be too earnest in prayer to the One Lord that He would again make His Name One throughout all parts of the Church: nor too strict in watching our hearts and lives, that we lose not the blessing held out to such charitable prayers.

SERMON XXXII.

THE UNIVERSAL LANGUAGE. II.

ZEPH. iii. 9.

"For then will I turn to the people a pure language, that they may all call upon the Name of the Lord, to serve Him with one consent."

OF all disappointments, there is none perhaps more trying to a really good and dutiful mind than that which is occasioned by the sad difference between the promises and prophecies of Holy Scripture and the actual state of the Christian world, as we see it with our eyes. The Scripture says, "[a] All shall know Me, from the least of them unto the greatest of them:" and we see too many, of whom it may be truly said, that they neither know nor care about God. The Scripture says, "[b] Nation shall not lift up sword against nation, neither shall they learn war any more:" yet wars and fightings have been going on these many ages among Christians, as if they were heathens. The Scripture says, "[c] The idols He shall utterly abolish:" yet we have too much reason to fear that a very large proportion of Christ's people every where put a kind of idolatrous trust in one or other of God's creatures, instead of depending on the great Creator only.

[a] Jer. xxxi. 34.   [b] Isa. ii. 4.   [c] Ib. 18.

And to come at once to the example which we already began to consider: the Scripture says that as there is One Lord, so His Name should be One; and that God would restore to all nations a pure language, to serve the Lord with one consent: but we see that some Christian nations are sadly separated from others; some teaching as sacred truth what others seem to reject, as heretical; and that, instead of gladly remembering one another in their prayers, they shut out on purpose all thoughts of mutual communion, the one sort fearing to be entangled in the heresy and error which they suppose prevails among the other. And this, as matter of fact, is equally certain, whether we blame all parties or none, whether we blame these or those, still the fact that we are divided and separated, remains, and seems at first sight contrary to the other fact, that God has promised all should be one.

This is most reasonably matter of great sorrow, self-abasement, and disappointment, to all who love God and His Church: but it need not be matter of doubt and perplexity, because, if we look a little further, we shall find that these same comfortable prophecies are all of them uttered with a condition. They are made to men as true children of the Church, true members of the Body of Christ: and therefore if persons, by wilful sin and unbelief, separate themselves inwardly and spiritually from that Body, the blessing is so far forfeited: they must not expect still to partake of all the glories of their Christian inheritance, any more than Israel might depend upon the finest wheat-flour and the honey out of the rock, without hearkening to God and walking in His ways.

As far as we can trace the reasons, looking back to former times, how the Church came to be so divided as she is, it is but too plain that it was the just judgement of Almighty God on Christians for abusing their privileges. For instance: near eight hundred years ago, there was a grievous separation between the Churches here in the West, and those of Asia and the East: which those who have looked into history say may be found clearly owing to the rash censures and selfish ways of certain great persons of those times, contending for the first place, and casting one another out of the Church. And again: we have all heard of the sad division which took place among the Western Churches about three hundred years ago, by which it has come to pass, that we in England and the greater part of our brethren in other countries are entirely separated from each other, as far as visible fellowship goes: still, we hope, being one in Christ Jesus, since we all hold the Faith of the Apostles and the Baptism and Communion of our only Saviour, yet cut off from the great privilege of sharing in one another's worship and Sacraments: possessed, we hope, of the Communion of Saints, but deprived of the outward exercise of that Communion.

Now whichever way we look, there can be no doubt of their having been grievous sin in all parties, both in the Church of Rome itself, and among ourselves who have been ever since separated from her: sin and irreverence, more than enough to account for so heavy a judgement on both sides. And the way to heal the mischief, and bring back the lost unity of the Church, without falling away from what is right in doctrine and worship, must surely be to repent of our sin and irreverence, and win back by earnest prayer and self-denial the forfeited blessing of one pure language, wherein we may all once more join in calling on the Name of the Lord, and serve Him with one consent.

Were we to look at all the points in which Christian Churches are divided one from another in doctrine and worship, I suppose we might easily perceive in every one, how sin and practical irreligion led in the first instance to the error and division. Take the example which the services of this time particularly remind us of. One of our great objections to the Church-services of many Christians abroad is that they are offered in a language unknown to most of the worshippers. We justly think that this appears contrary to the directions of the Holy Spirit by S. Paul: that a " person speaking in an unknown tongue should keep silence in the Church, except there be some one to interpret." But it is worth considering how it first began. The Latin language, in which the services are commonly performed in the Churches abroad, was the regular language of the several countries when they were first converted to be Christian. In course of time the language altered, while the services continued the same: and thus, almost before people were aware of it, the custom was established of worshipping in an unknown tongue. Now if care had been taken to teach all children the meaning of the several words and parts of the service, that service would not have been in a tongue unknown to them, although on other occasions the same language might not be known. And then, it may be, true reverence might have continued to use it in church, as putting the greater difference between a church and a house, the service of God and ordinary employments. But because those whose care it was, neglected to teach people the meaning of their prayers, the language came to be unknown, and much scandal and irreverence followed; which we in England, trying to amend, have seemed to separate from them, and no longer to be serving the Lord in the same language and with the same consent. Here is a plain instance, of the unity of the Church suffering, in consequence of the profane carelessness of those, who were intrusted to bring up the youth of those times.

The same kind of remark may be made on other matters, in which we are come to differ from our brethren abroad.

Well then, if sin have so divided and scattered Christians, is it not manifest that holiness must be the one only secret for bringing them together again: real holiness of heart and life, which will both set men, by some good instinct, against false doctrine, and will also give that virtue and prevailing force to their united intercessions and prayers for unity, which God (if one may so speak) shall hardly be able to resist? Some persons say, "never mind the divisions among Christians; there have always been such, and they cannot be helped: it is well enough, if in spite of them men go on holding a few, the very chiefest truths of the Christian religion." But the Bible holds out unity, we see, as one of the greatest prophecies: and the Prayer-book again and again most solemnly enjoins us to pray for it. Let us do so with all our hearts: being quite sure that there must be some deep and mysterious blessing, more than we know of, in the full unity of the Church. Otherwise we should not in so many ways have been invited and urged to make it the matter of our prayers. And surely, when we *do* feel a little of the blessing of Church unity, as He permits us to do now and then, in Church services especially, the joy and consolation is so great, that we may well believe it would be quite overpowering, too much almost for this world. When it is but one family dwelling together in unity, but one congregation joining heartily and rightly in the heavenly hymns and prayers of the Church; how keenly sometimes do we feel the blessing! It is like a cup running over. How much more, if we suppose it carried over the whole earth, and continued on in perfection, through eternity.

Surely strict lives are worth living, true self-denial is worth practising; surely in them, not after them only, is great reward, if they keep us so joined to Christ, that He will hear our prayers for unity, and do something, how faint and secret soever, at our supplications, for healing the wounds of His Church, and restoring her pure language.

SERMON XXXIII.

FESTIVAL JOY.

TUESDAY IN WHITSUN-WEEK.

ECCLES. ix. 7, 8.

" Go thy way, eat thy bread with joy, and drink thy wine with a merry heart; for God now accepteth thy works: let thy garments be always white, and let thy head lack no ointment."

THIS is one of those passages, so remarkable in the writings of Solomon, in which the words of sinful men in the world are taken up by the Holy Ghost, to be applied in a Christian sense. As they stand in Ecclesiastes, it seems very plain that they are intended to represent the sayings and thoughts of sensual, careless people, indulging themselves in their profane ways, their utter neglect of God and goodness, with the notion that this world is all. As if they should say, "When people are dead, there is an end of them: therefore all we have to do is to enjoy ourselves as much as possible; to eat our bread with joy, and drink our wine with a merry heart; to wear always festival garments, and anoint ourselves with the oil of gladness, while God still 'accepteth our works,' that is, while it is yet well with us, and we are capable of finding delight in life, according to the order of God's providence." It is much the same as the unbeliever's saying, in S. Paul, "[a] Let us eat and drink, for to-morrow we die."

But see the ever-watchful goodness and mercy of God. The words which the dissolute, wild-hearted sinner uses to encourage himself in his evil inconsiderate ways, He teaches us to take up, and use them in a very different sense : to express the inward joy and comfort which God's people may find in obeying Him. As thus : suppose a person giving himself up, with his whole heart, to the service and obedience of God : supposing him really withdrawing himself from the sins which had most easily beset him ; suppose him making some great sacrifice, parting with what he held very dear, or submitting to pain or grief for Christ's sake : then the Holy and merciful Comforter seems to say to him in the words of the text, "Go thy way now, thank God, and take courage ; the blessing of God is now restored to thee, and will be upon all thou hast, and upon thine ordinary employments and refreshments : now thou mayest eat thy bread with joy, and drink thy wine with a merry heart, for God now accepteth thy works." For, "whether we eat or drink, or whatever we do," if we "do all to the glory of God," we shall do it with His blessing and approbation : it will be so much more of happiness, joy, and thanksgiving to us.

Thus we may understand the words to teach the same lesson as the Apostle, when he says, "[b] Rejoice in the Lord alway, and again, I say, rejoice." They are God's gracious word of permission to those who fear Him, encouraging them to enjoy, with inno-

---

[a] 1 Cor. xv. 32.   [b] Phil. iv. 4.

cence, moderation, and thankfulness, the daily comforts and reliefs, with which He so plentifully supplies them, even in this imperfect world. They bring the same assurance from God as S. Paul gives to Timothy : " ^cEvery creature of God is good, and nothing to be refused, if it be received with thanksgiving."

Let us only think for one moment, what a heavenly light it would throw over our ordinary works and refreshments, if, being always careful to set about them with a good conscience, we could seriously bring it home to ourselves, that they are so many tokens of heavenly and eternal love ; so many reasonable grounds of hope, that God really accepteth our works.

But there is yet a higher, a Christian sense of these words, a sense in which they were taken of old by the holy Fathers of the Christian Church. The bread and wine, the white garments, the ointment for the head, are, according to this interpretation, figures and types of our Christian privileges, the blessings and favours of the kingdom of heaven. It is, then, as if the Holy Word had said to us, being, as we are, Christian men, members of the mystical Body of our Lord and Saviour, "Now you have been brought into the communion of saints; now God has set His seal upon you; now, to speak the Apostle's words, ' ^d ye are washed, ye are sanctified, ye are justified, in the name of the Lord Jesus, and by the Spirit of our God.' Go your way, then ; use your privileges with all reverence, joy and fear. Draw near as often as you can, to the holy feast of

^c 1 Tim. iv. 4.   ^d 1 Cor. vi. 11.

that Bread and Wine, which, to those who take it with penitent and obedient hearts, is the very Body and Blood of our Saviour Christ. Aweful as such an invitation is, you may yet draw near with holy cheerfulness, having God's seal and mark upon your forehead, and the earnest of His Spirit in your hearts."

And it would seem that if Christians were at all such as they ought to be, the words might be well and profitably understood with a particular reference to this sacred season of Whitsuntide.

For at this time, as you know, the Blessed Comforter came down, to set up the kingdom of Christ on earth; to dwell in men's hearts so as to unite them to Christ; by which union alone they can be partakers of the great things which the Gospel promises. This time, then, is the last of the Holy Seasons; it represents to us the full completion of God's unspeakable plan for the salvation of the world.

Supposing, then, any humble, faithful Christian to have rightly kept the former holy seasons: to have "worshipped and served Christ, for His Conception, in faith; for His Birth, in humility; for His Sufferings, in patience and irreconcileable hatred of sin; for His Death, by dying daily to sin; for His Resurrection, by rising again more and more unto righteousness; for His Ascension, by a heavenly mind:" may we not, without presumption, imagine him to hear the voice of his approving conscience, the certain yet silent whispers of the Holy Comforter in his heart, " Go thy way now, receive the fulness of the blessing of these sacred days, which thou hast so dutifully tried to observe. Let the light and warmth of Christmas, Easter, and Whitsuntide spread itself in a measure over the rest of thy year. Whatsoever God putteth in thine hand to do, in the way of holy devotion and true Church-communion, do it with all thy might, in the humble hope that God now accepteth thy works."

Such is the kind of comfort, which the sacred Scriptures encourage us, as Christians, to take to ourselves, at every new return of these great days, bringing home to us things which are the very foundation of our hope. It is a comfort which would be to us far more perfect than it is, and far plainer to be understood, if we were less unworthy of our privileges; if we had not too generally fallen from the righteousness of Jesus Christ, given to us at our Baptism. But even as it is, the words have a sound most comfortable to penitents, as well as to those who, by God's help, have kept themselves from wilful, deadly sin. They sound like words of absolution: "Go thy way, return again to that holy Table, from which thy transgressions had for a time separated thee: eat thy bread, and drink thy wine with a courageous and hopeful heart: for now there is hope that God accepteth thy works; that He hears thee, since thou hast left off inclining unto wickedness with thine heart. Thy case indeed is alarming, from the continual danger of a relapse; and thy loss at best is great, penitency instead of innocency being thy portion; yet go on steadily and cheerfully."

Thus, whether to souls that have as yet preserved the purity of their baptismal robe, or to humble penitent souls, desirous of recovering it, there are in Holy Scripture, if we had ears to hear them, most condescending invitations as well as warnings. Christ, in His Sacraments, is held out to them as their only but sufficient Hope.

Observe, however, the words which follow, which to the hearing of a thoughtful Christian convey a very serious admonition, telling us on what these unspeakable privileges depend, so far as our own conduct is concerned : "Let thy garments be always white, and let thine head lack no ointment." This also would be felt by the Christians of ancient times, as particularly suitable to the holy season of Whitsuntide. For that, as you know, was one of the solemn times of baptizing, and the new-baptized were always clothed in white, as a token of the "[e] fine linen, clean and white, the righteousness of saints," and of Jesus Christ; the wedding garment, which God had just put on them by making them members of His Son. To say, therefore, to Christians at Whitsuntide, " Let thy garments be always white," was the same as saying, " Take care that at no time you stain or sully the bright and clear robe of your Saviour's righteousness, which has just been thrown over you : according to the Apostle's saying, "[f] As many as have been baptized into Christ have put on Christ.' As much as possible keep it clear from all spot of wilful sin ; and if you have unhappily fallen, give yourself no rest, until by your true and deep repentance, all your life long, you have put the matter entirely in your Saviour's hand, to wash out even that wilful stain, if so it please Him, by His most precious Blood."

[e] Rev. xix. 8.   [f] Gal. iii. 27.

Again, says the wise man, "Let thine head lack no ointment:" and this again is an allusion which would come with a particular meaning in early times to the new-baptized Christians, and those who had been present at their Baptism. For both in that Sacrament, and in Confirmation, which comes next after it, they used in those days to anoint with holy oil. And oil is in Scripture the constant token of the gifts and graces of the Holy Spirit. Therefore, to say, "Let thy head lack no ointment," would mean, "Take care that thou stir up, cherish, and improve the unspeakable Gift, of which thou art now made partaker. Use diligently all the means of grace which Christ has provided for thee in His Kingdom, whereof thou art now come to be an inheritor."

Think not, that because we have received so great a blessing freely and fully, without any merit, without any exertion of our own, therefore we have but to go on quietly, taking no particular pains, and all will come right at last. Nay, the very greatness of the blessing is a call upon us to labour night and day, that we lose not, after all, the fruit of such exceeding mercy. It provokes the envy and spite of the Evil one, to take all the advantage he can of us: let it, therefore, encourage us to be more and more devout and watchful. What a shame for us to be negligent in prayer, who know that we have Christ's Spirit abiding in us, to help our infirmities, and pray for us and with us! What sin, what danger, what ruin, for us to be violently carried away with any worldly thing whatever, who know that "greater is He that is in us than he that is in the world!"

If we earnestly endeavour, and pray in Christ's Name, to have such thoughts as these, when we are reminded of our baptismal privileges, we may hope that the care of the Church in appointing these holy seasons will not be thrown away upon us: we may hope, next year, to accompany her in her mysterious round of holy feasts and fasts, from Advent to Trinity Sunday, with more dutiful and prepared hearts than we have done this year. But let us, above all things, beware of growing faint and cold, and treating these sacred things as matters of course. Let us remember that "we have opened our mouth unto the Lord," and we must not, we dare not, " go back : " but we shall undoubtedly go back, if we are not always labouring to go forward.

SERMON XXXIV.

CHRISTIAN MINISTERS, TOKENS OF CHRIST'S PRESENCE.

TUESDAY IN WHITSUNWEEK.

S. JOHN x. 9.

"I am the door: by Me, if any man enter in, he shall be saved, and shall go in and out, and find pasture."

PERSONS who attend to the Church-Services must have observed, that the lessons, epistles, and Gospels for Whitsunweek, especially those of this day, are selected in some measure with a view to the ministerial office, and to the doctrine of Holy Scripture concerning it. Yesterday's morning lesson, from the first epistle to the Corinthians, about the manifestation of the same Spirit by variety of gifts; and also the evening lesson about the seventy elders of Israel, who received a gift of the Spirit to assist Moses, have both of them an evident reference to that subject. So has one of the lessons for this morning, beseeching Christians to know those who are over them in the Lord, and admonish them, and to esteem them very highly in love for their work's sake. But most especially is this the case with the epistle and Gospel of the day: the epistle giving an account, how the Holy Ghost was given, and could only be given, by laying on of the hands of the Apostles; the Gospel pointing out those Apostles, as the persons trusted by the Chief Shepherd with the whole care of the sheep.

Nor are there wanting good and plain reasons, why this particular subject should be so much in the Church's mind, at this particular time.

First, this is, as you know, one of the Ember weeks; next Sunday, the Sunday of the Most Holy Trinity, is one of the Ordination Sundays. We are therefore to fast and pray for a blessing on those who shall be ordained. And that our fasting and prayer may be accompanied with worthier notions of the blessings we seek, it is well we should be reminded of certain portions of Scripture, telling us shortly, but very seriously, wherein lies the true greatness and sacredness of the ministry of Jesus Christ.

It is not that this ministry is sanctioned by the law of England, rather than any other, to instruct, and warn and guide us: it is not that the same ministry always was, and is still, a mighty instrument in God's hand, for all the best works that have been done in the world: it is not for the love of peace and order, knowing there must be some ministry in the Church, and thinking it best to hold by that which is established. These are all reasons of more or less weight; but neither in each separately, nor in all taken together, can they be truly called *the* reason, why the ministry is so very great and sacred. *The* reason is, that Christ only is the door of the sheep; that our spiritual life entirely depends on a real, though mysterious, union with Him; to which union the ministration of the Apostles, or of others ordained through them, is, ordinarily speaking, quite necessary.

This being so, all the reasons which would otherwise make us to be greatly concerned for the wellbeing of Christ's ministry among us, are unspeakably heightened, and made more important and more affecting. And, of course, no more serious introduction to hearty prayer for Bishops and Priests and Deacons, could have been contrived, than the reading of some of those Scriptures, which openly affirm these great things concerning the ministry of those whom Christ sends, as He has sent those three Orders.

But again, this subject of the Christian ministry is connected very closely with the blessing of Whit-Sunday; is indeed a material part of that blessing. For by that ministry the blessing is continued down to these, and to all times. It was to the Apostles that the Holy Spirit visibly came: through them the promise was made to the Church, that He should abide in us for ever; and therefore, if there were now no successors of the Apostles in the world, that promise would seem to have become a dead letter, to have passed entirely away from us. But thanks be to Almighty God, that is far from being the case.

For as in the first days of the Church, the visible gift of the Holy Ghost to the Apostles and some other disciples, was the external token, to the very senses of men, of His inward Presence and abode in their hearts; so now the presence of the Apostles themselves, by their successors, the Bishops principally, and under them the Priests of the Church, is a like external token, addressed also to the senses, of the same Spirit abiding in *our* hearts also. The Apostles knew for certain, that the promised Comforter was present in their ministrations, to regenerate His people first, and afterwards to strengthen and refresh them; because they saw the fiery tongues, they heard the sound as of a rushing mighty wind, they felt the power in themselves to speak with new tongues, and to work various other miracles besides. We, in like manner, the word sounds a bold one, but I verily believe it is no more than Scripture plainly warrants us in affirming, we are sure that the same Holy Spirit is present also in our ministrations, for the same gracious purposes: we are sure of it, because we know that the hands of those whom Christ commissioned for that purpose were solemnly laid on our heads, and the same commission, in part or in whole, given to us. So that we, as Bishops or Priests, do really stand in the place of the Apostles, and the word spoken to them is spoken to us.

Thus we see there is a double reason, why Scripture relating to the Ministry and the Succession should be read in this week particularly;

First, to assist our prayers for those who are shortly to be ordained:

Secondly, to remind us, that through this ministry we have our portion in the precious gifts, brought from heaven by the Holy Ghost.

This ministry is, in part, the token and the mean of the continuance of the indwelling Spirit in the people of God. It is our pledge, that we enter in by the door; according to that parable of our Lord which forms the Gospel for the day. As in the epistle to the Hebrews we are instructed, that the only entrance into the Holy of Holies is through the veil, that is, the flesh of our Lord: we must be new-born, and made members of His Body, (which, as the catechism teaches, we are in Holy Baptism,) before we can be said to belong to His Church and kingdom: so here, in His own parable, the Church is the sheep-fold, and our Saviour is the door. It is only through Him we must pass, if we would go in and out, and find pasture. No irregular ways, no ways of men, whatever good they may do us in other respects, will admit us to the fulness of the blessing of the Gospel of Christ.

It is much to be observed, that our Lord distinctly represents Himself as the door, by which both shepherd and sheep must enter. He that climbeth up some other way, is a thief and a robber: he only, that entereth in by the door, is the shepherd of the sheep. This is the leading idea of the parable.

And to give the key for explaining it, He adds afterward, "Verily, verily, I say unto you, I am the door of the sheep . . . I am the door: by Me if any man come in, he shall be saved, and shall go in and out and find pasture." By which it would seem, that it is quite as necessary for the shepherds, in their peculiar office, as it is for the sheep of the flock, to enter in by the door. There must be some peculiar token and mean of grace, sealing the ministers of Christ for their office, by immediate communication with Himself, like as there must be the holy Sacrament of Baptism, to seal every Christian for spiritual union with Christ.

This is what we should expect by the parable: and so in fact it has ever been in the Church. Men enter into the fold of our Lord and Saviour, as sheep, by Baptism; as shepherds, by Ordination. In both cases through Him, as the door.

Should it be said, by way of answer to this, that too many of those, who are duly ordained, have in all ages neglected or abused their privileges, and some have behaved rather like thieves, who come on purpose to steal, and to kill, and to destroy: and should the question be asked, as it sometimes is, "Are we to call these bad men shepherds, merely because they have been ordained, and deny the name to good and charitable teachers, merely because they have not been ordained?" the answer to this may be perceived, on well considering our Lord's way of speaking, concerning the sheep of His flock themselves. "By Me if any man enter in, he shall be saved, and shall go in and out, and find pasture." Yet we know that too many of those, who enter in by Jesus Christ, being baptized in their infancy, and so made members of Him, do not continue in that salvation: they neglect it; they receive God's grace in vain; they refuse to go in and out and find pasture; to walk quietly in the way of righteousness, and beside the waters of comfort; and yet all the while our Blessed Lord's saying holds true concerning them also: they were saved, but they have forfeited their salvation.

Thus He speaks of the sheep; and the like turn may with reason be given to His account of the shepherds. "He that entereth in by the door is the shepherd of the sheep. To him the porter openeth, and the sheep hear his voice, and he calleth his own sheep by name, and leadeth them out: and when he putteth forth his own sheep, he goeth before them, and the sheep follow him, for they know his voice." This is the account of the natural and intended effect of God's calling a man to be a shepherd and Bishop in His Church; but it may be forfeited as the baptismal privileges may: and yet this will no more interfere with the reality and necessity of Christ's call by ordination, than the bad lives of too many Christians interfere with the necessity of Holy Baptism, and the reality of the grace then given.

If the ministers of Christ are unworthy, and do not their duty, let them look to it: but still they cannot unordain themselves: they are yet ministers of Christ; and the Sacraments of our Lord, the tokens and means of our union with Him, are continued among us through them. Their going wrong does not destroy their commission, nor do away with the spiritual and heavenly state of things, of which their being among us is a token: it does not turn the Church into the world, the new heaven and the new earth into the old heathen or Jewish condition; it still leaves on every Christian the full burthen of his baptismal promises, and of those high and unspeakable privileges, which were sealed to him at the holy fount of regeneration. It still leaves him a member of Christ, a child of God, and an inheritor of the kingdom of heaven; bound by solemn oath to renounce what God hates, to believe what He teaches, to keep what He commands.

Such is the view which our Lord's parable of the sheep-fold, compared with what we read elsewhere in the Bible and Prayer book generally, would lead us to take of our own condition, so far as it depends on the presence of an apostolical ministry among us. Whoever truly believes it, and lays it to heart, will find that it will make an extreme difference in all his notions and conduct on Church matters.

I do not mean simply in keeping him from schism, and from any proceedings within the Church in the spirit and temper of schism, that is, of self-confidence: but I mean, particularly; in respect of those who really love the Church, and wish to obey it; who desire and endeavour to walk conscientiously in all Church-duties and ordinances. If such persons will use themselves to consider this outward kingdom of God as a pledge of the inward; the ministry and Sacraments as sure tokens of the Father and the Son dwelling in their hearts by the Holy Spirit; surely that is a way of thinking, which will in an unspeakable way ennoble and purify all they do, both in the Church and elsewhere; all their wishes, prayers, and performances.

Particularly in regard of devotional duties, and Church-services, it will not so much set men on any new practices, as it will put their old observances on new and high ground. Thus in our dealings with Christ's ministers, more especially with His Bishops, when any come near us, we shall be full of awe, considering them as living and visible tokens of Him, under whose Cloud of Glory, though we see it not, we live: we should receive them, as the Galatians are praised for receiving S. Paul, "[a] as an angel of God, even as Christ Jesus."

In our thoughts on public matters, and what is

---
[a] Gal. iv. 14.

called the union of the Church of God with the State in which we live, we should look chiefly, not to the visible and immediate good done, but to the great duty which lies on the kingdoms of this world, to bow themselves down to the Church and Kingdom of our Lord, and to offer up all their power and glory, as a sacrifice, through her, to God.

In our use of the Prayer-book we should remember, that this also, coming down, as it does in a great measure, nearly from the day of Pentecost, is, like the apostolical ministry, a sure token of God's wonderful presence in our hearts; far more, therefore, than any other set of prayers and lessons, however good and edifying, could be.

Finally, this view, if we will steadily try to act on it, will guide aright, and lift on high, the whole course of our outward religion, both in word and deed. It will help to make us feel, after our measure, that Christ is not only the Saviour of all men, once for all, by His precious Death on the Cross, but also a Saviour, a present and abiding Saviour, to each of us at every moment, by His Spirit inhabiting our souls and bodies. It will make every day Sunday, and Sunday like one of the days of eternity. It will make every place a Church, and the Church a kind of Heaven.

SERMON XXXV.

WHY THE WITNESS OF GOD IS REJECTED.

TRINITY SUNDAY.

S. JOHN iii. 11.

" Verily, verily, I say unto you, We speak that we do know, and testify that we have seen, and ye receive not our witness."

THESE are the words of the eternal Son of God, describing the manner in which His witness, and the witness of His Holy Spirit, would be too generally treated in the world. That behaviour, He says, would be boldly practised towards Him, which men can least endure, when practised towards themselves. His positive declarations would be treated as falsehoods: His words of earnest advice and warning taken no more notice of, by many, than if they had never been spoken at all.

Now, men know what they feel when they are used in that way, even by those who are as wise and as good as themselves. They cannot very soon forget or pass it over. How then can they think, without trembling, of behaving in the same disrespectful way to the Eternal Father, to the Judge of quick and dead, to the Almighty Spirit, ᵃ in Whom they and all creatures live, and move, and have their being?

ᵃ Acts xvii. 28.

They cannot suppose that God Almighty is, as it were, too high above us to care how we behave towards Him. For He has warned us in so many words, "[b] Them that honour Me, I will honour; and they that despise Me shall be lightly esteemed." That is, they who turn their thoughts, seriously and humbly, to the message of their God, brought from heaven by His Son Christ Jesus, and sealed afterwards by the gift of His Holy Spirit; those He will always bear in mind; they will find Him a kind and merciful God; they will have His blessing both in this world and in the next. But on the other hand, "[c] surely He scorneth the scorners:" they who will not remember Him, will find themselves left without Him in the world; and how then can ever anything turn out well and happily to them?

Neither can the scorners of the Almighty pretend, that the things, which He teaches and they refuse to hear, are such as do not nearly concern themselves. On the contrary, the witness of the Son of God, the Gospel, of which He speaks in the text, contains in it all the particulars, on which depend the life, being, and happiness of every one, both here and hereafter.

Can any thing possibly concern you more than to know, that you have an immortal soul, a living spirit which never can die, and a body which will rise again after death, never more to return to corruption? And further, that God Himself has prepared for this soul and body of yours a home of everlasting peace and joy: things more blessed than eye ever saw, or ear heard, or than ever entered into man's

[b] 1 Sam. ii. 30.   [c] Prov. iii. 34.

heart to conceive? These truths, by His Gospel, our Saviour brought to light. Before Him, they might be darkly guessed at by a few good and wise men: now they are known for certain facts by every child in a Christian country. Can you, dare you, pretend for a moment, that the certain knowledge of these things makes no difference to you? Can you, dare you say, you have any excuse for running after wild and low pleasures, in order to drown the cares and sorrows of the world, now that your Maker has made known to you a place of eternal comfort and recompense? Can you, dare you plead, when vexed and disappointed, that you "do well to be angry, even unto death," now that your eyes are divinely opened, and you have it in your power, if you will, to look on, over a very few years, to a place where [d]there will be no sorrow, nor crying, and where "God shall wipe away all tears from your eyes?"

But Jesus Christ brought also to light the doctrine of eternal death: the chief evil, as well as the chief good. They who live within reach of His Gospel are inexcusable if they do not know how grievously they and all mankind are fallen from that righteousness in which God created them; if they do not think much of the danger they are in, lest they lose their souls for ever and ever. "[e] The wicked shall be turned into hell, and all the people that forget God." Surely, however painful it may be, it must be good for a man to know this. Having been once informed of it by our Saviour, we cannot be as if we had never heard of it.

If, indeed, no more had been revealed to man,

[d] Rev. xxi. 4.   [e] Ps. ix. 17.

than that there is a portion in heaven provided for him by God Almighty, but that he, through sin, is in great danger of missing that happiness, and falling into a place where "their worm dieth not, and the fire is not quenched:" if God had only made known to us our condition, without distinctly telling us how it may be bettered, something might have been said for spiritual doubtfulness and despondency, though nothing at all for wilful sin and disobedience. But, in His infinite and unspeakable mercy, He has told us much more than this: He has not only set life and death clearly before us, but has said distinctly, "Choose life," and has taught us how to do so effectually. This is, emphatically, the Gospel of Christ: namely, the way, revealed by Him from heaven, by which lost and undone sinners may return, if they will, to their heavenly Father; may put off their sin, and save their souls alive. All which our Lord has fully revealed to us, by instructing us in God Almighty's method of dealing with us by His Son and Spirit.

First, whereas all mankind were guilty, before God, of deadly sin, all had sinned, and come short of His glory; He has revealed to us, in His Son Christ Jesus, the only Name by which it is possible for a sinner to obtain forgiveness of the past. The Son of Man has been lifted up in our sight, that whosoever believeth in Him should not perish, but have everlasting life. The Son, which is the Word of God, begotten from everlasting of the Father, Very and eternal God, of one Substance with the Father; He has taken our nature upon Him, has suffered what we deserved, and has purchased for us what we never can deserve; pardon and favour from a just and holy God.

Will any man say, "These are great and high matters: they may be true, but I do not understand them, and why should I trouble myself about them?" If there be any such person, I can only answer him by another question. Suppose you were a drowning man, and your best friend came in sight, endangering his own life to help you, and shewing how you might make sure of deliverance, if you would only look, and try to move, towards him with a steady confidence in what he told you. Would that be "no concern of yours?" Would you refuse all attention to him, because you could not exactly make out all that he was saying and doing on your behalf?

Yet, if we are Christians at all, we must believe that this is but a faint representation of the mercy made known to us on the Cross, and our great need of it. We must believe, that Jesus Christ is now and evermore our Saviour; that He has bought us with His own Blood, to be His, both soul and body, for ever; and, if we have any sense at all of gratitude for unutterable love, or any fear at all of the unutterable misery, which that love, slighted, is sure to bring after it, we must think ourselves more concerned in this, than we can possibly be in any thing else: we must see, that it is no high matter, fit for scholars only to consider, but plain common sense and common gratitude, which tells us, that Christ having "[f] died for all," we must not henceforth live unto ourselves, but unto Him Who died for us, and rose again.

[f] 2 Cor. v. 14, 15.

And how are we to live to, or for Him? In the same sort of way, as when a dutiful child is said to live to, or for his parent, or an affectionate wife to, or for her husband, by looking to Him habitually and continually, and making it the business of our life to please Him.

But how is this possible to be done, considering the frail bodies we have, the corrupt world we live in, and the bad habits, most contrary to His will, which too many of us are got into? These are sad and true considerations; and yet it *is* possible for us to please God; for hear the other part of the witness of His Son, the good tidings which He brought from heaven. "I will pray the Father, and He shall give you another Comforter, that He may abide with you for ever: even the Spirit of Truth."

The Holy Ghost, Who is Very and eternal God, of one Substance with the Father, proceeding from the Father and the Son, He is ever present with Christians, strengthening them, in the absence of their Redeemer, to walk, by faith in Him, so as to please God. He is ready with His helping hand, to lift our thoughts above earthly things, and fix them on the Son of God, Who ought to be all in all to us. He is ready to bless our prayers and Communions, our good and humble thoughts and purposes, by making us gradually purer and purer, more and more fit to be received into heaven.

If any one can be found who is careless about these blessings, (and it must be with shame acknowledged, that a great many seem as if they never had "heard whether there be any Holy Ghost,") they must be careless of all divine things; they do not mind whether they are saved or lost: but those who think on this doctrine at all, must allow, that it supplies all a Christian need know, all the help he need ask. Whether he be rich or poor, learned or ignorant, the assistance of this Holy Spirit may be obtained by him, on sincerely praying for it. And when men once know this, one is as capable as another of perceiving, what of course must be his own duty. The simplest may understand as clearly as the wisest, that the nearer God's Spirit comes to him, to help him in well-doing, the more shameful and intolerable is his conduct, if he go on still in his sins.

Such is the witness of Jesus Christ, of which He was speaking to Nicodemus, when He said, men would not receive it, though made known to them on the most certain of all evidence. "We speak that We do know, and testify that We have seen, and ye receive not Our witness."

You have heard the substance of what was spoken, that is, of the Gospel of our Lord and Saviour; and have seen how very nearly the whole of it concerns every one of us. Observe now, who those are that speak, and judge whether it can be safe to disregard them.

The Gospel, by which God speaks to us Christians, was not, like former messages, entrusted to prophets and Angels only: no, not to the highest Archangel in heaven. But "g God, Who at sundry times and in divers manners spake in times past unto the fathers by the prophets, hath in these last days spoken unto us by His Son;" His only Begotten, One with Himself in Nature and in Glory. He did not only come

g Heb. i. 1.

among us, in His good time, but actually became one of us; "was made Man;" condescended to all our innocent infirmities; to thirst and hunger; to weariness and painfulness; to shame and sorrow; to wounds and death; and all this, though He was continually in the habit of working the most astonishing miracles, enlightening the blind, cleansing the lepers, and raising the dead to life. It is no great thing surely that we ask, when we entreat you, for your souls' sake, not to turn a deaf ear to a message thus recommended to you: when we beg you to believe that, to prove which, Christ rose from the dead; and to have some care of those souls, to save which, He came down from heaven.

Again, when the Son of God, having ended all His humiliation, was to return to the Right Hand of His Father; when He was to take to Him His great power, and rule over the world and the Church, He did not trust us to His Apostles only, nor to any of the Angels in heaven, but He sent to us the Holy Ghost the Comforter, to be, in His stead, God's witness of eternal things. That gracious and condescending Spirit has ever since, night and day, in all corners of the Christian world, been endeavouring to turn the hearts of men, and prevail on them to regard the things which belong unto their peace; first, by the mighty works and wonderful prophecies of the Apostles and early Christians; and, in all following times, by the godly motions which He puts into men's minds, when they rightly use the Scriptures and the Sacraments; by the good examples which He raises up, and the holy lessons which He teaches, in the Church.

Do not imagine it can be a light thing, an excusable oversight, to slight the witness of the Spirit. He bears long with us; but He will "not always strive with man." The greater and more continual His condescension now, so much the more frightful and hopeless, be sure, will their sentence prove at last, who shall be found to have received such unspeakable grace in vain.

Yet our Saviour gives us to understand, that such, too commonly, would be the case: "We speak that We do know, and testify that We have seen, and ye receive not Our witness." So it was in our Saviour's days, and so, too often, it is now. The Holy, Blessed, and Glorious Trinity, Three Persons and One God, comes down, as it were, from heaven, with all His glorious attributes, to bear witness of the way of salvation, and men refuse to receive His witness; to be redeemed, renewed, saved by Him.

This is often, perhaps most often, done as a mere matter of course. Men take, as it were, their full swing of the world, indulge themselves without scruple in every passion of their corrupt hearts, and never so much as ask themselves why. When you do get them to think a little of religion, especially when they are put in mind, as on this day, of the Catholic Faith, without which they cannot be saved, namely, that they "worship One God in Trinity, and Trinity in Unity:" I say, when inconsiderate persons are put in mind of these things, they are apt to say, "It is all a mystery, a secret too high for us; it may be very well for people of learning and leisure, but we cannot understand it, and therefore we have nothing to do with it."

And it is very true, that you cannot understand how those Divine Persons, Father, Son, and Holy Ghost, should be Three, yet One God. You cannot conceive how it should be so: but then the most learned and leisurely person in the world cannot conceive it any better. "[h]Canst thou by searching find out God? canst thou find out the Almighty unto perfection?" This question of Job may be asked of one man as well as of another, and must receive from all the same answer: "[i]It is as high as heaven: what canst thou do? it is deeper than hell: what canst thou know?"

If, then, your not understanding God's Nature is a reason for your not thinking about it, it is equally a reason to every other man in the world; and all piety, all goodness, towards God, may as well be let alone together.

But the plain truth is, our not understanding the doctrine of Three Persons in One God is not the smallest reason whatever, why we should leave it out of our minds, nor the smallest difficulty whatever, in the way of acting on it.

This may be made plain by a familiar instance. Take that which S. Paul has referred to, and of which many, no doubt, have thought more or less: "That which thou sowest is not quickened, except it die." We put the seed into the ground, dry, dead, and hard as it seems to be, and a fresh living plant springs out of it. Can we at all understand this? Do we know how it takes place? Yet we do not account our ignorance a reason, why we should leave off tilling the earth. Why, then, should the like igno-

[h] Job xi. 7.   [i] Ib. 8.

rance, with regard to the manner in which the Three Divine Persons are One only, ever-glorious God; why should our not understanding this be any objection to our religiously remembering it?

Men know not, as the wise man says, how the bones do grow in the womb of her which is with child; but they do not think themselves the less bound to love and honour the mother that gave them birth.

Take it, therefore, for a certain truth, that the Catholic Faith, which you have heard to-day, of Three Persons in One God, to be worshipped, served, and obeyed in all things, this Faith is necessary to the salvation of all alike, rich and poor, learned and unlearned, within whose reach God's providence has set it.

But observe: it must be believed *faithfully*. You must depend on the Son of God as your Redeemer; you must welcome the Holy Spirit as your Comforter, with the same kind of constant feeling wherewith you depend on, and welcome, those whom you know to be your nearest and dearest friends. This you cannot sincerely do, as long as you wilfully continue in any thing that you know to be sin; for so long the thought of their being present, and watching your very heart, will make you uneasy.

Consider, however, before it be too late, what it must be to reject their witness, or (what comes, in the end, to much the same) to turn carelessly away from it. After all, you must die; and when you die, what pardon, what consolation can you hope for, if you have refused to let your Saviour plead for you to His Father, and hardened your hearts against the Holy Ghost, the Comforter?

SERMON XXXVI.

THE SECRET OF THE LORD.

TRINITY SUNDAY.

Ps. xxv. 13.

"The secret of the Lord is among them that fear Him: and He will shew them His covenant."

To tell a person our secrets, is generally considered to be the greatest token of entire friendship towards him. It shews that we have entire dependence upon him, and that we quite reckon on his feeling for us, and doing as we would wish him. It is the particular mark of friendship, the difference between servants and friends: as our Lord Himself pointed out to His disciples. "Henceforth," said He, "[a] I call you not servants, for the servant knoweth not what his Lord doeth: but I have called you *friends;* for all things that I have heard of My Father, I have made known unto you." And we know how naturally pleased we are, to be entrusted with the secrets of those above us; to have our elders and betters explaining to us what they mean to do, and why. It is a silent sort of praise, which almost every person feels glad to receive. We naturally think, that when people do so, they have confidence in us, both in our wisdom and in our honesty: and this of course pleases all men.

[a] S. John xv. 15.

All too are gratified with finding or imagining that they know something which others do not know; that they can explain what others cannot; that they are trusted while others are kept at a distance.

Now, we may reverently say, Almighty God has *His* secrets. Wonderful and mysterious truths and doings, the full and deep meaning of which not even the highest of His creatures can entirely understand. For S. Peter says[b], concerning the great truths of the Gospel, that even the "Angels desire to stoop down and look into them." Even those glorious spirits know less than they desire to know, of the great love of God in creating, redeeming, regenerating us. Much more of course must fallen man, here in his weak and low condition, be distant from the full knowledge of God's ways. But as He in His mercy reveals to those blessed ones continually more and more of what He is about, so there are certain persons among men whom He favours in the same way, trusting them, and telling them His secrets. Who, it may be asked, are those honoured and happy persons? We may judge a little who are likely to be so, by considering what sort of people among our fellow-creatures we are most apt to entrust with our own secrets. The great thing of all is *Love*. If we see any one deeply attached to us, if we have no doubt that he feels for us in every thing, we are presently inclined to trust him. We know then that he will feel for us, that he will attend earnestly to what we tell him, and will think earnestly of it afterwards; that he will put himself in our place, and really endeavour to judge the best he can for us, not

[b] 1 S. Pet. i. 12.

being carried away by any interest or passion of his own. This is what we know a person will feel if he truly loves us, and therefore to such an one we willingly tell our secrets; hoping, if we get nothing more by doing so, at least to obtain that relief, which goes along with a mere opening of a full heart.

But then is love the only thing we look for in a person, fit to be told of our secrets? Clearly not: for we do not trust children with them, nor other people who are as simple as children, though they love us never so well. Besides love, there must be, in a trustworthy person, a respect and reverence for ourselves, and for what we tell him, which will prevent his dealing lightly with it, or speaking of it rashly where he ought not. When people neglect this, and speak carelessly of all matters to any body who seems good-natured and friendly, they can hardly expect their secrets to be kept, and no one pities them, when trouble comes on them by those secrets being known. Thus you see that a mixture of love and something like fear is the temper which best prepares a man to be trusted with his neighbour's secrets. And the Scripture every where seems to teach, that it is much the same kind of character which makes a man fit to be entrusted with heavenly mysteries, with the secrets of God Almighty. "The secret of the Lord is among them that fear Him." "ᶜTo this man will I look, even to him that is poor and of a contrite spirit, and *trembleth at My word.*" "ᵈThou hast hid these things from the wise and prudent, and hast revealed them unto *babes.*" Those who approach God with a deep reverence, with an

ᶜ Isa. lxvi. 2.   ᵈ S. Matt. xi. 25.

earnest desire to please Him, and with a dread of offending Him; those are the persons, to whom He will, by degrees, reveal Himself more and more. He will open their eyes, that they may understand "ᵉwondrous things out of His law." It is not much learning nor cleverness, nor being quick and ready to recollect the *words* of Scripture, which enables men to think rightly of such aweful mysteries as this of to-day: but it is devotion and seriousness of heart. The Most Holy Trinity, Father, Son, and Holy Ghost, Three Persons, One God, reveals Himself in ways of His own, ways which no tongue can tell, no heart imagine, to the humble and meek, the contented and self-denying. Just such in the Old Testament are those, whom we find the Almighty favouring with especial knowledge of His will and purposes.

They were such as Noah, just and perfect, and walking with God: to whom accordingly God declared His purpose of sending a flood upon the earth. Or they were such as Abraham, walking by faith not by sight, counting not his own son too dear to offer up when God commanded; commanding his children and his household after him to keep the way of the Lord: whom consequently God honoured with the title of His friend, and concerning whom He said, "'Shall I hide from Abraham that thing which I do?" Or again, those to whom God loves to reveal Himself are, like Moses, very tender spirited and afraid of sin: with whom " God spake face to face, as a man talketh with his friend:" or they are like the Apostles, who in faith and fear followed Christ, giving up all that they had, and so by degrees He

ᵉ Ps. cxix. 18.   ᶠ Gen. xviii. 17.

shewed them all the hidden and wonderful things of His kingdom.

All these are witnesses, how our Lord from the beginning kept to the rule which He afterwards laid down in the Gospel: "[g]If any man will do His will, he shall know of the doctrine, whether it be of God, or whether I speak of Myself." "He that hath ears to hear," ears opened by sincere obedience and love, of him only, Christ said, "let him hear." The rest may answer well, and seem to know much, but they cannot really understand, they cannot really have the mind of Christ.

So again, you may observe, the Gospel tells us more of the heavenly secrets than the law does, for this very reason, because it brings men nearer to Christ. Grace and Truth go together: where God requires most entire love and fear of Himself, there He offers to shew Himself most openly. Hear our Saviour's own words. "Henceforth, I call you not servants, for the servant knoweth not what his Lord doeth: but I have called you friends: for all things that I have heard of My Father I have made known unto you." The offer is most gracious: to reveal to us the whole counsel of God: to keep back nothing; but to make known whatsoever the Son had heard of the Father. But see on what it depends, To have the benefit of it, we must be *friends* of our Saviour: He speaks the word Himself: "[h]Ye are My friends, if ye do whatsoever I command you." To know our Lord's secrets we must be His friends, and to be His friends, we must keep His commandments. His secret "is with them that fear Him."

[g] S. John vii. 17.   [h] Ib. xv. 14.

We may see how it is with children when they say the catechism. Without doubt they answer at once on points, which the wisest men of old, heathen and Jews, knew nothing about. They acknowledge the Most Holy Trinity, the Incarnation of Christ, the creation and fall of man, the Redemption of the world by the Death of the Son of God, the sanctification of the souls of Christians by His Holy Spirit dwelling in our hearts, the regenerating power of Holy Baptism, the Presence of Christ's Body and Blood in the Holy Communion. All these mysteries Christian children acknowledge, as often as they repeat the catechism: and who shall deny that if they be good children, they acknowledge them in true faith, however little they may seem to understand them?

At all events, we are quite sure of this, that if any such child be taken away, by God's merciful providence, without having broken God's seal and forfeited His baptismal blessing, it will presently know great things, greater than the wisest and most enlightened on earth. Such a child will depart and be with Christ in paradise. Such a child will know what the death of a Christian is, and what power in the Cross of Christ to support His little ones through that dark valley. Such will know, and will not only imagine, what such promises as these mean, "[i]He shall feed His flock like a shepherd, He shall gather the lambs with His arms, and carry them in his bosom:" and again, "Suffer the little children to come unto Me, and forbid them not: for of such is the kingdom of heaven." These, and many more sweet and aweful secrets are doubtless made known to the little

[i] Isa. xl. 11.

ones of Jesus Christ, as soon as they are taken out of this world. Being absent from the body and present with the Lord, they see His face with joy: and they know for certain, what it should seem the holiest can hardly know on earth, till near his end, that they personally shall be saved for ever; that they cannot possibly fall away. While parents and friends perhaps are mourning round their graves, and missing their innocent and happy looks, they are admitted in a moment, at once (we may believe), to such a knowledge of God's secrets as shall wipe away all tears from their eyes for ever. Thus it is with children: and so too with all who live humble and child-like before God, and do not cast away the treasure of their Baptism. However simple and ignorant they might seem here, how much soever they might want words or clear ways of thinking on what they believed, " the secret of the Lord is with them," all the while, and will be with them after death in a yet more blessed and unspeakable way.

One token of this great mercy, to be shewn after death to such as fear God, is the wonderful way, in which even now He guides them to understand His providence, and their own duty. It is astonishing how much even very simple persons, who have gone on steadily in the way of goodness, seem to know of the secret meaning of what happens to themselves and others. Circumstances which ordinary people see nothing at all in, they lay up like the blessed Virgin Mary; they keep and ponder them in their hearts: and so they come to be silently prepared, no one knows how, for trials and changes, which otherwise might be far too severe for them.

More especially with regard to their own duty, God's Holy Spirit will never forsake any exact conscientious humble Christian, who seeks Him heartily in prayer and obedience, but He will always be secretly at hand to guide such a one in the most difficult cases, so that he shall not fall into sinful error, "If any man will do His will," if he have made up his mind in all things, little and great, to do and suffer, as he knows God would have him, God will in time reveal to him the matters, of which as yet he may seem doubtful; or if not, he may have reasonable hope that the doubt is of no great consequence. This is the kind of anchor, sure and stedfast, for well-meaning people in times of doubt and perplexity. As e.g. in the case of the greatest of the perplexities of these latter times, not knowing for certain which is God's true Church. It was the case in our Lord's own time: there must have been a doubt among good Jews, when they first heard of the Blessed Jesus and His Apostles, how far they could join with Him, without forsaking the temple and the law of Moses. He therefore tells them the way out of this doubt. "Do His will, and you shall know of My teaching:" Serve Him truly, with a good mind and heart, in all things, and you will soon find that you are not far from the kingdom of God. Thus was fulfilled in our Lord's time the latter part of the promise in the text: they that fear the Lord; "He will shew them His covenant." He will not only "lead them in the right way" in matters concerning their daily conduct, but will also silently instruct them in matters of belief and rules of Church communion, so that errors, even deadly in themselves, shall not prove deadly to them: the sting of them shall be taken out by His overflowing grace: and bye and bye, when the darkness of earth is past, He will bring them to the full light, and they shall behold His righteousness.

Let no person's heart fail, because he does not see all this with his eyes. Let us not say, how should this be? Good people are not always knowing even in religious matters; and certainly knowing people are very far from being always good. This indeed is too true: but we must bear in mind that the knowledge promised in the Scriptures is an inward, secret, silent knowledge, and that to which it is promised is an inward, secret, silent disposition of the heart; neither are such as men can positively take notice of. They that are good, shall know of the doctrine, but we cannot say quite for certain who are good: we know not what secret unrepented sin may be yet lurking in a man's conscience, and causing his inward sight of holy truth to be false and dim, perhaps without his at all suspecting it himself: or his own heart may justly smite him, without others at all knowing of it; and so, for all his good report, he may be a very insufficient judge of divine things.

Again, they that are really good shall "know indeed of the doctrine." That is promised: but it is not promised that they shall be able to give an account of their knowledge; it is not promised that they shall have plenty of words, and a clear way of putting them together: they may truly know, yet not as yet be distinctly aware of their own knowledge: just as any little child knows that its parents are its best friends, and turns to them as a matter of course in its troubles: yet it never did nor could *say* to itself, "my parents are my best friends." So, whoever receives from the Church, the Creed, the Lord's prayer, and the ten commandments; and believes the Creed heartily, says the Lord's prayer devoutly, and practises the commandments diligently; that man has in him a great deal more knowledge than he himself is aware of: the whole "[k]law of his God is in his heart, and his goings shall not slide." Such persons have *that* in them, which by God's mercy will teach them the right way, when new difficulties come on, when they are called on to do anything, or to give advice to any one, suddenly. The Spirit which Christ promised is in them, to teach them and guide them into all truth. He will never leave them nor forsake them. They will never be left destitute of His aid, be the call never so sudden.

Would we then have a quiet heart, and be at rest in our faith and practice? Would we be free from distressing doubt? Would we have the best security, that can be had in this life, against false and wrong notions of holy Truth? Let us keep steadily, in thought, word and action, to that which we already know to *be* truth: humbly commit beforehand all we say and think about holy things to Him Who came down at Pentecost to sanctify God's chosen people: be very careful what we say about the things of God, and to whom we say it. Let us not think that what we say is of course right, because it sounds serious, and relates to some sacred subject. "Set a watch before your mouth, and keep the door of your lips:" "[l]be not rash with your mouth, and let not

[k] Ps. xxxvii. 32.   [l] Eccl. v. 2.

your heart be hasty to utter anything before God." Above all things, let us beware of getting into a way of saying what we do not mean, of uttering devout words as a matter of course, saying, "Lord, Lord," while we do not the things which He commands. "ᵐ Fear God and keep His commandments, for this is" the whole comfort, as well as "the whole duty of man."

^m Eccles. xii. 13.

SERMON XXXVII.

HEAVEN OPENED.

TRINITY SUNDAY.

Rev. iv. 1.

"*I looked, and behold a door was opened in Heaven.*"

WHEN we were little children, and first began to look upwards and around us, and wonder at the meaning of what we saw, I suppose one of our first thoughts was, to imagine what might be in the infinite deep of the blue sky, and to wish that we had eyes to see beyond it. We naturally asked ourselves, and others, who and what there is in that vast space, where our sight loses itself as soon as we begin to gaze. Our earliest notion indeed, when we were quite infants, was that we could even touch the firmament: thus little children will sometimes reach after the moon, and cry to have it given them; and it is only by slow degrees that we learn how very far distant we are from those heavenly things. By degrees only do we learn how conpletely sin has separated between us and our God: what a deep gulph is fixed between the glorious and happy place, and such as we were at our birth. At first we feel as if we could touch it: it seems to us no such very hard thing to be good and to please God. Bye and bye sad and shameful experience convinces us more and more that we were born in sin, the children of wrath: we feel more and more our distance from heaven, and long more and more to have the door opened, and look in and see who is there, how they are employed, and what hope there is of our joining them.

By nature the door of heaven is shut against us, because we are sinners, and nothing unclean can enter there. We cannot even look in, for our very looks are defiled and partake of sin. Our thoughts and imaginations grovel on the earth: they have no wings to mount up so high. Yet who can be quite contented with what he sees and experiences here? Which of us, in his better moments at least, has not longed for something better? Who has not now and then felt the longings of his childish days returning upon him, and wished that he might see heaven opened, and obtain some glimpse of a more perfect happiness than any which he has yet known? Surely those plaintive verses of the Psalm do but express what passes, from time to time, in every soul of man. "[a] Oh that I had wings like a dove; for then would I flee away, and be at rest. Lo then would I get me away far off and remain in the wilderness." And then the thought comes grievously over us, "It might be so, were it not for our many sins, and for the deep corruption which hangs about us; but now we are bowed down more or less by this body of death, who shall raise us up? Who can untie our chains, which in too many parts of our behaviour we have been wilfully forging for ourselves?"

To these sad fears and misgivings, whether of the natural unregenerate man, or of one who has sinned

[a] Ps. lv. 6, 7.

against grace and is trying to repent, God gives us in His Holy Gospel a very blessed yet awful answer. While we go about, thus weary and heavy laden, let us, though our eyes fail in the endeavour, let us still keep looking upwards, and in our measure we shall receive the same mercy, which Christ bestowed on His own beloved disciple. A door will be opened to us in heaven, that we may see something of the great unspeakable wonders of that glorious and happy place. Nay, this door has been opened to us: it stands continually open: it is not shut night nor day: if we had tried steadily to lead Christian lives, we should not need but to shut our eyes, and fall on our knees, and say the Lord's prayer, or use any other good and holy act of devotion, with a devout and attentive heart, and presently some one or more of the invisible things would be more or less brought before us, some of the wonders which shall hereafter be, or which now are, but out of sight, would be made present to us, for our warning or our comfort, or both.

To believing and penitent eyes, I say, the Gospel opens the door of heaven, and when they raise their eyes that way, and humbly look in, what is it they see?

The first look shews them Almighty God on His throne; as the Evangelist goes on to describe it: "Behold a throne was set in heaven, and One sat on the throne." God's Holy Spirit helps those who try to muse on Him in earnest: helps them to forget for a while those ordinary things which they see, and to fix their minds on Him Who is Invisible: Whom no man hath seen, nor can see, Who yet is close to each of us at every moment: Who is above all, yet through all, and in all. We behold Him with the eye of faith sitting on His throne in heaven, surveying and ordering all the things which He hath made, and we feel that, while He thus seeth all things, His Countenance is towards us individually, watching what we say, do, or think, as exactly as if there were no being besides for Him to regard. We tremble before His Almightiness, we are dazzled by His unspeakable light and purity, we say in the deep of our hearts, as one said of old, "Who can stand before this holy Lord God?" Yet, while our hearts are thus overwhelmed with awe, He helps us, in proportion to our true devotion and penitence, to rejoice in the midst of our trembling: to rejoice and give thanks for "His Name, which is great, wonderful and holy:" to be comforted in our sorrow and fear, and even amid the reproofs of our conscience, by the feeling that the great Father of all has not quite hid His face from us. He permits us to feel that we are not left alone in the world, not left to be the sport of blind chance or evil spirits: that He is with us, and offers to hold us with His Right Hand, if we will but cling to it. He yet allows us to be in some sort aware of His Presence, to call Him, however unworthily, by the gracious name of Father, to turn ourselves, however imperfectly, towards Him in all our troubles and perplexities.

This is what He vouchsafes to shew us on our first look into the door of heaven. Now let us look again, beseeching Him to fill our hearts with His glory and His greatness, that we may not look altogether unworthily. As the first look into heaven shews us One God sitting upon His throne, so the second, if so it please Him, may shew us in that One God, the Three Divine Persons, Father, Son, and Holy Ghost; distinct as Persons, yet in Nature undivided; of one Substance Power and Eternity, yet so differing from one another, as that " the Father," the first Person, " is of none, neither made, nor created, nor begotten; the Son is of the Father alone, not made, nor created, but begotten: the Holy Ghost is of the Father and of the Son, neither made, nor created, nor begotten, but proceeding." This most Holy Trinity, we understand by faith to be reigning evermore in heaven, and evermore present in all the works of God. The manner how, none can understand, not the wisest: but the truth and certainty, that so it is, all may believe, even the simplest: and great indeed, and unspeakable is the help and comfort which the faithful humble Christian derives from the contemplation and worship of this adorable Trinity. To an unbeliever or a scoffer, or to a mere worldly person, it cannot be explained: on such matters the most charitable way is to say as little as possible to such men: but the less men speak of them the more they will naturally think: for this doctrine of the Holy Trinity is like the secret of some great king, which, being made known by special favour to some holy and humble servant of his, fills that servant's heart, so that he cannot get it out of his recollection: and the less he is permitted to speak of it, the more he thinks of it, night and day. And the thought has a special power to keep him out of mischief: he considers with himself, that this Blessed Trinity is not only reigning in heaven, but also, by the grace of Holy Baptism, abiding in each one of our hearts. God has trusted us with this aweful secret: if we are not quite hardened, surely we must feel that we never can do enough to acknowledge this miraculous loving-kindness; we must feel that the Holy Trinity, abiding in us, and known to be so, is a seal and safeguard against all the enemies of our souls: according to the saying of the wise man: "[b] The Name of the Lord is a strong tower; the righteous runneth into it, and is safe."

As the first look into the open door of heaven shewed us the One God sitting on His throne, and the second, the Holy, Blessed, and Glorious Trinity of Persons, so the third may reveal to the eye of faith the Holy Manhood and Humanity of Jesus Christ, taken into God, and exalted to the Father's Right Hand. For thus we read in the continuation of S. John's vision: "I beheld, and lo, in the midst of the throne stood a Lamb, as it had been slain." It was, I suppose, the same sight as appeared to the blessed S. Stephen, when he was in the act of his martyrdom: "heaven opened, and Jesus the Son of Man standing on the Right Hand of God." What these great saints and martyrs saw thus openly in this vision, God in His great mercy permits all humble and penitent Christians to see by faith, when they pray to Him attentively. Only kneel down with a true heart, either in Church or at home, and say the good prayers which you have learned from those who are set over you, especially at the end, when you say, "Through Jesus Christ our Lord," and He permits you to look in, as it were, at the door of heaven, and

[b] Prov. xviii. 10.

see the great High Priest, Jesus Christ the Son of God, ever living to make intercession for you. To this you may turn, with this you may comfort yourself, on this you may depend, when your heart is in heaviness. Here, in this lower and outer world, you may have no place to flee unto; you may feel as if no man cared for your soul. But there is One within the veil, Who knows all and cares for all. He can be touched with a feeling of your infirmities, for He was Himself made in all points like as you are, sin only excepted. Only, if you would preserve and improve this unspeakable comfort, take care that you pray in faith, nothing wavering: take care and be not double-minded, but resolve with your whole heart that you will not again wilfully offend Him.

And as a great earnest and encouragement to the devout worshippers of Jesus Christ, behold what He allows us to see in the next look, which we are to-day invited to direct within the everlasting gates. The great High Priest Himself is not the only child of Adam Whom we by faith may behold in heaven: but with Him, and beneath Him, and wholly, and only for Him, we see those who are called His saints: the best, and most favoured, and most severely tried, of those who had served Him here on earth: in some sense or other, the Scripture represents them as even now rejoicing with Him in heaven. For S. John saw "round about the throne four and twenty seats, and upon the seats four and twenty Elders sitting, clothed in white raiment, and on their heads crowns of gold." These four and twenty are not Angels, for they were heard praising our Lord as follows, " Thou wast slain, and hast redeemed us to God by Thy

Blood." They are therefore holy souls, redeemed by Christ's Blood: and the number of twentyfour seems to signify that they are the saints first of the Jewish, and afterwards of the Christian Church: the first twelve answering to the twelve tribes, the second to the twelve Apostles. All these, brethren of our own, and naturally and originally weak and sinful as we are, we may now think of as making part of the blessed company of heaven, and joining with the Holy Church throughout all the world in most high praise and honour, offered day and night to the Father, the Son, and the Holy Ghost. Our Church instructs us so to think of the saints in heaven, in the hymn called the Te Deum, which we use every day in the morning service. "The glorious company of the Apostles, the goodly fellowship of the prophets, the noble army of martyrs, praise" and acknowledge the Three Persons in One Godhead: "the Father, of an infinite Majesty; His honourable, true, and only Son; also the Holy Ghost, the Comforter."

And this goes on day and night, they are never weary of their holy and happy work. With them it is not as with the best of men on earth, to have heaven's door opened, and see into those blissful abodes, now and then only, by rare glimpses, seldom coming and soon gone; but those favoured spirits have no door between them and the glory of their God and Saviour; they behold Him with open face, in His Light they see light, they are satisfied with the plenteousness of His house, and He gives them "drink of His pleasures as out of a river;" out of the well of life, which can never fail.

These are the great and blessed things which Almighty God permits us dimly to behold, whenever by devout meditation we are enabled to look in for a moment at the door which His Son has opened for us in heaven: the Lord of all sitting on His throne; the Holy Blessed and Glorious Trinity, Father, Son, and Holy Ghost: Jesus Christ, the Son of God Incarnate, as a Lamb, which had been slain, standing "at His Father's Right Hand to succour all them that suffer for Him;" and round about Him the chief of His saints, the first fruits of His redeemed. All this and more He permits and invites us to behold, with our mind's eye, in the times of solemn prayer, and at all times when we are able and willing to give ourselves up to such high and holy thoughts.

Why is it that we too commonly find so little in ourselves to answer to this gracious invitation? It would seem as if we had but to shut our eyes to the world, and this glorious Vision would presently appear; being, as it is, always close to every one of us, had we but sight to behold it. But in the first place, we are unwilling to shut our eyes; too generally there is something or other here, to which we so cling that we will not give up the sight of it, no, not for those sights which make the saints blessed in heaven. And next, when we are at length brought to make such an endeavour, when we do in earnest try to think only of heaven, we find too surely the visions of this world still haunting us: our works, our diversions, our cares, our friends, our companions, keep flitting across our minds, like so many earthly clouds, and will not leave us alone, to meditate peaceably on those joys and glories. In a word we must be pure in heart, in order to see God. We must labour and pray continually to be disengaged, in heart at least, from these lower matters, if we would taste and see how gracious the Lord is, and how good and blessed a thing to be always in His Presence. "[c]Every man that hath this hope in him, purifieth himself, even as He is pure." Without such endeavours, real, hearty, and persevering, any pleasure we may seem to feel in meditating on God and on everlasting joy, will prove but a dangerous dream, perhaps even a snare of the Evil one. This way, therefore, let all our care be turned; to keep our hearts and fancies pure, that when we have leisure we may be free to look in at the door of heaven; and when our earthly work ceases, we may turn ourselves of course that way, and never turn back again.

Now to the Holy Blessed and Glorious Trinity &c.

[c] 1 S. John iii. 3.

SERMON XXXVIII.

THE ANGELIC HYMN, HOLY, HOLY, HOLY, OUR COMMUNION HYMN.

TRINITY SUNDAY.

Isa. vi. 3.

"One cried unto another, and said, Holy, Holy, Holy, is the Lord of hosts: the whole earth is full of His glory."

About seven hundred years before our Lord came down among men, there was, as is supposed, a silence of prophecy for a time, on account of the sin of king Uzziah, who had intruded on the priest's office. God being angry withdrew Himself, and made no answer to the inquiries of His people: even as He had withdrawn Himself from Saul. But when Uzziah died, it pleased Him to break that silence: and in a very wonderful way. He chose Isaiah to be His prophet, and called him by a glorious and aweful vision. He " saw the Lord sitting on a throne, high and lifted up:" as it were a great King, Who reigneth for ever, preparing to judge His people. His train, His glory, filled the temple: as when He had been used to appear to Moses or to Solomon, in brightness that could scarcely be endured. Above it stood the Seraphim, the bright and burning Angels, all on fire with divine love: " each one had six wings: with one pair he covered his face, and with one pair he covered his feet, and with one pair he did fly:" teaching us, perhaps, among other things, with what intense fear and awe we ought to come near the great God of heaven and earth, and how ready we should keep ourselves to hasten wheresoever He may command. And one of these blessed beings kept on crying to another, and saying, "Holy, Holy, Holy, is the Lord of hosts: the whole earth is full of His glory." Their employment was to keep up continually their hymn of praise to the Most High: the one side taking it up when the other ceased; and so answering one another, and keeping up the strain day and night: somewhat in the same way, as when the Psalms are sung or said by course in our churches: which custom Isaiah was probably used to in the temple. And now both he and we after him have the comfort of knowing, that when we are so employed, we are for the time companions of the Angels in heaven: praising God as they do by alternate chanting of holy words: yea, often, even in the very same words which they use: "Holy, Holy, Holy, is the Lord of hosts: the whole earth is full of His glory." For that divine verse is both in our daily service, and also our service for the Holy Communion. It is in our daily service, as it is a part of the hymn of S. Ambrose, commonly called the *Te Deum:* "To Thee Cherubin, and Seraphin, continually do cry, Holy, Holy, Holy, Lord God of Sabaoth; heaven and earth are full of the Majesty of Thy glory." It is also in our Communion Service, in the most joyful part of it, when we have been absolved from our sins, and stand up to give thanks to God: "with Angels and Archangels, and with all the company of heaven, we laud and magnify His glorious Name, evermore praising Him and saying, Holy, Holy, Holy, Lord God of hosts, heaven and earth are full of Thy glory." Well may the Church use it as her sacramental hymn, as she has always done, no doubt, since she was a Church: seeing that not only was it taught to the prophet Isaiah in so wonderful a way, but also to the Apostle S. John. When he saw a door opened in heaven, and the Lord sitting on His throne, then also he heard the four beasts, i. e. the Cherubim, joining in the same anthem which Isaiah had heard from the Seraphim. "[a] They rest not day and night, saying, Holy, Holy, Holy, Lord God Almighty: which was, and is, and is to come." Whenever therefore we recite the Te Deum, and more especially whenever we receive the Holy Communion, we have the happiness of knowing that, at that very time, some or all of the blessed company of heaven are reciting the very same words. They do it by course, taking up the words one from another: for so it pleases God that His creatures should praise Him. So we read of His works here on earth, that "[b] one day telleth another, and one night certifieth another:" and again concerning the continual succession of His people: "[c] One generation shall praise Thy works unto another, and declare Thy power."

But whether the song be uttered in heaven or in earth, whether it be Angels or men who sing, whether it be heard by prophets before Christ's Incarnation, or by Apostles after His Ascension into Heaven, still it is the same song, "Holy, Holy, Holy, is the Lord."

[a] Rev. iv. 8.   [b] Ps. xix. 2.   [c] Ib. cxlv. 4.

Holy is the Father of our Lord Jesus Christ, the Fountain of all being in heaven and in earth: Holy is the Only-Begotten Son our Lord Jesus Christ, God of God, Light of Light, Very God of Very God, being of One Substance with the Father: Holy is the Blessed Spirit, the Comforter, proceeding eternally both from the Father and the Son: and these three Holies are One Lord God of Hosts, "which was, and which is, and which is to come."

The hymn is the same, only there is a little difference between the last words of it as they stand in Isaiah, and as we use them in our services now. Isaiah heard the Seraphim sing, "the whole earth is full of His glory:" but as we now recite it, it stands, "heaven and earth are full of Thy glory." Because Isaiah's soul was carried on especially to the time of our Lord's Incarnation and humiliation on earth, but the Church now considers Him as reigning in heaven after His Sufferings. It is the same Saviour, the same salvation, only more complete and more perfect now than it was then.

Now, then, my brethren, on this great and wonderful Day, appointed for especial meditation on the great secret of the Most Holy Trinity, Three Persons in One God; I ask you, by God's help, seriously to consider with me, what a thing it is to be invited continually to take part with saints and Angels in such a hymn as this; what a blessing, if we use it rightly: what a shame and condemnation, if we neglect or abuse it. Suppose that by your own fault you were a friendless wanderer and outcast, turned out of your home, and not knowing where to lay your head: and suppose that in your wanderings you should come suddenly to a place, from which you heard strains of the sweetest and most heavenly music, set to words full of comfort; so that you could not but feel assured in your heart, "Here is the cure of all my miseries: if I can once be admitted here, and allowed to remain, I know I shall be always in peace and in joy:" should you not anxiously look after the entrance into that happy place? Should you not rejoice if you found the door open, and press towards it as eagerly as you dared? And would it not be a blessing, more almost than you could believe, if you heard yourself called by name and invited to come, with an assurance that the music and all the joys of the place were expressly intended for you? Well, this is just our case: your case, my brethren, my case, the case of us all, in respect of that great Angelical hymn. We are outcasts from Paradise, wanderers about the world, unable of ourselves to find any true rest and consolation: and behold, a door is opened in heaven, and we are invited to look in and see things which shall be hereafter, and to hear the song of the saints and Angels, and join in it: we know also in the bottom of our hearts, that thus and thus only can we ever be happy. What will you do? Will you turn away from the gracious voice, the voice of the Gospel, the voice like a trumpet talking with you, the voice which would welcome you to the holy and joyful place? Or will you not rather listen to it with all your ears and all your hearts, and for that purpose stop your ears to all the mean harsh sounds of this earth, and get as near heaven's gate as you can? And when you hear the gracious sound inviting you from within, "Come unto Me, all ye that travail and are heavy laden, and I will refresh you," will you churlishly turn back? Will you not obey it with humble joy and thankfulness? It is true, you feel and own yourselves quite unworthy: how can you help it? You know too well, how sadly your garments are soiled by your long and inexcusable straying in the wilderness of the world: yet trusting in His pardon so mercifully, so largely offered, you may venture in: only taking care to wait at the door long enough for a reasonable hope that the stain and soil has begun really to be worn away by your true penitence. O, venture in: do not depart, with so many, alas! who ought to stay: but do you offer and present yourselves at Christ's Altar to receive the Holy Sacrament of His Body and Blood. There we kneel down, we confess our sins, we bow down our heads to receive Christ's Absolution, pronounced over us by His appointed Minister. He says, "Lift up your hearts:" and we make answer, that "we lift them up unto the Lord." O let us take care that this may be a true answer: let us at least endeavour at that moment to get rid of all vain, trifling and worldly thoughts, and to see with our mind's eye somewhat of that astonishing vision, which He in His favour shewed to Isaiah and to S. John. In heart let us try to behold Him sitting on His throne, and all the host of heaven standing before Him, and let us hearken to them, how they cry continually one to another, " Holy, Holy, Holy is the Lord of hosts: the whole earth is full of His glory." That glorious Angelical hymn is meant by our gracious God to be our hymn also. We are to take part in it: mean and unworthy as we are; He created us, He died for us, and He would have us to praise Him accordingly.

But mark this well, my brethren. The word by which we praise Him is "Holy." We do not repeat three times the title Almighty, or Eternal, or All-wise; or any other of the manifold Perfections of God. But He chooses rather to be called Holy. That is now His title for ever, and His memorial to all generations. O how plainly does this speak to every one of our consciences, and warn us not to draw near with unclean, unprepared, unholy minds! The Angels and saints, who take up this song in heaven, are all of them holy, very holy: they are full of holiness, each according to his measure. He Who knoweth whereof we are made, knows that *we* cannot as yet be like them: yet He expects that we should wish, pray, endeavour to be so: without so much holiness at least as *that*, "[d] no man shall see the Lord." That is the first and principal thing for those who would partake in the song of the Angels, and come worthily to the Holy Communion.

Again, whereas the word "Holy" is three times repeated, it is requisite that the worthy communicant should come in such faith as is implied in that threefold repetition: faith in God the Father, God the Son, God the Holy Ghost, Three Persons and One God. We are not to imagine any difference nor inequality in any of their Divine Perfections: but to offer ourselves up, both our souls and bodies, alike to the Father, to the Son and to the Holy Ghost: humbly hoping and earnestly labouring, that in His good time we may be permitted (like Moses) to see more of this great sight, how the Father and the Son and the Holy Ghost are Three yet One: Three in

[d] Heb. xii. 14.

Person, One in Substance, and in all Divine Perfections. That will be joy indeed; but in the mean time He invites us to live and be saved by hope: and He promises to keep us safe under the seal of the Most Holy Trinity, which He put on us at our Baptism. He accepts our song of praise, though as yet we do not understand it. He allows us to say or sing it after the blessed Angels, as children repeat some holy lesson after grown people, with far less understanding than they, but still with a dutiful and obedient mind : and bye and bye, the deep meaning of our own sayings will dawn upon us. For the present, we must all be content to be ignorant : ignorant, not only in comparison of the Angels, but in comparison also of many of our brethren, who know far more than we do : but what of that? We may take our part, such as it is, in the great angelical hymn, and not grudge our neighbour his part. We may take our assigned portion, be it high or low, of thankful service to God here in this world, and we may add our Amen, said or chanted, to the response of some great congregation : and we need not fear its being lost or drowned, as too insignificant to be heard in such a sea of voices. He will hear it, He will treasure it, He will take account of it at the last Day.

Especially He will observe and set down, whether such as join in His holy assemblies are free from jealousy towards another : whether they praise Him, each in his station, with an unenvious, ungrudging mind. The blessed Angels, we know, do so: they make answer to one another, each in the part which He has assigned them : they know their place and have no desire to change it. When will it be so among us? When shall we see but a single congregation worshipping Him in such perfect charity, that neither the lower and more suffering members repine, nor yet the more comely and honourable be lifted up? Certainly, if ever such a thing might be on this side the grave, it would go a way towards making the Holy Church, what it was always meant to be, a heaven upon earth.

The heavenly company, S. John says, "rest not day and night;" they are never tired of glorifying the Holy Three in One: and we, for our short life here, why should we think it so hard to *continue* honouring God by holy obedience? Why should we be so soon weary of remembering loving and serving Him? Let us, this good day, make one good resolution: that we will never again give way, knowingly, to sloth, inattention, tediousness of spirit. We will not, by our own consent, neglect our part in the great never-ceasing Anthem.

And if it be a lowly part, yet let us believe, that no part of such a service can be really low and mean: since to wait, in the humblest station, on the great God in His temple, is plainly far higher preferment than to be the prime favourite of the greatest earthly king. This is a great point indeed: that we should know in our hearts the dignity of our common calling. This is, I suppose, what S. Paul asked so earnestly for his converts the people of Ephesus: that they might know "the riches of the glory of Christ's inheritance in the saints; and the exceeding greatness of His power to us ward who believe," that they might "ᵉ be able to comprehend with all saints what is

ᵉ Eph. iii. 18, 19.

the breadth, and length, and depth, and height; and to know the love of Christ which passeth knowledge." Could *our* eyes but be opened for one moment to see the high company we are in, and the glorious work we are about, when we are praising God in His Church, surely it would be harder for us to go back to the miserable, contemptible follies which now too easily prevail against us. *We* could not then so lightly pass in a moment from holy things to unholy. *We* should be frightened and ashamed, when the temptation came, to look out for the praise of men, or to favour ourselves in respect of bodily and sensual comfort. The thought would keep fresh in *our* heart, "Am I not a Christian? a companion of Cherubim and Seraphim in glorifying God? How then dare I give myself up to be carried away by such childish unworthy things?"

This is one use which God would have us make of those glimpses of heavenly glory, which from time to time He shews His faithful ones, whether in Church services, or otherwise. They should help to put down the earthly mind and to encourage the heavenly mind. Endeavour, I beseech you, to use them so: and your reward will indeed be great. Instead of *hearing* only of God, how He was seen in visions by the prophets, you will then see Him, as He is. You will see Him face to face: and it will be, to all eternity, your glory and your joy!

SERMON XXXIX.

THE HOLINESS OF GOD, TOWARDS US AND IN US.

TRINITY SUNDAY.

REV. iv. 8.

" They rest not day and night, saying, Holy, Holy, Holy, Lord God Almighty, which was, and is, and is to come."

"THEY rest not day and night." It is remarkable that these are the very same words which, further on in the book of Revelations, are used to describe the torments of the damned. "ᵃ They have no rest day nor night, who worship the beast and his image, and whosoever receiveth the mark of his name." As much as to say, that after the sabbath of the grave is over, and the body is once more awakened and joined to the soul, there shall be no more sleep for ever. The good shall never rest from their happiness, nor the wicked from their torment. The one is as certain as the other.

And yet in another sense, the condition of the saints in heaven is entire and perfect peace and rest: as it is written, "ᵇ Great is the peace that they have who love Thy law:" and our Lord's own promise is, "Peace I leave with you, My Peace I give unto

ᵃ Rev. xiv. 11.   ᵇ Ps. cxix. 165.

you." Rest is their reward, and yet here we read, "They have no rest day nor night." From care, from wearisome labour, from anxiety, from all pain and disquiet of mind and body, they are at rest for ever; but it is not the rest of sleep or of mere inactivity: it is resting from all lower works, that they may be at leisure to think of God, to adore and praise Him, to draw nearer and nearer to Him, in heart and spirit, for ever. "They rest not day and night, saying, Holy, Holy, Holy, Lord God Almighty, which was, and is, and is to come."

My brethren, this is indeed too high and hard a subject for sinful mortals, swallowed up with the cares of this lower world. We cannot enter into it, more than very faintly: but even the little we may understand would be enough, were we but willing, to lift our souls far above the things that we see, and make us long, as the Psalmist did, for the wings of a dove, that we might flee away, and enter into that rest. For consider. When it is said that those blessed spirits are for ever crying out, "Holy, Holy, Holy, Lord God Almighty;" none of us, of course, is so childish as to think only of the mere saying or singing the words over and over again. Of course we understand that the heart goes along with the words: that each one of the heavenly spirits, in every moment of the solemn services which they are continually performing, is evermore thinking more and more deeply on the meaning of those aweful words. That is, the employment of happy souls, now and for evermore, is to see God, and know Him, and love Him, more and more perfectly. "They rest not day and night," because the work they are upon, is so great and high that it can never be ended, and so full of joy and comfort and refreshment, that they can never tire of it. The Wisdom of God, that is, God Himself, says, "c They that eat Me shall yet be hungry, and they that drink Me shall yet be thirsty:" as much as to say, that in heaven it is far otherwise than it is in regard to those things which most delight our frail hearts. Here, we very soon come to enough of a good thing, and from enough we presently go on to too much: but of that true joy in heaven God will so make us partakers, if we do not prove unworthy, that while we feel we always have enough, yet more and more will ever be most welcome to us. In one word, the joy of the saints is in God, and therefore it has no end, for God is without end. "They rest not day and night," nor ever desire to rest, from praising Him.

And what is it, for which, most of all, they praise and honour and adore Him, and desire to draw near to Him? It is His Holiness: their endless song is, "Holy, Holy, Holy, Lord God Almighty." Holiness, in Scripture, seems to mean that perfect Goodness of God, whereby He is most opposite to all sin and imperfection. "d God is Light," says S. John, "and in Him is no darkness at all:" as if he should say, "God is Goodness, and in Him is no evil at all." "This," the same S. John adds, "is the message which we have heard of Him, and declare unto you." This is the great message of the Gospel, that God will have nothing to do with sin, and that He has made Himself a way, by His Son and Spirit, for freeing us His people from all sin for ever. The joy then which

c Ecclus. xxiv. 21.   d 1 S. John i. 5.

we hope bye and bye to taste in God's Presence, is altogether a pure joy; a joy in holiness, a joy in Him who is most Holy. You cannot taste it, you can have no true notion of it, as long as you give yourself up to any kind of sin. A person who had gone on for many years, singing entirely out of tune, would be very ill-prepared to join in any perfect harmony: so are we unprepared for heaven, if we are living in any respect unholy lives. The chant of the Angels is not for such: they could not join in it, they could not understand it, even though by some miracle they were taken up where the Angels are. Oh may the good Spirit of God write this lesson deep in our hearts, and save us from the madness of thinking to be ever happy without being holy!

May He teach us also to have in perpetual remembrance what He has taught us of Himself, and of the great things which He has done for us: that we may love Him and serve Him and follow Him, His very self, not an image of our own contriving, which we vainly fancy to be like Him. For so the heavenly anthem instructs us, by repeating the word "Holy" three times, no more and no less: that we might know Him Who is Holy, Him Whom the saints and Angels are for ever praising, to be Three Persons, yet One "Lord God Almighty, which was, and is, and is to come." Much in the same way does the Church instruct us, every year, by the return of this Feast of Trinity. After we have been keeping our solemn days of remembrance of the wonders of God's mercy, one by one, this Day is appointed to gather them, as it were, all together, and to acknowledge

Him Who wrought them, to be Three Persons in One God. We know it is His will, that we should do so: for so, in the beginning of our Christian life, it pleased Him to reveal Himself to us, causing us to be baptized in the Name of the Father, and of the Son, and of the Holy Ghost: and so in the crown and end of that life, when we shall see Him as He is, we are to praise Him with the word, Holy, thrice repeated, in acknowledgement of the same Three Divine Persons. From beginning to end, and all along, we are to look upon Him as Three in One, each of the Three, Infinite in Holiness. And therefore, from time to time, as long as we live, we must praise Him in such hymns as the Creed of S. Athanasius, and as the Gloria Patri at the end of the Psalms. And when we endeavour, in our weak way, to join devoutly in such hymns, we may with humble courageous hope think of the Angels who are now and ever singing them in heaven, and of the promise given to the faithful, "ᵉI will hear thee, and thou shalt praise Me." The beginning, the middle, and the end, of our praise, our joy, and our love, must be for Him Alone, Who is Holy, Holy, Holy, Three Persons, One Lord God Almighty.

Consider, how in the work of our salvation each one of these Three glorious Persons has severally manifested His own infinite Holiness, His hatred of sin, and love of all kinds of goodness. God the Father, Who made us and all the world, made us pure and without spot of sin, and so declared how perfectly Holy He is. And when we had sinned, He again declared Himself Holy, by passing that

ᵉ Ps. l. 15.

fearful sentence, which turned us out of Paradise, out of God's Presence. And now being minded, in His unspeakable mercy, to forgive us, He requires no less a sacrifice than His Only-begotten Son, to reconcile Him to sinners, and obtain them His blessing. Alas! my brethren, what have we done? to think lightly of any known sin, and to think well of ourselves after we had knowingly sinned, while yet we had learned so much of the Holiness of the Eternal Father: that He has prepared Hell for the impenitent, and will not save even the penitent but by the Blood of His only Son!

Think now of the word, Holy, repeated the second time; and think withal of the holiness of the Only-begotten Son, our Lord Jesus Christ: how pure and undefiled He was, without blemish and without spot, and how His very enemies and murderers were compelled to cry out, "I find no fault in this Man." Think, why He took our nature upon Him at first. It was because of His tender love towards us, joined with His entire hatred of sin. He sought to save us, but He knew and felt that our sins were so very bad, that the only way for us to be forgiven would be for Him to stoop from heaven to earth, become one of us, and bear our sins in His own Body on the Tree. So Holy is He, so unchangeably set against sin, that He will dismiss those who have not repented in time, and who will appear before Him at the Judgement seat;—He will send them away once for all, His own redeemed He will send away, if impenitent,—into everlasting fire. How then can we hope to be ever in His favour, so long as we permit ourselves to be entangled in any known sin?

Think, once more, of the Third Person of the Blessed and Glorious Trinity: think, Christians, of God the Holy Ghost, the good and gracious Spirit of the Father and the Son, how He condescended, as on Whitsunday, to come down and abide in men's hearts, for this very express purpose, that we might be able to fight the Lord's battles manfully against sin and wickedness. Think how near, how close He is to you: dwelling in the silence and solitude of our very hearts, counting your body His temple, your members as so many limbs of Christ's own Body: hating sin entirely, and making you feel, when you are tempted, that He *really does* hate it. Think seriously, think earnestly of this. Is it not so, that when evil comes in your way, you feel a certain inward whisper, deep down in your own hearts, "Why will you do this? God sees it, and entirely hates it." You perceive this, and you call it, perhaps, the voice of conscience, and you know that it is a very serious thing. But will you now set your heart in earnest upon this certain truth, that such inward whisperings, in you who are baptized, are indeed the voice of God, not at a distance, but dwelling in your own soul and body? What a horror then, what a sin and misery must it be, to go on with anything amiss, in despite of that still small voice!

And remember this also, that when we say, the Holy Ghost is dwelling in Christians' hearts, we do not so mean it, as if the Father and the Son were away. For these Three Persons, as the text teaches, are One "Lord God Almighty." Their works are inseparable; so that where One is, there, in Presence and in Power, are all Three: as our Lord Himself gave us to understand, when He was taking leave of His disciples before His Death. "'If a man love Me, he will keep My words: and My Father will love him, and We," i. e. the Father and the Son, "will come unto him, and make Our abode with him." The Father and the Son will come by the Holy Ghost to every Christian who does not throw away the blessing, and will dwell within him, so that his soul and body shall be night and day full of God, a true temple of the Holy and Glorious Trinity. Do not turn away from this thought, because you cannot understand how it should be so. Do not forget it, because the wonderful Presence is all out of sight. Your own soul is out of sight: but yet you know very well what must become of you, if you forget and neglect your own soul. In like manner, be careful, I beseech you, to worship and adore the Living God, the Trinity in Unity, vouchsafing to abide in your hearts. And remember that, when you let your will go after any thing sinful, you offend and affront not God the Holy Ghost only, but God the Father likewise, and God the Son : for where the Holy Ghost is, there are also the Father and the Son, in all their glory, love, and holiness: and so, when a Christian man sins willfully: when he tells a lie, or looks on what is forbidden, it is as if he said to the Father Who made him, "⁸depart from me, for I desire not the knowledge of Thy ways:" it is, as if he said to the Son Who redeemed him, "I will not have you to reign over me: depart from me, for what have I to do with Thee?" If this is almost too shocking to think of, what must it be to live in the habit of saying such words, in heart,

---

ᶠ S. John xiv. 23.   ᵍ Job xxi. 14.

to the Most High God? And yet, in heart and in meaning, we do say such words, every time that we consent to what He has forbidden.

This is indeed very terrible to think of: but on the other hand what joy and gladness is it, when we reflect on what Holy Scripture tells us of the Presence of the Blessed Trinity in all our endeavours to do good and obey our Saviour! S. Paul says, "[h] I can do all things through Christ which strengtheneth me:" and again, "[i] Not I, but Christ liveth in me; and the life which I now live in the flesh I live by the faith of the Son of God, Who loved me, and gave Himself for me." The Apostle says not this of himself only, but of every one, even the simplest believer. The prayers and alms and other good deeds, the faith and patience of such an one, are not his own, but Christ's. They belong not to the man himself, but to the Holy, Blessed and Glorious Trinity, which has abode in him ever since his Baptism. They are therefore good and acceptable before God, as being the works, not of corrupt human nature, but of the Holy and good Spirit of the Father and the Son. The simplest action wrought by a Christian in Christ's Name with a good mind, is thus turned into something very precious and holy, and will in no wise lose its reward.

I do not of course mean, that good Christian people will themselves know, when they do things in this acceptable way, and so as to have a blessing laid up for them in heaven. The better they are, the more they will humble themselves, and of course, so much the less will they know of their own goodness.

[h] Phil. iv. 13.   [i] Gal. ii. 20.

Still however there will generally be in the bottom of their hearts, a secret indescribable peace, a calm courageousness of spirit, a deep conviction of their Lord's unfailing mercy, which will carry them through this world far happier, on the whole, than they could be any other way: and bye and bye, in the other world, they will find how all things have worked together for their good. They will then perceive how their constant endeavours to be indeed holy here, have prepared them for the constant solemn services, the praising God in His Holiness hereafter. They rest not here, but according to their measure are trying day and night to be holy: therefore to them it will be in comparison no strange thing, to find themselves hereafter wholly taken up with such anthems as that in the text, "Holy, Holy, Holy, Lord God Almighty:" wholly employed in gazing on God, their Creator, Redeemer and Sanctifier: and in receiving light from His Light, holiness and righteousness from His adorable Perfections.

So be it, O Lord, with us, Thy unworthy servants: for His sake, Who died to purchase the blessing for us!

SERMON XL.

HEAVEN CREATED FOR US, WE RE-CREATED FOR IT, BY THE HOLY TRINITY.

TRINITY SUNDAY.

Ps. xxxiii. 6.

"*By the Word of the Lord were the heavens made, and all the hosts of them by the Breath of His Mouth.*"

WHY should the history of the creation of the world be read in the Church on Trinity Sunday? Because Trinity Sunday, coming after all the great days, doth as it were complete the Church's witness of God's manifestation of Himself in the Gospel: and the creation of the world, and more especially that of man in God's own image, was the beginning of that manifestation. The making heaven and earth out of nothing, which is what we call creation, was, as far as we are told, the first work whereby the Holy Trinity began to reveal and make Itself known. From all eternity God Almighty, the Father, the Son and the Holy Ghost, had dwelt in His own Light, "[a] the Light which no man can approach unto," rejoicing in the glory and blessedness of His own Eternal Being, the bliss and glory, of which the Son saith, He had it with the Father before the world was; living and reigning with Him in the unity of the Holy Spirit.

[a] 1 Tim. vi. 16.

Thus it was, until it pleased the Father by His Word and Spirit to create this visible world, and also the invisible world of Angels and spirits. God the Father, the First Person in the Trinity, is especially called the Maker and Creator of the world, because He *is* the First Person, the Root, the Fountain, the Beginning of all: as the holy Creed says "He is made of none, neither created, nor begotten." "*Of* Him are all things," therefore He is especially our Creator: but not without His Son and His Spirit: as we read, "The Spirit of God moved upon the face of the waters;" and God spake by His Word or Son, the Second Person in the Everlasting Trinity, and said, "Let there be light, and there was light:" and so all along, all through the six days of creation God said, "Let it be so, and it was so." It was His Word, His Son, by Whom He brought all into being. "[b]All things were made by Him; and without Him was not any thing made that was made." By Him, i. e. by Jesus Christ, "[c] were all things created, that are in heaven, and that are in earth, visible and invisible, whether they be thrones, or dominions, or principalities, or powers: all things were created by Him and for Him." Thus Scripture teaches that all things were created by the Son; and of the Spirit's part in the beginning of the world it saith, "The Spirit of God moved upon the face of the waters;" and again, "[d] Who hath measured the waters in the hollow of his hand?—Who hath directed the Spirit of the Lord, or, being His counsellor, hath taught Him?" And thus in part we understand the word put into the mouth of the Psalmist, "By the word

---

[b] S. John i. 3.   [c] Col. i. 16.   [d] Is. xl. 12, 13.

of God (i. e. by His Son Jesus Christ our Saviour) were the heavens made, and all the hosts of them by the Breath of His mouth," i. e. His Spirit; of Whom another Psalm told us last Sunday, "ᵉ When Thou lettest Thy Breath go forth, they shall be made; and Thou shalt renew the face of the earth."

By this we understand that the same holy Saviour, Who is all in all to us sinners, is the great Lord, Creator and Upholder of all things; able therefore to make all work for good to them that love Him; and that the same Holy Ghost, in Whom we trust to be our Sanctifier, is the very Being, Who first began to brood like a Dove over the earth, when it was without form and void, and to prepare it for all the order and beauty, that God intended to bring out of it: whereby we know that He is able to sanctify us to the uttermost, able to change the fallen and corrupt heart, and new-create it, after the image of God, unto righteousness and true holiness.

Further (and this, my brethren, is the point to which I would especially draw your attention to-day) as the very first words of the Bible tell us how that "in the beginning God created the heaven:" so the Psalmist in the text teaches that " by the *Word* of God were the heavens made, and all the hosts of them by the Breath (or Spirit) of His Mouth;" i. e. the Blessed Son and Spirit were with the Father in the beginning, and bore Their part with Him in the creation of the heavens. The heavens, I say, and the very heaven of heavens; not only this deep blue sky, this firmament with its sun, moon, and stars, so vast bright and awful to look up to, but the

ᵉ Ps. civ. 30.

highest heavens and their inhabitants, the Angels and Archangels, the Cherubim and Seraphim, the Thrones, Dominions, Principalities, Powers, and whatever else there may be beyond sight and thought; all, of which the Apostle speaks, were the work and are the property of Jesus Christ, our Redeemer, and of the Holy Spirit our Guide and Comforter; and, belonging to Christ and His Spirit, they do in a manner belong to each good Christian. "All," saith he[f], "are yours," as surely as "ye are Christ's." Now, my brethren, consider a moment; what a great unspeakable thought is this! Suppose the child of some great rich person, the son and heir of such a monarch as Nebuchadnezzar, taken up to some high hill, in the midst of a grand city like Babylon, and told, "Now cast your eyes around: all these lands and houses and gardens, all these streets and palaces, and the treasures and wealth of every kind which they contain, all belongs to your father: he means it for you; it will be all yours, if you will only be dutiful, and please him." What would be the thoughts of that person? We do not perhaps know exactly: the heart of man is very wayward, and none of us, I suppose, can tell quite for certain, what his own thoughts would be in such a case: but one thing, I imagine, *is* quite certain: we should any one of us, if we believed the saying, think a great deal of it: we should regard it as making a great difference in our condition: we could not forget it: we could not be, as if we never had heard it. Well: but this very thing is true: the word, not of a man but of God, has really come to each one of us with this very assurance, not

[f] 1 Cor. iii. 21. 23.

concerning any earthly estate, or domain, but concerning the glorious heaven which we see above us. Our Lord saith, as it were, to each one of us, "Is not this the great and glorious home which I have builded for the house of the kingdom of My people; I have builded it even for thee, by the might of My power, and for the honour of My majesty?" He hath said—we heard it a very little while ago: "[g]I go to prepare a place for you. And if I go and prepare a place for you, I will come again, and receive you unto Myself; that where I am, there ye may be also." As in the beginning He, Who is the Wisdom of the Father, established the visible heavens; as He said, "Let there be a firmament, and lights in the firmament;" so He is now, by His Intercession in His kingdom, preparing the spiritual and invisible heavens to be our everlasting home. And when it is prepared, and we prepared for it, He "will come again, and receive us unto Himself; that where He is, there we may be also." He will take His Church, purified from earth and sin, released for ever from danger and suffering, He will take it up with Him through the everlasting gates, which will be lifted up for Him and the hosts of His redeemed, and they will follow after Him, and abide with Him, and see His Face for ever.

But in the mean time they too (we cannot be reminded of it too often) must have had their preparation on earth. For this is our Lord's word, confirmed by His oath: "[h] Verily, verily, I say unto thee, except a man be born again, he cannot see the kingdom of God." Not every one is fit to be one of

[g] S. John xiv. 2. 3.   [h] Ib. iii. 3.

the Lord's host, the host of heaven, the happy company who shall follow their Saviour through the everlasting doors, when He shall ascend the second time; but those only who shall have been marked with His mark, and transformed into His likeness, here on earth: and that is a work which none but His Spirit can accomplish: therefore we understand how the prophet should say, all the host of heaven were made by the Breath of the Lord's Mouth. As the Angels, the good and pure spirits, were created in the beginning by the Holy Spirit, or Breath, of the Father and the Son, so we sinners, if ever we are to become good and pure, and come to heaven, must be new-created by the same Holy Spirit. His grace is that blessed and heavenly Fire, which our Lord came to send upon earth; to kindle upon one defiled soul after another, and purge and refine it as gold and silver, that it may be a worthy offering to the Father, through the merits of Christ, now in Communion, and hereafter at the Day of Judgement. By the Word of the Lord, i.e. by His Son Jesus Christ, are the heavens even now being prepared for each good Christian, and all the host of them—all the saints and penitents who are one day to be received there, are being prepared by the Breath of His Mouth, i.e. His Holy and life-giving Spirit.

Do we believe these things, my brethren? Do we really believe in the Life everlasting, purchased for us by the Blood of Christ, prepared for us by His Intercession, sealed to us by His Holy Spirit? Yes, we believe it, one and all, we dare not deny it: we know and feel in the bottom of our hearts that it is the only way to be happy. But alas! my brethren, what signifies our belief, if we permit ourselves to go on, almost or altogether, as if we had never heard of these things? Our Lord is in heaven preparing a place for us; the Holy Spirit is here on earth to prepare us for the place; and we; what are we ourselves doing? Here, in this our village, we are one thousand Christian souls: how many of us, being of sufficient age, are seriously trying to obey the godly motions of the good Spirit? We are all in Christ's school: how many of us are learning His lessons? O how can we give ourselves up to these ordinary things: a little more money, a little more worldly credit, a little more amusement and pleasure: while thrones are being got ready for us in the royal palace of heaven, and the Holy Comforter close at hand, offering to shew us the way, and help us along it? Observe how it is when a person is possessed, as happens not uncommonly, with a longing to be a sailor or soldier, or in any other special profession: or with a strong attachment to any particular person. In such a case, men live upon the hope which possesses them: it occupies their minds night and day: it brings every thought into captivity: it is their meat and drink: as He said, Who set us the great example of like zeal in the only sufficient cause, "ⁱ My meat is to do the will of Him that sent Me, and to finish His work." O why should not we follow Him? Why should not we, every one of us, seek and obtain grace to live upon the thought of heaven and of Christ preparing it for us, as men, earnest in any earthly desire, live upon the remembrance of the person or thing that they long for? Let no man

---

ʲ S. John iv. 34.

say, "It is not in me : I long for such a Christian mind, I think those most happy who have it; but I cannot feel it, and I cannot force myself to do so." Of course, no man can change his own heart: but he may wish and pray that God would change it: and in the mean time he may, by God's help, carefully keep himself in word and deed from the things which he knows God hates.

To such as faithfully endeavour this, He Who is the Truth has promised full success. As surely as a father would give good gifts to his children, so surely will your heavenly Father give the Holy Spirit to them that ask Him. And He can and will change the heart, and teach you to love what now you cannot care for. The very season of Whitsuntide reminds us what a change He wrought in the blessed Apostles. They had been "unstable as water," forsaking their Lord as soon as ever they understood that He was really to suffer : but when the Holy Comforter had descended on them, they were all on fire with boldness and fervent zeal, to do and suffer all His Will: and he was happiest who could give up most for his Lord. He is the same Spirit that He was then, and we in our measure have the same need that they had. As He gave strength and energy to S. Peter and the rest, so He hath ever since, and will to those who shall come after, making each generation of faithful men in its turn His hosts, His soldiers, His angels, to serve Him duly in His Church, and wage war courageously against His enemies. Only, as was said to the hosts of the Lord when they entered on the wars of Canaan, "ᵏ Only

ᵏ Josh. i. 7.

be ye strong and very courageous." Christian courage—*that* is the virtue, the want of which ruins so many good beginnings. Young persons, we will suppose, have learned what is right, their hearts are more or less touched; they make good resolutions, and enter on a better way of life: bye and bye comes a strong temptation to commit what seems but a little fault: they know it is wrong, but they dare not be so very particular as to shrink from what so many others do: it is so very unpleasant to be scorned or pointed at: in short they are cowardly and give way: and when they have done so once, it is but too easy to do it a second and a third time. Now all this sin and misery would be effectually stayed, if persons would first make a good and brave resolution to resist the first temptation with all their might; and secondly, if they would humbly and regularly ask the aid of God's good Spirit to keep their resolution. Again, it is a point of Christian courage, in which we are most of us sadly wanting, to do the right thing, when we know it, *at once;* not to stand parleying and doubting about it, but to strike your blow *at once,* like a valiant soldier, who knows what his commander expects of him, and what will most baffle his enemy. For want of this it is that so many fall into a kind of irresolute, half-obedience; even if they do a good deal of their duty, they lose many a blessing for want of doing it at the right time: but a good *and brave* man will, as I said, act *at once.*

A third point of Christian courage is the not fearing to engage ourselves beforehand, by strong resolutions and promises before God, when we are quite certain of our duty. Fear not, by the help of the Holy Spirit, to pledge yourself to what is right, and to keep your pledge.

Fourthly, and very particularly, courage requires of you to do without the countenance of men. It is plain common sense : man cannot help your soul in your need: man cannot change your heart, nor obtain forgiveness of your sins. Why will you think so much of man, when you have the Eternal God offering Himself to be your help and your refuge ? Have pity on your own soul: do not so throw it away: and have pity, too, on the souls of those whom you are tempted to follow in the wrong way: your weakness is *sure* to do them harm; your firmness *might* do them a very great deal of good. Finally, pray and strive to be courageous under long weariness and disappointment. Let nothing daunt, nothing dishearten you, when you may reasonably hope you are following Christ. Remember what He endured, and grudge not tedious waiting, grudge not missing your earthly comforts, the sense of being helped, sympathy from others, good done to them, and the like: never mind missing all this, if such be His will.

Wherever you are, and whatever you are about, remember, in all dangerous trials especially, that you carry about you, as a holy spell and charm (if we may use such a word) rather let me say, as a saving seal and token of protection from the Lord, the Most Holy Name of the Trinity ; the Father, the Son, and the Holy Ghost, into which Name you were baptized. With this, the weakest of us will be strong: strong enough against the fiercest and most subtle temptation, like David coming to Goliath in the Name of the Lord God of Israel. You cannot fail, if in heart and act you be true to yourself and to God.

Too sadly I feel, that as in former years, so it will be also in this: too many will be found to have heard the word of God, speaking to them in His great and holy seasons, one after another, with little or no real fruit. But whether men hear, or whether they forbear, we must not cease to warn: and you know in your hearts, every one of you, that it will be well in the end for those who take our warning; for every one of them, and for them only.

SERMON XLI.

THE THREEFOLD CORD.

TRINITY SUNDAY.

Eccles. iv. 12.

"A Threefold cord is not quickly broken."

This must be an old proverb, taken from something very familiar, and applied by the wise king, or rather by the Holy Spirit guiding him, to a very deep and high meaning. How deep and high, we shall better understand, if we go back, as the Church does this day, to the very beginning of our Bibles. He made man in His own Image, and having made him, He left him not long by himself, but made woman also, to be an help meet for him. These two works were works of so great importance, that the Almighty Lord is spoken of as even taking counsel about them: considering beforehand how He should order them. God said, "Let us make man in Our Image, after Our likeness:" and again God said, "It is not good that the man should be alone: I will make him an help meet for him." As persons who are very much in earnest, very full of any matter, often, in setting about it, talk to themselves, without knowing that they do so: so our great Creator here takes counsel with Himself, to shew us what a weighty business He is taking in hand. The first thing on which He thus counsels with Himself, is the making man after His own Image, the second is the not leaving him alone. Now we know that this saying, "It is not good for man to be alone," relates in the first place to Holy Matrimony, but no doubt it relates also to the need which men have of one another, and each one of far better help than his own, in all the concerns, both of this life and of the next. See how this is set out at length by the wise man. "[a]Two are better than one, because they have a good reward for their labour. For if they fall, the one will lift up his fellow: but woe to him that is alone when he falleth, for he hath not another to help him up. Again, if two lie together, then they have heat: but how can one be warm alone? and if one prevail against him, two shall withstand him." Now all this we all understand at once as far as relates to the concerns of this life, how impossible it is for us to do without one another: and the dullest of us can at once discern, what a lesson it all teaches of love and good-fellowship, and the duty of all caring for one another, since God has made us so, that we cannot go on at all without one another. All this we understand by the instances given of two being better than one. But what is this which comes after? "A threefold cord"—Why "threefold?" Not merely because, union being strength, the more there are in union, the greater the strength: not merely that as two are better than one, so three are better than two, although that might often be true in earthly matters; and cordage, we know especially is always threefold at least, else it will be quickly broken; but, as I said, there is a deeper meaning in this, as there is, I believe, always in the Scripture, when the number three is mentioned at all parti-

[a] Eccles. iv. 9—12.

cularly. It always takes us back, if we consider it well, to the number of the Divine Persons, the Holy, Blessed, and Glorious Trinity. Thus in the text, it is as if Solomon should say, " It is not good for man to be alone : two are better than one : but a threefold cord—that is best and strongest of all, for this is the very nature of man, according as he was at first created." He was made in the Image of God; and God, though He is One, is not alone. He is not single nor solitary, but Three in One, and so hath been and will be, for ever and ever. And man, being made at the first in God's Image, after His likeness, was not altogether single and solitary. Man, at the beginning, was in a certain sense three in one, and in that, as in some other respects, was made after his Creator's likeness. You may ask, how was Adam, when first created, an Image of the eternal Three in One ? Different answers might be given to this, all more or less true ; but I will mention only one answer, and that I will take out of S. Paul. S. Paul prays God for the Thessalonians, that their "[b] whole spirit and soul and body may be preserved blameless unto the coming of our Lord Jesus Christ." Their spirit and soul and body : see here three parts, three separate principles, forming together one man : not one man of any sort, but one spiritual Christian man. For S. Paul, had he been writing to the heathen, would not, I imagine, have said anything about spirit, because the heathen had not the Spirit. Thus stands the doctrine, as I understand it : As God is Three Persons in one Substance, the Father, the Son, and the Holy Ghost, so Adam when first created had three principles (so to call them) in one person, the

[b] 1 Thess. v. 23.

same three which the Apostle here mentions; the body, formed out of the dust of the earth; the soul or breath of temporal life, breathed into his nostrils by the Lord God after He had formed him, whereby, as we read, "the first man Adam was made a living soul;" and the Spirit, the Lord and Giver of Life, given to the same Adam to join him in unspeakable communion with his Creator, making him in some way partaker of heavenly life, as his having a soul made him partaker of this earthly life. Thus man was made in the Image of God, in that being one he was three, made up of body, soul and spirit, and so he continued during his time of innocence. Too soon, alas! he sinned, grievously sinned, and what was the consequence? He lost the Image of God, in which he was at first so happily created; he lost it, as in other respects, so in this particularly, that the Holy, Life-giving Spirit departed from him, and so he consisted no longer of body, soul and spirit, but of body and soul only: the threefold-cord was not broken, but in a manner untwined: one of the lines, the principal one was removed, two only remained, and they were soon to be untwined also: he was no more an image of the Trinity.

In this sad condition we are every one of us born, without any portion or part in that blessed Spirit, Who is the only Lord and Giver of eternal life. This was our ruin by nature, what then is our restoration by grace? What but our being new-created in the Image of God which we have lost? what but our receiving anew the Blessed Spirit Whom we drove away from us? This might not be, until a Sacrifice had been offered for us, able indeed to take away sin: and such Sacrifice none might offer in heaven or in earth but He Who was made one of us that He might offer it, God the Son, the Lamb of God slain from the foundation of the world. He, by His meritorious Cross and Passion, purchased for us remission of our sins, and the gift of His good Spirit which we had lost and forfeited, to unite us to the Divine Nature, to create us anew after the Divine Image, by giving us His own gracious Self, causing us to become spirit soul and body, a likeness of the Holy Trinity again. This blessing He purchased for us all on the Cross, but He gives it to each one of us at Holy Baptism, when He sends His Spirit into our hearts to make us members of Himself. At our Baptism, unless we hinder it by our sins, the original Image of God, in which Adam was created, is restored and renewed in us, and, as I said, we are once more made body and soul and spirit, instead of being only soul and body, as we had been ever since Adam's sin. And this is the threefold cord, which cannot be broken; though by wilful sin and unbelief on our part, it may be again untwined, and too often is so. We are sure it cannot be broken, we are sure the good work wrought for us in Baptism cannot be undone except by our own sin, because it is the work of the Blessed Trinity, it depends on the inseparable union of the Three Divine Persons with each other, and on that other inseparable union of the Nature of God with the Nature of Man in the Person of Jesus Christ. If the Father, the Son, and the Holy Ghost can cease to be of one Substance, Majesty and Glory; if Jesus Christ our Saviour can cease to be for ever both God and Man; then may the Holy Spirit depart from the souls and bodies of Christ's redeemed and regenerated, without wilful sin of theirs. But not else:

the threefold cord, I say it again, may be untwined but cannot be broken.

All our holy services and Sacraments are divinely ordered to assure us of this. Our Faith, uttered in the Creed of the Church, whether it be the Apostles' Creed or the Nicene Creed or, as to-day the Creed of S. Athanasius, begins with the Trinity and ends with life everlasting; and the one is as sure as the other; the threefold cord binds us to the Throne for ever. Our Baptism, what is that but the seal of the Trinity, Almighty God the Father, the Son and the Holy Ghost, giving us Himself, to come unto us and make His abode with us, giving us His Name, the name of Christian, to be unto us a strong tower, into which we may run and be safe? The benedictions or blessings of Holy Church are all uttered in the Name of the Trinity: when she dismisses us after Holy Communion, it is with the blessing of the Father, the Son and the Holy Ghost, that we may not lose the good thing we have received: when she absolves us after confession of sin, it is still in the same Name, to make sure of the untying of our bonds: when she would place a guard on our marriages, that no unclean or morose spirit may enter in and spoil them, her word is, "God the Father, God the Son, God the Holy Ghost, bless, preserve and keep you:" and not only in Church services, but in all very serious matters it has ever been usual among Christians to provide, as well as they might, for their good success, by putting them under the care of the Divine Trinity, beginning or ending them in the Name of the Father, the Son, and the Holy Ghost. Again, that our Psalms and hymns and solemn thanksgivings may be indeed to God's praise and glory, we bind them also to His Throne by that other threefold cord of the Gloria Patri: professing thereby, before men and Angels, that all our worship and devotion is dedicated to Him Who is Three in One, and to Him alone, for ever and ever. The Faith, the Name, the worship of the Most Holy Trinity, meet us every where in the Prayer-book, and will not let us turn with dependence towards any body or anything else. O my brethren, let us hold fast by it, for there is no other cord to lay hold of: if we let this go, we shall assuredly make shipwreck of our souls. And how may we hold fast by it? The seal of the Trinity will be in a manner worn out of our foreheads, the Name of the Trinity will be no protection to us, if we do not keep entire the Faith of the Trinity. Many false prophets are abroad, saying this or that against it: let us at once refuse to listen to them; let us put their books in the fire; if they attempt to discourse with us, let us say, "I cannot talk with you;" and above all things let us pray: for only the sacred Trinity Itself can teach and secure our faith in the Trinity. Let us pray, as we do this day, that as He hath "given us grace by the confession of the one true Faith, to acknowledge the glory of the eternal Trinity, and in the power of the Divine Majesty to worship the Unity, so He may evermore keep us stedfast in that good Faith." We shall do well to consider that holy collect as a safeguard, an antidote against all poison of profane unbelief, to last us through all the long months until the holy seasons begin again. And He Who knows how frail we are, how our nature shrinks from trials and troubles, He permits us to hold by the same threefold cord for protection against *them* also: He permits us to say to Him, not only "keep us stedfast in this Faith," but also, "defend us evermore from all adversities." What is this but putting the seal of the Trinity upon our friends and families, our bodies and estates and all our earthly interests, as well as upon our souls? Thus we put our very life and limbs and all the comforts and conveniences of our life, and more especially we put all who are near and dear to us, under the protection of the Father the Son and the Holy Ghost, till the holy seasons begin afresh. And what can we do more or better for them?

Now all this which I have put you in mind of, out of Holy Scripture and out of the Prayer-book, of holding fast this threefold cord, which may be let go, but never can be broken: all this our profession of relying on the Blessed Trinity is clearly one of two things: it is either the most blessed of realities or the most fearful of all pretences and mockeries. There is no middle way: it must be one or the other: to every one of us the faith we profess in the Trinity is either salvation or increased damnation. It is far too aweful to be treated lightly, to be dealt with as a matter of course. It is the threefold cord which alone sustains us and keeps us from dropping into the great deep of a miserable eternity: as it often happens at sea, that persons clinging to a single rope (which rope is always at least threefold) are preserved from drowning by that and nothing else. If they let it go, they are lost. Do you not see what madness it would be for one in such a case to begin playing with the rope, and trying whether he might not possibly let it go for a moment and seize it again, or with how few fingers he might hold it, or to indulge any other childish fancy about it? And if there chanced to be a spiteful enemy at hand, who kept throwing within one's reach things which he knew one would be tempted to lay hold of, would it not be common sense to make a strict rule with one's self, that, come what would, one would not take hold of any of them, seeing that in order to do so, one must either in whole or in part let go the rope which alone kept one from drowning? Just such an enemy is the devil: just such common sense is Christian, evangelical self-denial, the rules which serious men, taught by our Saviour, impose upon themselves, that they may not be tempted to let go the Threefold cord, faith, living faith in the Blessed Trinity, for the sake of laying hold of any thing, pleasant, wise, strong, rich or glorious, which that Wicked one may cast in their way. Do not then listen to any one, who would persuade you not to be strict and particular. Be sure there is something very wrong, when you hear or read, or your own heart whispers to you, "Such great exactness, such continual watching, cannot surely be altogether necessary. If I keep from grievous notorious sin, and have real good feelings at times, and look to Christ only as my Saviour, I need not fear but it will come right at last." Do not, I say, get into this way of thinking: for only imagine how it would sound to one hanging by a rope over a precipice, were some one from below to call out to him, "You need not hold so very hard, nor keep such continual hold: you may let go for a moment and rest yourself, or pick that beautiful flower from the rock: see it is just within your reach." Would he be a friend or an enemy who should so counsel?

Be sure then, dear brethren, that he will be your

best friend, who shall, by God's help, most effectually prevail upon you, not, of course to be dismal and melancholy, but to be always in earnest, always careful, always religious, in your cheerfulness as well as in your graver thoughts, in your business as well as in your devotion, in your pleasure as well as in your business: to keep up through the rest of the year, any good thoughts and purposes which His grace may have put into your hearts during the holy Seasons which end with this day. For this is in fact nothing else but keeping hold of the Threefold cord which your Saviour put into your hands, when He baptized you into the Name of the Father, the Son, and the Holy Ghost. It is watching over the precious seal, the Threefold stamp, which He then and there fixed on our foreheads. Very soon He will be here, to see if we are holding by that cord, if we are watching to preserve that mark. As He then finds us, so will He judge us. How will it then be, when He shall ask, "Why have you let go My Threefold cord, why have you suffered My Threefold seal to wear out?" and you shall have nothing to say, but, "It was too much trouble to mind them?"

Thanks be to God.

NEW AND CHEAPER ISSUE

OF

The Library of the Fathers

OF THE HOLY CATHOLIC CHURCH, ANTERIOR TO THE DIVISION OF THE EAST AND WEST.

Translated by Members of the English Church.

Already Issued.

	£	s.	d.
ST. ATHANASIUS AGAINST THE ARIANS. 1 vol.	0	10	6
With very full illustrative notes on the history of the times, and the faith in the Trinity and the Incarnation. The most important work published since Bishop Bull.			
——————— HISTORICAL TRACTS . . .			
St. Athanasius is *the* historian of the period.	0	10	6
——————— FESTAL EPISTLES . . .			
The work recently recovered in the Syriac translation.			
ST. AUGUSTINE'S CONFESSIONS, with Notes . .	0	6	0
Containing his early life and conversion. The notes illustrate the Confessions from St. Augustine himself.			
——————— SERMONS ON THE NEW TESTAMENT. 2 vols.	0	15	0
Clear and thoughtful expositions of Holy Scripture to the poor of Hippo, with rhetorical skill in fixing their attention.			
——————— HOMILIES on the PSALMS. 6 vols.	2	2	0
Full of those concise sayings on Christian doctrine and morals, which contain so much truth accurately expressed in few words.			
——————— ON THE GOSPEL AND FIRST EPISTLE OF ST. JOHN. 2 vols. . . .	0	15	0
At all times one of the favourite works of St. Augustine.			
——————— PRACTICAL TREATISES . .	0	6	0
Chiefly on the doctrines of grace.			
ST. CHRYSOSTOM'S HOMILIES ON THE GOSPEL OF ST. MATTHEW. 3 vols.	1	1	0
——————— HOMILIES ON THE GOSPEL OF ST. JOHN. 2 vols.	0	14	0
——————— HOMILIES ON THE ACTS OF THE APOSTLES. 2 vols.	0	12	0
St. Chrysostom, besides the eloquence of his perorations, is remarkable for his care in developing the connection of Holy Scripture.			
——————— TO THE PEOPLE OF ANTIOCH	0	7	6
The celebrated homilies, where St. Chrysostom employed the fears of the people at the Emperor's displeasure to call them to repentance.			
ST. EPHREM'S RHYTHMS ON THE NATIVITY, AND ON FAITH	0	8	6
From the Syriac. A very devout writer of the mystical school, and full on the doctrine of the Incarnation.			

LIBRARY OF THE FATHERS, (*continued*).

	£	s.	d.
ST. CYRIL (Bishop of Jerusalem), CATECHETICAL LECTURES on the CREED AND SACRAMENTS .	0	7	0
ST. GREGORY THE GREAT, MORALS on the BOOK OF JOB. 4 vols.	1	11	6

Called the Magna Moralia, from the depth of the observations on human nature of one who lived in close communion with God.

	£	s.	d.
ST. IRENÆUS, THE WORKS OF	0	8	0

Translated by the late Rev. JOHN KEBLE.

	£	s.	d.
ST. JUSTIN THE MARTYR. Works now extant .	0	6	0
TERTULLIAN'S APOLOGETICAL AND PRACTICAL TREATISES	0	10	6

The treatises, especially the Apologetic, have, over and above, much historical information on early Christianity. They are full of those frequent sayings of deep practical truth, for which his name is almost proverbial.

The following Homilies of S. Chrysostom are about to be reprinted, as revised by Mr. Field's Text.

ST. CHRYSOSTOM'S HOMILIES ON ST. PAUL'S EPISTLE TO THE ROMANS. 1 vol.

———————————— GALATIANS AND EPHESIANS. 1 vol.

———————————— PHILIPPIANS, COLOSSIANS, AND THESSALONIANS. 1 vol.

The Homilies on the Corinthians and the Pastoral Epistles may still be had in the original bindings at the following prices:—

	£	s.	d.
ST. CHRYSOSTOM'S HOMILIES ON ST. PAUL'S EPISTLES TO THE CORINTHIANS. 2 vols. .	0	18	0
———————————— TIMOTHY, TITUS, AND PHILEMON. 1 vol.	0	7	6

The Epistles of S. Cyprian, and the Treatises of S. Pacian, may still be had in the original bindings.

	£	s.	d.
THE EPISTLES OF ST. CYPRIAN, WITH THE TREATISES OF ST. PACIAN	0	7	6

St. Cyprian, besides his great practical wisdom, states the doctrines of grace as carefully as if he had lived after the Pelagian heresy. He was a great favourite of Dean Milner. He is a witness of the early independence of the several Churches.

THE TREATISES OF ST. CYPRIAN *will shortly be reprinted.*

	£	s.	d.
ST. CYRIL (Archbishop of Alexandria), COMMENTARY UPON THE GOSPEL OF ST. JOHN. Vol. I. . .	0	12	0

Profound and accurate on the Doctrine of the Incarnation.

In preparation.

THE FIVE BOOKS AGAINST NESTORIUS, together with the SCHOLIA ON THE INCARNATION.

LIBRARY OF THE FATHERS, (continued). 3

ORIGINAL TEXTS.	£	s.	d.
ST. AUGUSTINI Confessiones	0	7	0

(This edition has been revised with the use of some Oxford MSS. and early editions.)

ST. CHRYSOSTOMI in Epist. ad Romanos . . .	0	9	0
———————— ad Corinthios I.	0	10	6
———————— ad Corinthios II.	0	8	0
———————— ad Galatas et Ephesios . . .	0	7	0
———————— ad Phil., Coloss., Thessal. . .	0	10	6
———————— ad Tim., Tit., Philem. . . ·	0	8	0
———————— ad Hebræos	0	9	0

(For this edition all the good MSS. of St. Chrysostom in public libraries in Europe have been collated, and the Rev. F. Field having employed his great critical acumen upon them, the English edition of St. Chrysostom is, so far, the best extant, as Sir H. Savile's was in his day.)

THEODORETI Commentarius in omnes B. Pauli Epistolas, Edidit C. MARRIOTT. Pars I. continens Epistolas ad Romanos, Corinthios, et Galatas	0	8	0
———————— Pars II. ad Ephes., Philip., Coloss., Thess., Heb., Tim., Tit., et Philem.	0	6	0

(In this edition gaps were supplied, and the Text improved, by aid of two Paris MSS., the one of the beginning of the tenth, the other of the eleventh century (which were brought to Paris from Constantinople after the time of Sirmondus). Dr. Cramer's "Catenæ" also furnished some good readings, in addition to those of Nösselt in Schulze's edition of his works.)

Edited by P. E. PUSEY, M.A.

THE THREE EPISTLES (ad Nestorium, ii., iii., et ad Joan. Antioch.) OF S. CYRIL, ARCHBISHOP OF ALEXANDRIA. With an English Translation. 8vo., in wrapper, 3s.

(The Text has been revised from the extant MSS. of any value.)

To Subscribers only, 10 vols., 8vo., cloth, 12s. per volume.

A NEW EDITION OF THE WORKS OF S. CYRIL, ARCHBISHOP OF ALEXANDRIA. Vols. I. and II., containing the COMMENTARIES UPON THE TWELVE MINOR PROPHETS; Vols. III., IV., and V., containing the COMMENTARY ON S. JOHN; and Vol. VI., containing THE THREE EPISTLES; THE BOOKS AGAINST NESTORIUS; EXPLANATION AND DEFENCES OF THE TWELVE CHAPTERS AND THE SCHOLIA, (*A Brief Treatise on the Doctrine of the Incarnation in Simple Language,*) can be delivered to Subscribers now; the remaining volumes will be issued in due course.

Subscribers' Names should be sent to James Parker and Co., Broad-street, Oxford, of whom Prospectuses may be obtained.

SERMONS BY THE REV. E. B. PUSEY, D.D.

PAROCHIAL SERMONS, Vol. I., for Season from Advent to Whitsuntide.

1. The End of All Things.
2. The Merciful shall obtain Mercy.
3. Prepare for Seasons of Grace.
4. God with Us.
5. The Incarnation a Lesson of Humility.
6. Character of Christian Rebuke.
7. Joy out of Suffering.
8. God calleth thee.
9. The Fewness of the Saved.
10. Fasting.
11. Review of Life.
12. Irreversible Chastisement.
13. God's Presence in Loneliness.
14. Barabbas or Jesus.
15. Christ Risen our Justification.
16. The Christian's Life in Christ.
17. Our Risen Lord's Love for Penitents.
18. How to detain Jesus in the Soul.
19. The Christian's Life hid in Christ.
20. Increased Communions.
21. Heaven the Christian's Home.
22. The Christian the Temple of God.
23. Will of God the Cure of Self-Will.

TWENTY-THREE SERMONS. 8vo., cloth, price 6s.

PAROCHIAL SERMONS, Vol. II.

1. Faith.
2. Hope.
3. Love.
4. Humility.
5. Patience.
6. Self-Knowledge.
7. Life a Warfare.
8. The Besetting Sin.
9. Victory over the Besetting Sin.
10. Prayer heard the more through delay.
11. Re-creation of the Penitent.
12. The Sin of Judas.
13. The Ascension our Glory and Joy.
14. The Teaching of God Within and Without.
15. The Rest of Love and Praise.
16. Faith in our Lord God and Man.
17. Groans of Unrenewed and Renewed Nature.
18. Victory amid Strife.
19. Victory through Loving Faith.
20. The Power and Greatness of Love.
21. Our Being in God.
22. The Sacredness of Marriage.

TWENTY-TWO SERMONS. 8vo., cloth, price 6s.

PAROCHIAL SERMONS, Vol. III.

Reprinted from the Plain Sermons by Contributors to the "Tracts for the Times." Revised edition.

1. Sudden Death.
2. Conversion.
3. The Cross borne for us and in us.
4. Real Obedience, in all things.
5. Christian Life a Struggle, but Victory.
6. The Value and Sacredness of Suffering.
7. The Christian's a Risen Life.
8. Victory over the World.
9. Obedience the Condition of Knowing the Truth.
10. Pray without ceasing.
11. Conditions of Acceptable Prayer.
12. Distractions in Prayer.
13. Baptism the Ground and Encouragement to Christian Education.
14. Holy Communion. — Danger in Careless Receiving.
15. Holy Communion. — Privileges.
16. Christian Kindliness and Charity.
17. Obeying Calls.
18. The Transfiguration of our Lord the Earnest of the Christian's Glory.
19. Christian Joy.
20. God's Glories in Infants set forth in the Holy Innocents.

TWENTY SERMONS. 8vo., cloth, price 6s.

PAROCHIAL SERMONS, preached and printed on Various Occasions.

1. The Day of Judgment. 6d.
2. Christ the Source and Rule of Christian Love. 1s. 6d.
3. The Preaching of the Gospel a Preparation for our Lord's Coming. 1s.
4. God is Love. 5. Whoso Receiveth One such Little Child in My Name Receiveth Me. 1s. 6d.
6. Chastisements Neglected, Forerunners of Greater. 1s.
7. The Blasphemy against the Holy Ghost. 1s.
8. Do All to the Lord Jesus. 6d.
9. The Danger of Riches.
10. Seek God First and ye shall have All. 1s. 6d.
11, 12. The Church the Converter of the Heathen. Two Sermons. 6d.
13. The Glory of God's House. 6d.

THIRTEEN SERMONS. 8vo., cloth, 6s.

The above Sermons may also be had separately.

SERMONS PREACHED AT ST. SAVIOUR'S, LEEDS, On Repentance and Amendment of Life, with a Preface by Dr. PUSEY.

1. Loving Penitence.
*2. The Nature of Sin.
*3. The Sinner's Death.
*4. God's Merciful Visitations.
*5. The Last Judgment.
*6. Hell.
*7. Love of Christ for Penitents.
*8. The Returning Prodigal.
*9. Death to Sin in the Death of Christ.
*10. Virtue of the Cross.
11. Looking unto Jesus the Groundwork of Penitence.
12. Looking unto Jesus the Means of Endurance.
13. Union with Christ, &c.
14. Hopes of the Penitent.
15. Bliss of Heaven, "We shall be like Him."
16. —— "We shall see Him as He is."
17. —— Glory of the Body.
18. Progress our Perfection.
19. Daily Growth.

NINETEEN SERMONS. 8vo., cloth, price 7s. 6d.

The Sermons with an asterisk prefixed are not by Dr. PUSEY.

SERMONS preached before the UNIVERSITY of OXFORD, between A.D. 1859 and 1872.

1. Grounds of Faith difficult to analyze because Divine.
2. God is our Light in all Knowledge, Natural or Supernatural.
3. Prophecy a Series of Miracles which we can examine for ourselves.
4. The Prophecy of Christ our Atoner and Intercessor in Isaiah liii. 12.
5. The Christ the Light of the World to be rejected by His own, to be despised, and so to reign in glory.
6. Power of Truth amid Untruthfulness in Jewish Interpretation of Prophecy.
7. Causes which Blinded the Jews to the Prophecies that Jesus should suffer.
8. The Gospel could not be True unless it had certain Truth.
9. Jesus the Way, the Truth, and the Life.
10. The Doctrine of the Atonement.
11. Christ the Lord our Righteousness.
12. Human Judgment the earnest of Divine.
13. The Terror of the Day of Judgment as arising from its Justice.
14. Grieve not the Spirit of God.
15. Value of Almsgiving in the Sight of God.
16. The World an Ever-living Enemy.
17. On Human Respect.
18. Each has his own Vocation.
19. To Believe in Jesus the Teaching of the Holy Ghost.

NINETEEN SERMONS. 8vo., cloth, price 6s.

SINGLE UNIVERSITY SERMONS.

The Holy Eucharist, a Comfort for the Penitent. Preached 1843. 1s.

Entire Absolution of the Penitent. Two Sermons. Preached 1846. 1s. each.

The Presence of Christ in the Holy Eucharist. Preached 1853. 1s.

Justification. 1s.

All Faith the Gift of God. Real Faith Entire. Two Sermons. Preached 1855. 2s.

Patience and Confidence the Strength of the Church. Preached 1841. 1s.

Everlasting Punishment. Preached 1864. 6d.

Miracles of Prayer. Preached 1866. 8vo., sewed, 1s.

Will Ye also go away? Preached 1867. With Preface and Appendix. 1s.

This is My Body. Preached 1871. 8vo., sewed, 1s.

The Responsibility of Intellect in Matters of Faith. Preached 1872. With an Appendix on Bishop Moberly's Strictures on the Athanasian Creed. 8vo., sewed, 1s.

Sinful Blindness amidst Imagined Light. Preached 1873. 8vo., 1s.

Christianity without the Cross a Corruption of the Gospel of Christ. Preached 1875. With a Note on "Modern Christianity a Civilized Heathenism." 8vo., 1s.

God and Human Independence. Preached 1876. 8vo., 6d.

LENTEN SERMONS,

Preached chiefly to Young Men at the Universities, between 1858 and 1874.

1. Life the Preparation for Death. 6d.
2. Why did Dives lose his Soul?
3. Almost thou persuadest me to be a Christian.
4. Balaam — Half Conversion Unconversion.
5. The Losses of the Saved.
6. Eve—The Course of Temptation.
7. Man's Self-Deceit and God's Omniscience.
8. Our Pharisaism. 6d.
9. Personal Responsibility of Man.
10, 11. The Prodigal Son.
12. Repentance, from Love of God, Life-long. 1s.
13. David in his Sin and his Penitence.
14. The Grace of Christ our Victory.
15. The Conflict, in a Superficial Age.
16. The Gospel, the Power of God.
17. The Prayers of Jesus.
18. The Means of Grace the Remedy against Sin.
19. The Thought of the Love of Jesus for us, the Remedy for Sins of the Body. 6d.
20. Continual Comfort the Gift of God.
21. Suffering, the Gift and Presence of God.
22. Jesus the Redeemer, and His Redeemed.
23. Jesus at the Right Hand of God.
24. Isaiah — his Heaviness and his Consolation.

TWENTY-FOUR SERMONS. 8vo., cloth, price 6s.

Sermons 1, 8, 12, and 19 may also be had separately.

ELEVEN ADDRESSES DURING A RETREAT OF THE COMPANIONS OF THE LOVE OF JESUS, engaged in Perpetual Intercession for the Conversion of Sinners. Eleven Sermons. 8vo., cloth, 3s. 6d.

WORKS by the Rev. E. B. PUSEY, D.D.

THE MINOR PROPHETS; with a Commentary Explanatory and Practical, and Introductions to the Several Books. 4to., sewed, 5s. each part.

Part I. contains HOSEA—JOEL, INTRODUCTION.
Part II. JOEL, INTRODUCTION—AMOS vi. 6.
Part III. AMOS vi. 7 to MICAH l. 12.
Part IV. MICAH i. 13 to HABAKKUK, INTRODUCTION.
Part V. HABAKKUK, ZEPHANIAH, HAGGAI.
Part VI., completing the Work. *In preparation.*

DANIEL THE PROPHET. Nine Lectures delivered in the Divinity School of the University of Oxford. With Copious Notes. *Third Edition.* (*Seventh Thousand.*) 8vo., cloth, 10s. 6d.

THE DOCTRINE OF HOLY BAPTISM, as taught by Holy Scripture and the Fathers. (Formerly "Tract for the Times," No. 67.) 8vo., cloth, 5s.

THE DOCTRINE of the REAL PRESENCE, as contained in the Fathers from the death of St. John the Evangelist to the 4th General Council. 1855. With the SERMON. 8vo., cloth, 7s. 6d.

THE REAL PRESENCE, the doctrine of the English Church, with a vindication of the reception by the wicked and of the Adoration of our Lord Jesus Christ truly present. 8vo., 7s. 6d.

The ROYAL SUPREMACY not an arbitrary Authority, but limited by the laws of the Church of which Kings are members. Ancient Precedents. 8vo., 7s.

The COUNCILS of the CHURCH, from the Council of Jerusalem to the close of the 2nd General Council of Constantinople, A.D. 381. 1857. 7s. 6d.

AN EIRENICON. VOL. I. Letter to the Author of the "Christian Year," "The Church of England a Portion of Christ's One Holy Catholic Church, and a Means of Restoring Visible Unity." *Seventh Thousand.* 8vo., cloth, 7s. 6d.

—————— VOL. II. First Letter to Dr. NEWMAN, "The Reverential Love due to the ever-blessed Theotokos, and the Doctrine of her 'Immaculate Conception.'" 8vo., cloth, 7s. 6d.

—————— VOL. III. Second Letter to Dr. NEWMAN, "Healthful Re-union as conceived possible before the Vatican Council." (Formerly entitled, "Is Healthful Re-union Impossible?") 8vo., cloth, 6s.

MARRIAGE with a DECEASED WIFE'S SISTER, together with a SPEECH on the same subject by E. BADELEY, Esq. 3s. 6d.

GOD'S PROHIBITION of the MARRIAGE WITH A DECEASED WIFE'S SISTER (Lev. xviii. 6) not to be set aside by an inference from His limitation of Polygamy among the Jews (Lev. xviii. 18). 8vo., 1s.

COLLEGIATE and PROFESSORIAL TEACHING and DISCIPLINE. 8vo., cloth, 5s.

The CHURCH of ENGLAND leaves her Children Free to whom to Open their Griefs. A Letter to the Rev. W. U. RICHARDS. With Postscript. 8vo., cloth, 5s.

LETTER to the LORD BISHOP of LONDON, in Explanation of some Statements contained in a Letter by the Rev. W. DODSWORTH. (*Fifth Thousand.*) 16mo., 1s.

RENEWED EXPLANATIONS in consequence of MR. DODSWORTH'S Comments on the above. 8vo., 1s.

Other Works published by Dr. Pusey.

SERMONS FOR THE CHRISTIAN YEAR. By the late Rev. JOHN KEBLE, Author of "The Christian Year."

 ADVENT TO CHRISTMAS-EVE. 8vo., cloth, 6s.
 CHRISTMAS AND EPIPHANY. 8vo., cloth, 6s.
 LENT TO PASSION-TIDE. 8vo., cloth, 6s.
 HOLY WEEK. 8vo., cloth, 6s.
 EASTER TO ASCENSION DAY. 8vo., cloth, 6s.

To complete the "Christian Year," there are, further, being selected—
 Sermons from Ascension to Trinity Sunday, 1 vol.
 For the Trinity Season, 2 or 3 vols.
 For Saints' Days, 1 vol.
 For Septuagesima to Lent, 1 vol.

VILLAGE SERMONS ON THE BAPTISMAL SERVICE. By the Rev. JOHN KEBLE. 8vo., cloth, 5s.

TRACTATUS DE VERITATE Conceptionis Beatissimæ Virginis, pro Facienda Relatione coram Patribus Concilii Basileæ, A.D. 1437. Compilatus per Rev. P. FRATREM JOANNEM DE TURRECREMATA, S.T.P., Ordinis Prædicatorum, Tunc Sacri Apostolici Palatii Magistrum. Small 4to. (850 pp.), cloth, 12s.

TRACT XC. On certain Passages in the XXXIX. Articles, by the Rev. J. H. NEWMAN, M.A., 1841; with Historical Preface by E. B. PUSEY, D.D.; and Catholic Subscription to the XXXIX. Articles considered in reference to Tract XC., by the Rev. JOHN KEBLE, M.A., 1851. 8vo., sewed, 1s. 6d.

DEVOTIONAL WORKS edited by Rev. E. B. PUSEY, D.D.

The SUFFERINGS OF JESUS. Composed by FRA THOMÉ DE JESU, of the Order of Hermits of St. Augustine, a Captive of Barbary, in the Fiftieth Year of his Banishment from Heaven. Translated from the original Portuguese. In Two Parts, Fcap. 8vo., cloth, 7s.

The SPIRITUAL COMBAT, with the PATH of PARADISE; and the SUPPLEMENT; or, the Peace of the Soul. By SCUPOLI. (From the Italian.) 3s. 6d.
———————— Cheap Edition, in wrapper, 6d.
———————— fine paper, limp cloth, 1s.

PARADISE for the CHRISTIAN SOUL. By HORST. Two Vols. *Fourth Thousand.* Fcap. 8vo., cloth, 6s. 6d.

The YEAR of AFFECTIONS; or, Sentiments on the Love of God, drawn from the Canticles, for every Day in the Year. By AVRILLON. (*Second Thousand.*) Fcap. 8vo., cloth, 6s. 6d.

A GUIDE for PASSING LENT HOLILY, in which is found for each day, Advice as to Practice, a Meditation and Thoughts on the Gospel for the Day, and Passages from the Holy Scriptures and the Fathers; with a Collect, and One Point in the Passion of our Lord Jesus Christ. By AVRILLON. Translated from the French, and adapted to the use of the English Church. *Fourth Edition.* Fcap. 8vo., cloth, 6s.

A GUIDE FOR PASSING ADVENT HOLILY. By AVRILLON. Translated from the French, and adapted to the use of the English Church. *New Edition.* Fcap. 8vo., cloth, 5s.

The FOUNDATIONS of the SPIRITUAL LIFE. (A Commentary on Thomas à Kempis.) (*Third Thousand.*) By SURIN. 4s. 6d.

The LIFE of JESUS CHRIST in GLORY. Daily Meditations from Easter Day to the Wednesday after Trinity Sunday. By NOUET. (*Third Thousand.*) Fcap. 8vo., cloth, 6s.

LENT READINGS from the FATHERS. Fcap. 8vo., cloth, 5s.

ADVENT READINGS from the FATHERS. *New Edition.* Fcap. 8vo., cloth, 3s. 6d.

MEDITATIONS and select PRAYERS of ST. ANSELM. *New Edition.* Fcap. 8vo., cloth, 5s.

From the "Paradise for the Christian Soul."

OF DEVOUT COMMUNION. (*Third Thousand.*) 18mo., 1s.
LITANIES. In the words of Holy Scripture. Royal 32mo., 6d.

In the Press.

MANUAL for CONFESSORS, by M. l'Abbé GAUME. Translated from the French.

www.ingramcontent.com/pod-product-compliance
Lightning Source LLC
Chambersburg PA
CBHW020541300426
44111CB00008B/752